The Great Book of
Questions AND Answers

This edition published in 2007 by Arcturus Publishing Limited
26/27 Bickels Yard, 151–153 Bermondsey Street,
London SE1 3HA

Copyright © 2007 Arcturus Publishing Limited

ISBN: 978-1-84193-691-8

Printed in China

Created by: Q2A Media
Editors: Ella Fern and Fiona Tulloch
Cover design: Q2A Media/Steve Flight

The Great Book of
Questions AND
Answers

Capella

Contents

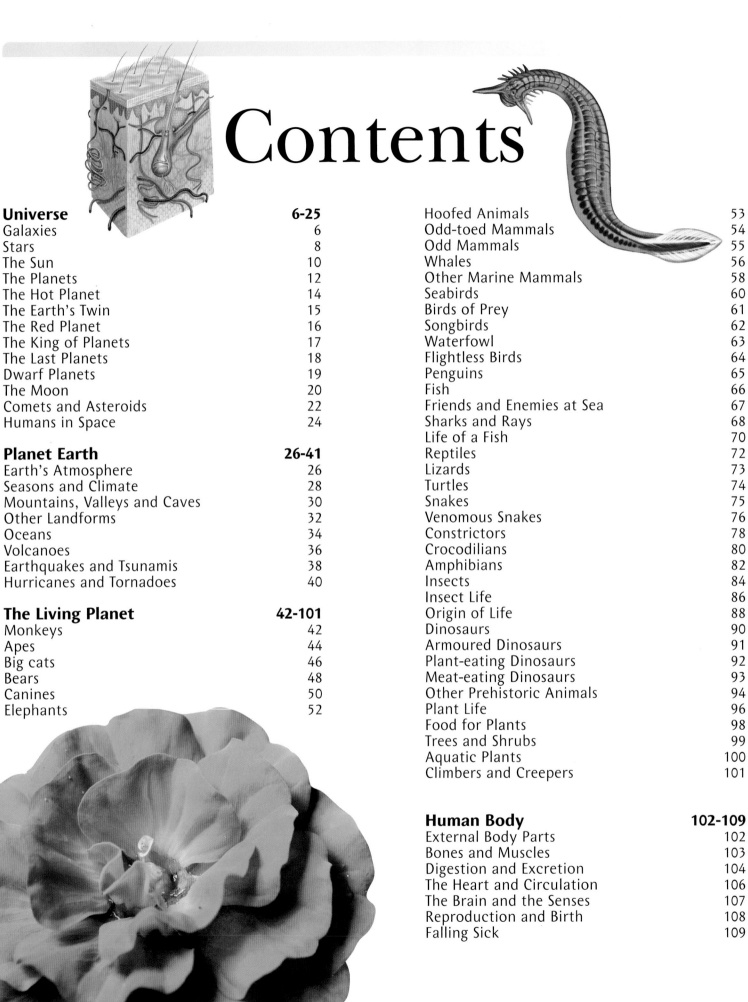

Galaxies

The universe is a huge open space made up of billions of galaxies and an even larger number of stars. Our galaxy is called the Milky Way. Our solar system, including the Sun, the planets and their moons, forms just a tiny part of the Milky Way.

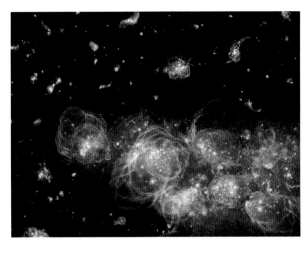

▲ **Early universe**
Scientists think that the early universe was a dense cluster of matter, that has kept expanding from the Big Bang until now and is continuing to expand.

Quick Q's:

1. What is the Big Bang theory?

The Big Bang theory suggests that the universe as we know it today was created after a huge explosion or 'bang'. Georges Lemaitre proposed the theory of the Big Bang in 1927, and in 1929 Edwin Hubble expanded on his work.

2. Which is the largest galaxy?

Scientists do not know exactly. The largest galaxies we know of are giant elliptical (oval) galaxies located in the middle of a whole group of galaxies. One of the largest is in the central galaxy in the cluster Abell 2029.

3. How big is the Milky Way?

The Milky Way is huge. It takes the Sun about 250 million years to orbit once around the centre of the Milky Way.

4. What is Messier Object 31?

The Andromeda Galaxy is also known as Messier Object 31, or M31. This galaxy is more than twice the size of Milky Way. But it is still not the largest galaxy we know of.

Q **How was the universe formed?**

A The universe was born more than 15 billion years ago. It is believed that the universe began as a small ball of fire. This fireball grew larger and larger until one day it exploded, to form the universe that we know.

Q **How big is the universe?**

A No one knows how big the universe really is. There are at least 100 billion galaxies that we know of. However, this number keeps growing as better telescopes are developed and we see more and more galaxies. On top of that, the galaxies are moving away from each other, causing the universe to expand. Some scientists believe that the universe will never stop expanding, while others think that one day it will begin to shrink until it becomes a fireball again.

Q **What is a galaxy?**

A A galaxy is a group of billions of stars, dust and gas bound together by gravitational force. A galaxy can either be on its own or in a cluster. Galaxies come in different shapes and sizes. Scientists have divided them into three categories based on their shapes – spiral, elliptical (oval) and irregular (no shape).

▼ **Expanding universe**
Scientists think that stars and other elements in the universe are continuing to move away from each other due to the force of the original Big Bang.

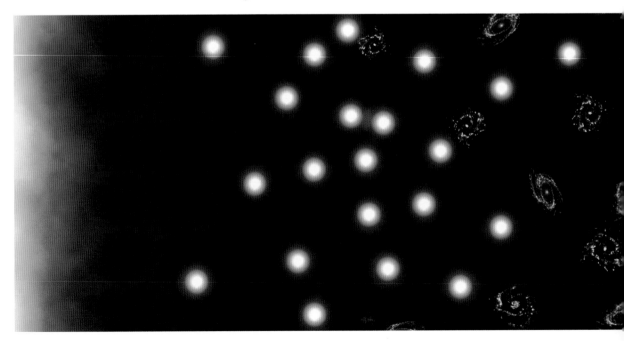

Q How did the Milky Way get its name?

A In ancient Greek and Roman myths, it was believed that the goddess Hera (Juno) spilt milk across the sky and called the white streak it left a 'river of milk'. The Romans called it *Via Lactea* or a 'road made of milk'. This is how our galaxy came to be named the Milky Way.

Q Is the Milky Way a part of a cluster of galaxies?

A The Milky Way and three of its neighbouring galaxies are part of a larger cluster known as the Local Group (because they are closest to Earth). The neighbouring galaxies in the Local Group are called Andromeda, and the Large and Small Magellanic Clouds. Of the 35 galaxies in the Local Group, only these three can be seen with the naked eye.

▶ **Milky Way**
An artist's impression of our galaxy, the Milky Way, based on observations made by modern telescopes. Our Sun is a small star on one arm of the galaxy.

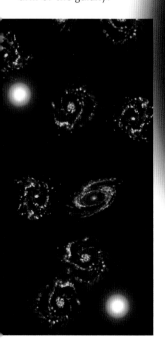

A galactic crash

Sometimes, galaxies crash into one another due to the force of gravity. But the stars in them are too far apart to cause any real damage. Our own galaxy is on a collision course with its neighbour Andromeda. The collision will take place in about five billion years and the two will merge to form an elliptical (oval) galaxy.

Try these too...

Stars (8–9), The Sun (10–11), The Planets (12–13), Comets and Asteroids (22–23), Scientific Revolution (150–151)

Stars

A star is a huge ball of gas and dust that gives out both heat and light. When the gases in the star burn out, it dies. A star can live for millions, even billions, of years depending on its size. Each galaxy in the universe is made up of several billion stars.

Quick Q's:

1. How many stars are there in the universe?

We know of about 70 sextillion (7 followed by 22 zeros) stars in the universe. However, we are only able to see about 8,000 of these.

2. What are giant and dwarf stars?

Scientists classify stars as giant or dwarf stars on the basis of their size. The Sun is a dwarf star. Supergiant stars – the biggest in the universe – are at least 400 times bigger than the Sun.

3. What is a cluster of stars?

Stars are usually found in groups called clusters. Some clusters are made up of loosely packed stars, while other stars are packed tightly together to form a dense cluster.

4. What kind of stars are binary stars?

Pairs of stars are called binary stars. Binary stars revolve around the same centre of gravity.

5. Which is the brightest known star?

The Pistol Star is the brightest known star in the universe. It is about 10 million times brighter than the Sun.

Q What is a protostar?

A Stars are born in clouds of dust and gases, mainly hydrogen. More and more gas is pulled together by gravity to form a cloud. After a while the cloud begins to spin. This makes the gas atoms bump into each other at high speeds, creating a great deal of heat. As the cloud becomes hotter a nuclear reaction takes place inside, and the cloud begins to glow. This glowing cloud is called a protostar. The protostar continues to contract until it becomes a star.

Q How long does a star live?

A A star glows for millions of years until the gases in its outer layer begin to cool, and the hydrogen in the inner core is slowly used up. The cool outer layer starts to glow red. When this happens the star is called a red giant. The red giant continues to lose its brightness until it fades away. Depending on its size, a red giant may die in an explosion, get compressed to form a black hole or become a white dwarf.

Q What is a white dwarf?

A A small star usually shrinks to form a dense white dwarf. The size of a white dwarf is similar to the size of Earth. There are many white dwarfs in our galaxy but they are too dim to be seen. Sirius B is one of them.

▶ **White dwarf**
An enhanced image of white dwarf stars, which have already shrunk to a size comparable to that of the Earth. These stars are too dim to be detected without modern telescopes.

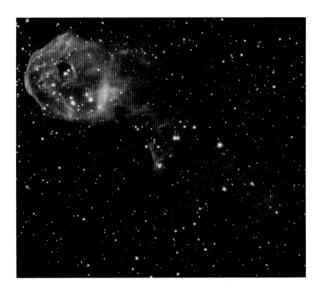

▲ **Protostar**
An artist's impression of the original ball of dust and gases that combine to form a protostar.

Q What is a supernova?

A A supernova is a vast explosion in which an entire star is destroyed. After the explosion, extremely bright light is emitted for several days. Supernovas appear a billion times brighter than the Sun. Sometimes, a supernova explosion can go on for weeks or even months. Supernovas mostly occur in distant galaxies. The last supernova to take place in the Milky Way occurred in 1604. It was observed by the famous astronomer Johannes Kepler. The brightest supernova to be recorded so far is 1993J in the galaxy M81. It was seen on 26 March 1993. But because the stars are so far away, we may see a supernova explosion long after it takes place.

Q What is a black hole?

A Black holes are extremely compact space objects that were once massive stars. Sometimes a huge star begins to shrink until it is smaller than an atom. This is called a black hole. The centre of the black hole is called 'singularity'.

The gravity near this point is so strong that any object that gets too close to the black hole is pulled into it. Even light gets sucked into it, which is why we can't see a black hole. Scientists use special instruments to detect a black hole's presence. They examine the effects it has on the objects near it.

▼ Black hole
Nobody can actually see a black hole, because the extremely strong gravity inside them does not even allow any light to escape, let alone anything else. This is an artist's impression of what a black hole may be like.

▼ Dwarf stars
When stars reach the end of their lives, their fires start to die out, and then they become dwarf stars due to the gravitational pull of the matter inside.

Heavenly pictures

By drawing imaginary lines between the stars in the sky, you will notice the shapes of animals or objects familiar to you. You might see a crab, a dragon, a bear or other patterns. These star patterns are called constellations. Astronomers have identified 88 constellations in all. The more famous ones are the Great Bear, the Little Bear and Orion, also known as the Hunter. The constellations also include characters from Greek mythology and the 12 signs of the zodiac.

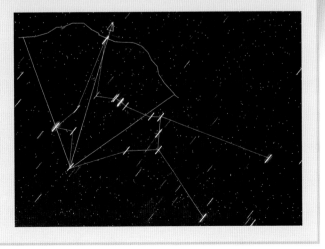

Try these too...

Galaxies (6–7), The Sun (10–11), The Planets (12–13), The Moon (20–21), Humans in Space (24–25), Earth's Atmosphere (26–27), Scientific Revolution (150–151), Computer Revolution (162), Matter (178–179), Light (180–181), Heat (184–185), Electricity (186–187), Forces and Motion (190–191), Communication and Satellites (192–193)

The Sun

Our solar system is made up of the Sun, eight planets, three dwarf planets and many asteroids, comets and other space rocks. The Sun is the largest object in the solar system and is located right at its centre. The planets, dwarf planets, asteroids and comets travel around the Sun in an ellipse. Our solar system was formed about 5 billion years ago, and the surface of the Sun is about 4.6 billion years old.

Quick Q's:

1. What are sunspots?

Sunspots are storms on the surface of the Sun. These storms appear as huge, dark spots in satellite pictures and so are called sunspots.

2. How hot is the Sun?

The Sun's surface temperature is about 5,760 °C (10,400 °F), while its centre is an incredible 15 million °C (28 million °F) – that is more than 150,000 times hotter than boiling water!

3. How far is the Sun from us?

The Sun is about 150 million kilometres (93 million miles) away from the Earth.

4. What is the corona?

The corona is the glowing atmosphere of the Sun that extends millions of kilometres into space. The corona is 200 times hotter than the Sun's surface!

5. Is the sun worshipped by people?

The sun has been worshipped as a god since ancient times by the Greeks, Romans and native Americans.

Q. How was the Sun created?

A. Before it was formed, the Sun and the rest of the solar system was a huge mass of hot gas and dust called a solar nebula. This nebula spun faster and faster until the clouds of gases, dust and ice particles clumped together and exploded, forming the sun.

Q. Why does the Sun glow?

A. The Sun is made up of huge amounts of hydrogen and helium gases. Nuclear reactions at the centre of the Sun emit a large amount of energy that makes the Sun glow. That same energy travels through space and reaches us as heat and light.

Q. What is a solar eclipse?

A. A solar eclipse occurs when the Moon comes between the Sun and the Earth, blocking the Sun from our view. In a total solar eclipse, the Moon blocks out the Sun from our view completely. In a partial eclipse, however, a part of the Sun is visible. During an annular eclipse, we can see a small ring of the Sun glowing around the Moon. When the Moon is nearer to the Earth it appears larger and therefore covers the Sun completely, although it is actually much smaller than the Sun. However, in an annular eclipse the Moon is too far away from the Earth to block the Sun out totally and therefore a ring of sunlight is seen.

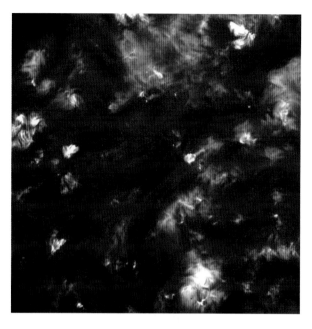

▲ **Flaring up!**
Solar flares on the surface of the Sun. Solar flares were observed for the first time in 1859.

Q. What is a solar flare?

A. Sometimes the Sun produces a huge amount of magnetic energy that sends out jets of gas into space. These jets of gas are called solar flares and cause a sudden increase in the brightness of the Sun. Solar flares are often followed by the release of electrically charged particles like protons and electrons. These are called solar winds and are known to travel at a speed of about 500 kilometres (300 miles) per second.

▼ **Blocking the Sun**
In an annular (ring-shaped) eclipse, the Moon covers only the middle portion of the Sun, causing a bright ring of light to appear around the Moon.

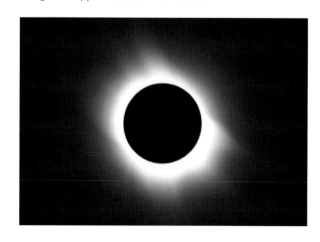

Q Is the Sun really a star?

A The Sun is a medium-sized star known as a yellow dwarf. It is younger and smaller than most stars in the universe, but is very bright and extremely hot. In about five billion years, when all the hydrogen in its core has been used up, the Sun will change into a red giant star. After that, the Sun will evolve into a white dwarf before finally dying out.

Q How did we learn about the Sun?

A We have sent several solar missions into space to study the Sun and its characteristics. The first detailed observations were made by NASA's Pioneer missions that were launched between 1959 and 1968. The Solar Maximum mission of 1980 made a detailed study of solar flares. The Solar and Heliospheric Observatory (SOHO) launched in 1995, has been continuously collecting data regarding the Sun for the last ten years.

In different directions!

The Sun takes about 26 days on average to rotate on its axis. Since it is made up of gas, different parts of the Sun rotate at different speeds. The surface closest to the equator rotates faster than that closest to the polar regions. The Sun's surface near the poles takes almost 36 days to complete one rotation.

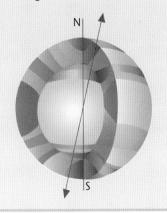

▾ A joint effort
The SOHO was launched jointly by the European Space Agency and NASA. For over ten years, SOHO has been studying the outer layers of the Sun.

▸ Surface of the Sun
There is constant activity visible on the surface of the Sun, as it pulses and glows due to the heat and light produced by the nuclear reactions within.

Try these too...

Galaxies (6–7), The Planets (12–13), The Moon (20–21), Earth's Atmosphere (26–27), Scientific Revolution (150–151)

The Planets

Planets are large masses of matter that orbit around a star. Our solar system consists of eight planets – Mercury, Venus, Earth, Mars, which are called inner or rocky planets, and Jupiter, Saturn, Uranus and Neptune, which are the outer planets, or gas giants.

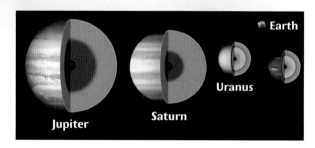

Quick Q's:

1. How did the planets get their names?

All the planets are named after Roman gods. Venus is named after the Roman goddess of love. The surface features of Venus are also named after various goddesses. For example the planet has a deep canyon named Diana, after the Roman goddess of hunting.

2. How many rings do Jupiter and Uranus have?

Jupiter has three thin rings that cannot be seen even with the most powerful telescopes. Uranus has as many as 11 rings.

3. How many moons does Venus have?

Apart from Mercury, Venus is the only other planet in the solar system that has no moon.

4. What about Pluto?

Until recently, Pluto was the ninth planet in our solar system. But in 2006, it was officially reclassified as a dwarf planet, because it is so small and its gravitational field is not as strong as that of the major planets.

Q How were the planets formed?

A After the gaseous cloud called the solar nebula collapsed upon itself due to the strength of its own gravity and formed the Sun, the dust and particles around it clumped together to form the planets. The heat of the Sun melted the ice particles nearby and eventually these rocks grew larger to form the four rocky planets. Some ice particles were too far away from the Sun to be melted. These ice pieces combined with gases to form the planets called the gas giants.

Q What are the features of a rocky planet?

A The rocky planets are made up of rocks and metals like iron and nickel. They are smaller than the gas giants but are very heavy. It is because of their weight that rocky planets rotate much slower than the gas giants.

▼ **Rocky planets**
Among the rocky planets, the Earth appears blue from outer space because over 70 per cent of its surface is covered with water.

▲ **Birth of planets**
The planets in our solar system were born when dust and particles around the Sun clumped together.

▲ **Gas giants**
The four outer planets, the gas giants, are much larger than the Earth.

Q What makes gas giants unique?

A The gas giants are bigger in size but lighter, as they are mainly made up of gases and ice particles. In fact, Saturn is so light that it would float if placed in water! Gas giants also spin extremely quickly and they have rings around them. These planets do not have a hard surface. Jupiter and Saturn have a semi-liquid centre that is covered by a layer of liquid gas.

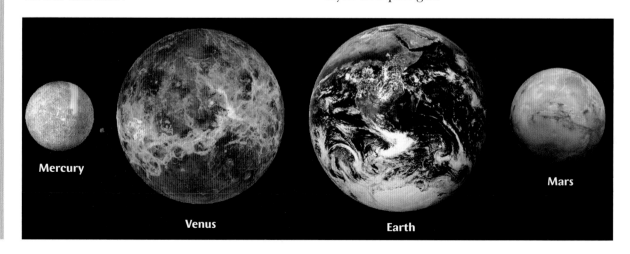

Mercury
Venus
Earth
Mars

Q What are the distinguishing features of each of the rocky planets?

A Mercury is the closest to the Sun and therefore its temperature can be as high as 467 °C (873 °F). Venus is covered with carbon dioxide containing droplets of sulphuric acid. This traps the Sun's heat and makes Venus hotter than even Mercury. Mars, the red planet, is considered to be the only planet after Earth where life could exist. As far as we know, the Earth is the only planet that supports life.

Q What are the special characteristics of the gas giants?

A Jupiter is the largest planet. It rotates faster than any other planet and has the most moons. Saturn is set apart by its beautiful rings, made up of dust particles and pieces of ice. Uranus is a strange planet where seasons last for more than 20 years, while Neptune is the windiest planet in the solar system.

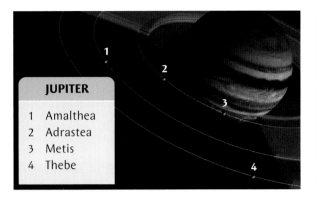

JUPITER

1 Amalthea
2 Adrastea
3 Metis
4 Thebe

▲ **Jupiter's moons**
Jupiter, the largest planet in the solar system, has so many moons that we are constantly discovering new ones. This image shows some of the bigger moons and the gossamer rings around the planet.

▼ **The solar system**
The relative sizes of the eight planets and the three dwarf planets are shown in this diagram of the solar system. Jupiter is the largest planet. The Sun, of course, is much larger than any of the planets.

Try these too...

Galaxies (6–7), The Sun (10–11), The Hot Planet (14), The Earth's Twin (15), The Red Planet (16), The King of Planets (17), The Last Planets (18), Dwarf Planets (19), The Moon (20–21), Earth's Atmosphere (26–27)

Saturn's moons

At least 46 moons orbit Saturn. Each moon is unique. Enceladus is among the shiniest objects in space. Titan's atmosphere is thicker than Earth's. Here are the big moons, seen from behind the moon Dione.

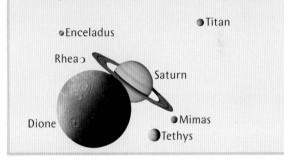

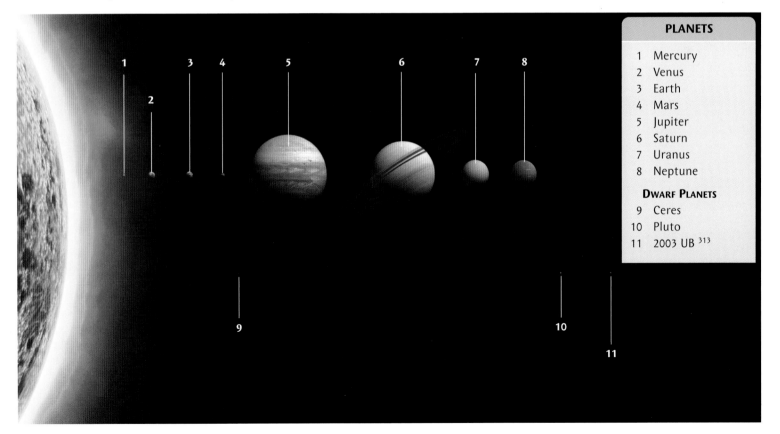

PLANETS

1 Mercury
2 Venus
3 Earth
4 Mars
5 Jupiter
6 Saturn
7 Uranus
8 Neptune

DWARF PLANETS
9 Ceres
10 Pluto
11 2003 UB[313]

The Hot Planet

Mercury is the planet closest to the Sun. It is also very small – about the size of Earth's moon. It is named after the Roman messenger god because it moves very quickly.

▲ **Sandy surface**
Mercury has a surface that is full of hills and steep canyons, all of it covered with a mixture of sandy substances. The core of the planet is metallic, like all the rocky planets.

Quick Q's:

1. How long does Mercury take to orbit the Sun?

Like all planets, Mercury goes around the Sun in an elliptical (oval) orbit. It takes about 88 days to complete one orbit.

2. How long is a day on Mercury?

Mercury goes around the Sun very fast, but rotates very slowly on its axis. Therefore a day on Mercury is equal to 176 Earth days!

3. Why does Mercury have huge craters?

As Mercury has very little atmosphere, meteors do not burn up in the air. Instead, they fall on the surface, creating huge craters.

4. What colour is the sky above Mercury?

If you were to look at the sky from Mercury, even during the day, it would appear black. This is because there is no atmosphere to spread the Sun's light.

5. Which is the largest crater on Mercury?

The largest crater is the Caloris Basin. It is about 1,300 kilometres (808 miles) in diameter. It is also one of the biggest craters in the solar system.

Q **Why are nights on Mercury freezing cold, although it's the planet closest to the Sun?**

A Unlike Earth, Mercury is not surrounded by a thick protective blanket of air called the atmosphere. This means that the heat from the Sun escapes, leaving the planet freezing at night. While the temperature during the day can be as high as 467 °C (873 °F), at night it drops to -183 °C (-297 °F).

Q **What is the surface of Mercury like?**

A If you were to land on mercury, you would find a surface very similar to that of the Moon. It has dust-covered hills, cliffs and is dotted by craters. The planet also has a thick metallic core and a sandy crust.

solar panel

Sun shade

◀ **Mercury close-up**
From up close, the surface of Mercury can be seen to be pitted with huge craters. Any meteor that comes near Mercury falls on the surface and creates a crater, as there is no atmosphere to burn the meteor up.

Q **What space probes have been launched to Mercury?**

A Mercury, being so close to the Sun, is very difficult to explore. Space probes are unable to withstand the heat of the planet. Only one space probe, Mariner 10, has visited Mercury so far. It photographed nearly half of the planet's surface. A new probe, Messenger, is on its way to Mercury. It was launched on 3 August 2004 and is expected to return, after photographing the whole planet, in March 2012. Another space mission will begin in 2013.

TV cameras

◀ **Looking at Mercury**
The Mariner 10 space probe is the only one to have got anywhere near Mercury so far. It is sending photographs of the surface of Mercury regularly now.

The Earth's Twin

Venus is the second planet from the Sun. It is also Earth's closest neighbour and its size, composition, gravity and distance from the Sun are similar to the Earth's. Venus is so similar to Earth, that it is often considered to be its twin. However, in reality, Venus is very different.

Q Why is Venus hotter than Mercury?

A Venus has a thick atmosphere, much thicker than the Earth's. The atmosphere is mainly carbon dioxide. This greenhouse gas traps large amounts of heat within the planet. That is why Venus is hotter than Mercury, though Mercury is closer to the Sun.

Q Why is a day longer than a year on Venus?

A Venus goes around the Sun at a very high speed. It takes only about 225 days to complete one orbit. However, it spins much more slowly on its axis, taking about 243 days to complete a rotation. Therefore, days on Venus are longer than years.

▶ **Mapping Venus**
Scientists have sent a number of space missions to Venus to find out more about its size, atmosphere, interior and surface, especially its volcanoes.

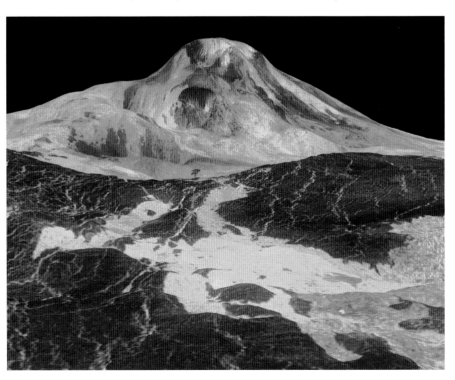

Q Are there volcanoes on Venus?

A There are more volcanoes on Venus than there are on Earth. About 80 per cent of the planet's surface is made up of smooth volcanic plains, and there are two major mountain ranges with volcanoes that may be active. The peak of Maxwell Montes, the highest mountain on Venus, lies 11 kilometres (7 miles) above the surface of the planet. Mount Everest rises only about 9 kilometres (6 miles) above sea level.

Try these too...

The Sun (10–11), The King of Planets (17), The Moon (20–21), Comets and Asteroids (22–23), Earth's Atmosphere (26–27), The Poles – The Arctic and Antarctica (122–123)

▼ **Volcano on Venus**
There is far more volcanic activity inside Venus than inside Earth; so, Venus has many more volcanoes.

Spinning backwards

All the planets rotate from west to east on their axes, apart from Venus, which spins in the opposite direction. On the surface of Venus, the Sun appears to rise in the west and set in the east. The planet might have been hit by a huge space rock, reversing the direction of its spin.

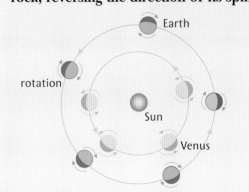

rotation

Earth

Sun

Venus

The Red Planet

Mars is the fourth planet from the Sun and is named after the Greek god of war. It is also called the red planet because it glows red in the sky. The presence of rust (iron oxide) on its surface gives the planet its colour.

Quick Q's:

1. Can you see Mars from the Earth?

On a clear night, Mars can be observed with the naked eye. Between July and September the Martian surface can be observed clearly through a telescope.

2. How many moons does Mars have?

Mars has two moons called Phobos and Deimos, which orbit very closely to its surface. Both moons are believed to be asteroids that were captured by the gravity of Mars as they came close to it.

3. Is there life on Mars?

The atmosphere of Mars is 95 per cent carbon dioxide, 3 per cent nitrogen and 1.6 per cent argon. Traces of oxygen and water have also been found. Some scientists have claimed to have found traces of methane. This gave rise to the speculation that there may be life on Mars, since methane is a gas produced by many animals. But other scientists pointed out that methane is also produced by the mineral olivine, which can be found on Mars.

Q **What is the surface of Mars like?**

A The surface of Mars is divided into the northern plains flattened by lava flows, and the southern highlands marked by huge craters. The planet boasts Olympus Mons, the largest volcano in the solar system.

Q **Is there water on Mars?**

A Scientists have found signs of water in rock layers. In 2006, the scientists saw new deposits of sediment on the surface of Mars. These sediments had not been there six years earlier. According to scientists at NASA, this is the strongest evidence so far that water still flows occasionally on the surface of Mars, though other scientists say the sediments could have been deposited by carbon dioxide frost or movement of dust. Samples of the minerals haematite and goethite have also been found in Mars. These minerals are sometimes formed in the presence of water.

▶ Martian moon
The two moons of Mars are quite small compared to our Moon. They may be asteroids caught by the gravity of Mars.

◀ Red planet
The surface of Mars looks reddish brown due to the presence of iron oxide.

The scientists have also found signs of frozen water near the South Pole of Mars. It is believed that huge floods flowed through Mars about 3.5 billion years ago. The water from the floods may have once collected in huge basins.

Q **Why are seasons on Mars longer than on Earth?**

A Mars and Earth are tilted on their axis in the same way. Therefore, Mars has almost the same kind of seasons as Earth. However, because a Martian year is equal to two years on Earth, each Martian season lasts twice as long as the seasons on Earth.

Q **What kind of weather would you find on Mars?**

A The temperature varies from -140 to 20 °C (-220 to 68 °F). The polar ice caps on Mars increase and decrease in size alternately in winter and summer. Mars also has dust storms, which can cover the entire planet.

▼ Olympus Mons
The tallest volcano in the solar system, Olympus Mons towers 27 kilometres (16.88 miles) above the surface of Mars.

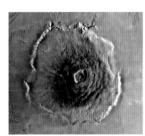

◀ Look out for Mars
From 27 August 2006, Earth and Mars have been closer to each other than they have been in the last 60,000 years! It has begun to appear brightly in the night sky, as seen here while looking south-east from Poodle Rock in the Valley of Fire State Park, Nevada, USA. Now Mars will be the brightest object in the night sky after the Moon and Venus.

The King of Planets

Jupiter is the first of the gas giants and the fifth planet from the Sun. It is the largest of all planets. In fact, more than a thousand Earths could fit inside it!

Q How did Jupiter get its name?

A The planet is named after the king of the Roman gods. It is indeed the king of the planets, not just because of its massive size, but also because it rotates the fastest. It is the fourth brightest object in the sky, after the Sun, the Moon and Venus.

Q How many moons does Jupiter have?

A Jupiter has more than 60 moons. Galileo Galilei, the famous Italian astronomer, saw the four largest moons of Jupiter in 1610. They were named Io, Europa, Callisto and Ganymede. By the 1970s nine more moons were discovered and today we know of 63.

Q What is the Great Red Spot?

A Jupiter is a planet of storms. The biggest storm area is called the Great Red Spot. It has been raging for at least 340 years. It is so big that it can be seen from the Earth through a telescope.

Q How many explorations have been made to Jupiter?

A Many explorations have been made to the king of planets. Pioneer 11 took the first close-up images in 1974, studied the atmosphere and detected Jupiter's magnetic field. Space probe Galileo, launched in 1989, orbited Jupiter. In 2000, the Cassini probe took the best ever photos.

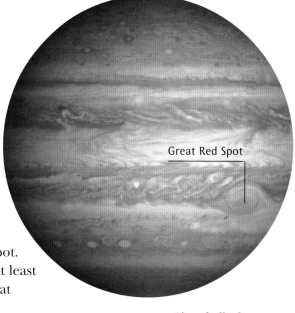

Great Red Spot

▲ Giant ball of gas
There are constant storms on Jupiter, during which the winds can roar five times faster than the fastest hurricane on Earth. Some of the big storms are seen here in brown.

Try these too...

The Sun (10–11), The Planets (12–13), The Last Planets (18), The Moon (20–21), Comets and Asteroids (22–23), Scientific Revolution (150–151), Communication and Satellites (192–193)

Volcanic moon

Io, one of the four largest moons, lies very close to Jupiter. There is a great deal of pressure on this small moon, since it is constantly being pulled by the gravity of Jupiter and the other large moons. This tug of war generates a lot of heat, so Io is covered with active volcanoes.

▼ Planet spotter
The Galileo space probe was the first to make an entire orbit around Jupiter.

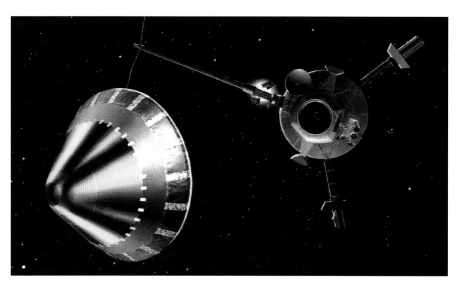

The Last Planets

Next to Jupiter are Saturn, Uranus and finally Neptune. Saturn is the second largest planet in the solar system. Like Jupiter, Saturn and Uranus are made up of gases. All three planets have rings, but it is Saturn's rings that are the most spectacular.

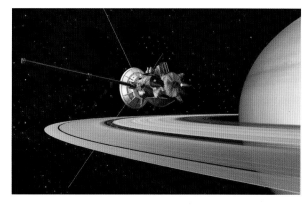

▲ Probing far
The Cassini space probe is expected to send us better photographs of the far planets.

▲ Saturn's rings
Saturn has seven large rings, each made up of thousands of smaller rings. These are among the brightest objects you can see through a telescope.

Q Why do Saturn's rings shine?

A Saturn's rings consist of dust particles and pieces of ice that can be quite large. The ice pieces reflect light, causing the rings to shine.

Q What gives Uranus and Neptune their blue colour?

A Both planets contain methane. Sunlight is reflected by clouds under the methane layer. Only the blue portion of the reflected light passes through the methane layer, so they appear to be blue.

▼ Strange rotation
Uranus rotates from top to bottom as it orbits the Sun.

Q Why do seasons on Uranus last for over 20 years?

A Uranus has a very peculiar orbit, unique in the solar system. The planet is tilted in such a way that its poles face the Sun directly, so that Uranus spins from top to bottom. It acts like a cylinder that is rotating on its ends instead of rotating on its sides. Scientists believe that another planet-like object might have crashed into Uranus, knocking it over on to its side. The long seasons are caused by the planet's unusual orbit.

Q Are there winds on Neptune?

A Neptune is the windiest planet in our solar system. Winds on this planet can reach speeds of about 2,000 kilometres per hour (1,200 miles per hour). That is more than ten times the speed of the strongest hurricane on Earth.

▼ Cloudy over Neptune
The clouds over Neptune are always being blown about by the strong winds on the planet.

Quick Q's:

1. How big are Saturn's rings?

Saturn's rings can be up to 1 kilometre (0.6 miles) thick and stretch for over 280,000 kilometres (175,000 miles).

2. When were Saturn's rings discovered?

Saturn's rings were first observed by Galileo through a telescope in 1610.

3. Who discovered Uranus?

Uranus was the first planet to be seen through a telescope. It was discovered in 1781 by astronomer William Herschel.

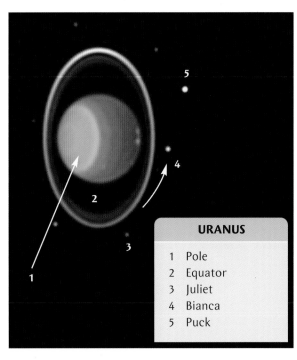

URANUS	
1	Pole
2	Equator
3	Juliet
4	Bianca
5	Puck

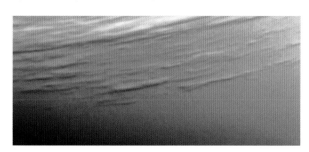

Dwarf Planets

In 2006, the International Astronomical Union (IAU) made a decision that changed the way we organize our solar system. The IAU announced the removal of Pluto from the list of planets. They reclassified Pluto as a dwarf planet. Instead of nine, we now have only eight planets in our solar system.

Q How is a dwarf planet different from other planets?

A According to the IAU's new definition, a planet is a space object that orbits the Sun and has a nearly round shape. Its gravity must be strong enough to clear all other space objects (except satellites) out of its orbit. Dwarf planets also orbit the Sun and have a nearly round shape. But other space objects nearby are not cleared by the gravity of the dwarf planets. They are not big enough for their gravitational fields to do this. Dwarf planets are different from satellites, which orbit a planet and not the Sun.

◀ **Distant Sun**
An artist's impression of how the Sun would look from the surface of Eris, the furthest of the dwarf planets in the solar system. The Sun gives almost no heat at that distance and looks like a bright star.

Q How many dwarf planets are there in the solar system?

A Apart from Pluto, Ceres and Eris (UB313) have also been classified as dwarf planets. Until recently, Ceres was called the largest asteroid. It has a diameter of about 950 kilometres (600 miles) and is in the asteroid belt between Mars and Jupiter. Eris is the largest of all the dwarf planets. It has a diameter of about 3,000 kilometres (1,850 miles).

Q Are there any other dwarf planets?

A Scientists are considering including Pluto's moon Charon among the dwarf planets. Charon does not actually go around Pluto – they revolve around each other. The planetoid Sedna and the asteroids Vesta, Pallas and Hygiea are also being considered.

▲ **Promoted**
Since 2006, Ceres is classified as a dwarf planet. Before that, it was simply the largest of the many asteroids that lie between the orbits of Mars and Jupiter.

Try these too...

The Sun (10–11), The Planets (12–13), The Red Planet (16), The King of Planets (17), The Last Planets (18), The Moon (20–21), Comets and Asteroids (22–23), Scientific Revolution (150–151), The New Millennium – 21st Century (163)

Thrown off orbit

Pluto was called the ninth planet for 76 years. After 2006, it was reclassified as a dwarf planet.

1 Sun	6 Jupiter
2 Mercury	7 Saturn
3 Venus	8 Uranus
4 Earth	9 Neptune
5 Mars	10 Pluto

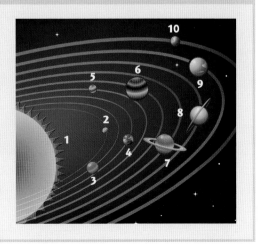

▼ **Pluto's moon**
Pluto (left) and its moon Charon actually go around each other, rather than Charon going around Pluto. Scientists may soon reclassify Charon as dwarf planet.

The Moon

There are many moons in our solar system, which orbit planets, just like planets orbit the Sun. Earth has one Moon, Mars has two small moons, Mercury and Venus don't have any, while Jupiter has at least 63! The Earth's Moon is made up of rocks, both solid and molten.

Quick Q's:

1. Does our Moon have a scientific name?

Astronomers call the Earth's Moon Luna, to distinguish it from the natural satellites of other planets.

2. If the Moon is cold and dark, how does it give off light?

The Moon does not give off light of its own. It simply reflects the sunlight that falls on it.

3. Why can't we see the Moon during the day?

During the day the bright light of the Sun blocks the soft glow of light reflected by the Moon.

4. What are spring tides and neap tides?

When the Sun, the Moon and the Earth are in a straight line, the gravitational force of the Sun strengthens that of the Moon causing tides that are higher than usual. These are called spring tides (although they have nothing to do with the season of Spring). When the Sun and the Moon are at right angles to the Earth, weaker tides, called neap tides, are caused. Tides are important to wash away the debris off the coasts.

Q **Why is the Moon's surface filled with craters?**

A The Moon does not have an atmosphere. Therefore, meteors and asteroids from outer space crash into its surface making craters. Tycho crater, one of the biggest lunar craters, is more than 85 kilometres (50 miles) wide.

Q **What does the term 'Blue Moon' mean?**

Blue Moon refers to the second Full Moon to appear in a month. It is very rare indeed. There are other definitions of Blue Moon as well, but this is the most widely accepted definition nowadays.

Q **How does the Moon cause tides in our oceans and seas?**

A Tides are caused by the gravitational force exerted by the Moon on our planet. This force causes the ocean to bulge out in the direction of the Moon, making the tide rise. As the Earth is also pulled towards the Moon, the ocean on the side facing away from the Moon also bulges out. So it is high tide there as well. In the region between the two bulges (high tides) the water level decreases, causing low tides. Tides are higher in the tropics due to the bulge of the equator. Many forms of life on the coast are tailored to the cycle of tides.

▶ **High and low**
The gravitational pull of the Moon on the Earth causes tides in the oceans and seas of the Earth.

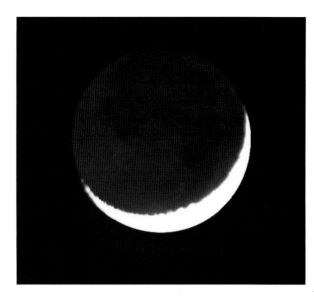

▲ **Crescent Moon**
As the Moon orbits around the Earth, we see only a part of it that is lit up by the Sun, depending upon the angle made by the Earth, the Moon and the Sun.

Q **Why does the Moon appear crescent-shaped at times?**

A The shape of the Moon as seen from the Earth keeps changing. The changing shapes of the Moon are called phases. When the side of the Moon that faces the Earth is turned away from the Sun, we are unable to see the Moon. This phase is called the New Moon. As the Moon travels in its orbit around the Earth, we start to see a small portion of the Moon that is lit up by the Sun. This is called the Crescent Moon. The lit up portion seen by us slowly increases, and we see a Half Moon, then a Three-quarter Moon. When the Moon completes a half orbit around the Earth, we can see the entire disc lit up by the Sun – the Full Moon.

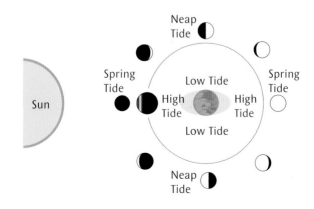

The dark side

Did you know that we see only one side of the Moon at all times? This is because the Moon takes the same amount of time to rotate on its axis as it takes to go around the Earth. The side we see is called the near side, while the one that is never seen is called the dark side. The first time people on Earth got to see the dark side of the Moon was when the first astronauts made an orbit around the Moon, and took photographs. The astronauts lost touch with Earth when they were on the dark side, because the moon blocked their radio signals.

▲ **Phases of the Moon**
We see different parts of the Moon lit up by the Sun, depending upon how much of the Moon that is lit up is facing towards us or facing away from us. This is repeated in a cycle every 28 days.

Try these too...

The Sun (10–11), The Planets (12–13), Humans in Space (24–25), Oceans (34–35), Forces and Motion (190–191)

Comets and Asteroids

Along with the Sun, the planets and their moons, several other objects made up of small pieces of rock, metal and ice are also a part of the solar system. These objects are asteroids, comets and meteors.

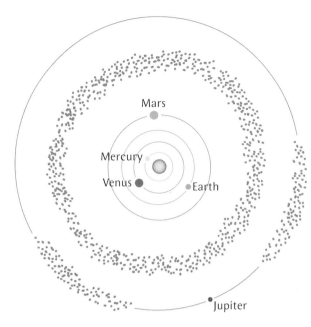

▲ Asteroid belt
Most of the asteroids in our solar system can be found in a belt between the orbits of Mars and Jupiter.

Quick Q's:

1. What are sungrazers?

Some comets crash into the Sun or get so close to it that they break up into tiny pieces. Such comets are called sungrazers.

2. Where are asteroids found in the solar system?

Most asteroids are found in a region between Mars and Jupiter, which is known as the asteroid belt.

3. Do asteroids have moons?

The asteroid Ida has a tiny moon, Dactyl. This was discovered by the spacecraft Galileo in 1993.

4. When will Halley's Comet be seen again?

Halley's Comet takes about 76 years to complete one orbit around the Sun, so it is expected to be seen again in 2061.

5. Why does a comet have a tail?

A comet is made up of ice and other material. As it nears the Sun, these materials heat up. Solar wind and pressure from the Sun's radiation push them outwards to form a tail that always points away from the Sun.

Q Are asteroids planets?

A When the solar system was formed, some fragments of rock were left spinning in space. These huge space rocks that orbit the Sun are called asteroids. Like other planets, asteroids are also made of metals like iron and have moons. Some of them are called minor planets.

Q Are asteroids dangerous?

A An asteroid can be thrown off its orbit by the gravity of larger planets, or if it comes too close to another asteroid. Once it is off its orbit, the stray asteroid often strikes the surface of other planets and moons. This causes widespread destruction and creates huge craters. In fact, some scientists think that an asteroid struck Earth about 65 million years ago, causing the extinction of the dinosaurs.

Q Are shooting stars really stars?

A Shooting stars are actually pieces of burning rock called meteors. A meteor is formed when a piece of debris in the solar system, called a meteoroid, enters the Earth's atmosphere. As the meteor rubs against the air in the Earth's atmosphere, it gets hotter and hotter until it burns up in a streak of light.

▸ A meteor
We can see a meteor without a telescope when it enters the Earth's atmosphere. Sometimes, a number of meteors are seen within a very short period of time. They leave a streak of light, which disappears very quickly. This is called a 'meteor shower', also known as 'meteor storm'.

Q How is a comet's tail formed?

A A comet is a mixture of ice, gas and dust. Like asteroids, they too travel around the Sun. As a comet nears the Sun, the ice on its surface melts and a jet of gas and dust particles is released to form a tail. Comet tails can be as long as 10 million kilometres (6.2 million miles).

Q Do meteors ever fall on Earth?

A Sometimes small fragments of a meteor, called meteorites, crash on to the surface of the Earth. Some are so big that they make craters where they fall. Many meteorites have been found on the Earth's surface. The best known of these is the Barringer Impact Crater in Arizona, USA. This crater was created by an iron meteor that fell on the Earth about 50,000 years ago. The meteor was almost 40 metres (130 feet) in diameter and slammed into the surface at a speed of about 11 kilometres per second (6.8 miles per second), creating a crater that was more than a kilometre wide.

The great Siberian explosion

On 30 July 1908 people living near Lake Baikal in Siberia saw a strange bluish light travel across the sky, followed by a loud explosion and shockwaves that knocked people off their feet. The explosion took place near the Stony Tunguska River and was probably caused by a meteor. It flattened about 80 million trees. The meteor may have broken up about 10 kilometres (6 miles) above the Earth's surface, so it did not leave a crater.

▲ Huge crater
The Barringer impact crater in the USA was created by a meteorite impact 50,000 years ago.

◀ Regular visitor
Halley's Comet orbits around the Sun once every 76 years, and is the most famous comet in human history.

Q Where do comets come from?

A Comets originate in two different areas of the solar system. Comets from the Kuiper Belt beyond Neptune are called short-period, since it takes them less time than other comets to go around the Sun. Comets from the Oort Cloud take as long as 30 million years to complete one orbit and are therefore called long-period comets. There are about a trillion comets in the Oort Cloud. The Oort Cloud itself is at the edge of the solar system, almost a quarter of the way from the Sun to the next star, Proxima Centauri.

Try these too...

The Sun (10–11), The Planets (12–13), Humans in Space (24–25), Earth's Atmosphere (26–27), Scientific Revolution (150–151), Forces and Motion (190–191)

Humans in Space

Ever since ancient times, humans have wanted to know more about the skies above them. They invented stories to explain the presence of the stars, the Moon and the Sun. Today, advanced technology helps us to travel into space and expand our knowledge about the world beyond our planet.

▲ **First woman in space**
Valentina Tereshkova was the first woman in space, aboard Vostok 6 on 16 June 1963.

Quick Q's:

1. What was the first living being to orbit Earth?

The first creature to orbit the Earth was a dog named Laika, aboard the Russian spacecraft Sputnik 2 on 3 November 1957.

2. Who was the first person in space?

On 12 April 1961, Russian cosmonaut Yuri Gagarin was the first person to travel in space, aboard the spacecraft Vostok 1. Gagarin orbited the Earth once on this historic flight, which lasted 1 hour and 48 minutes.

3. Which was the first ever space station?

Salyut 1 was the first space station. It was launched on 19 April 1971.

Q **How do space shuttles fly into space?**

A A space shuttle consists of two rocket boosters, three engines, an external fuel tank and two smaller fuel tanks. It also has an orbiter, which puts the shuttle into orbit. The rockets are used to propel the shuttle into space. When the shuttle is about 45 kilometres (28 miles) high, the rockets fall off into the ocean and the three main engines of the shuttle take over. Just before the shuttle goes into orbit, its engines are shut down and the external fuel tank is discarded.

Q **Why can't I fly into space in an aeroplane?**

A All objects, even aeroplanes, are glued to the surface of the Earth by gravity. If you wanted to escape this unseen force, you would have to travel at a speed of at least 40,000 kilometres per hour (25,000 miles per hour). Only space shuttles are designed to achieve this speed. A mixture of liquid hydrogen fuel and liquid oxygen is burned under high pressure to help the shuttle's rockets reach this speed and push it out of the Earth's atmosphere into orbit.

▲ **Weightless games**
On board a spacecraft, astronauts dance in zero gravity, as one colleague holds down a keyboard to play it.

Q **Is there no gravity in space?**

A All objects in space exert some gravitational force on each other. However, the gravitational force exerted by some objects, like the Moon, is much less than that of the Earth. When humans are in space they float around in the air, because there is not enough gravity to keep their feet on the ground.

▼ **Take off**
These three images show the space shuttle at its base (left), at the moment of take off (centre) and on its way to space (right).

Q Could I see the Sun rise and set from space?

A Astronauts aboard a space shuttle orbiting the Earth actually see 16 sunrises and sunsets every day! This is because once in orbit, a space shuttle goes around the Earth at a speed of more than 28,000 kilometres per hour (17,400 miles per hour) and takes only 90 minutes to complete one orbit.

Q Is it possible to live in space?

A Today astronauts spend a great deal of time in space stations. A space station is a floating space base. It is like a spaceship designed so that astronauts can live in outer space for weeks, months or even years at a time. Unlike a spacecraft, a space station cannot take off or land on planets. Other vehicles are used to transport people and materials to and from the station. Space stations are used for studying the effect of long-term space flights on the human body as well as for space research.

Q Is sending humans into space the only way to learn more about it?

A Apart from sending astronauts into space, we also use satellites, probes and telescopes to study space. Like moons, man-made satellites revolve around planets and help us learn more about them. A probe is an unmanned spacecraft sent into space to study objects other than the Earth. We have even put huge telescopes into orbit. The Hubble Space Telescope, sent into orbit in 1990, is the best-known among these. It is better to have a telescope in space than on Earth, because then there is no atmosphere to distort the image received by the telescope. However, the biggest telescopes are too big to be sent to space.

▲ **Many sunrises and sunsets**
When astronauts are on board a spacecraft and orbiting the Earth, they are moving much faster than the Earth, so they can see the Sun rise and set many times in a day. The normal human biological cycle can be upset by this, so astronauts are given special medicines to help them sleep.

Try these too...

The Planets (12–13),
The Red Planet (16),
The Moon (20–21)

Looking back in time

The Hubble Space Telescope works like a time machine that can travel into the past. It took pictures of the universe when it was barely a billion years old – the universe is at least five billion years old now, though some scientists put its age as high as 14 billion years. The Hubble Space Telescope can look into the past because it takes billions of years for light from the far ends of the universe to reach the telescope. When the light reaches it an image is captured, and we can see what happened in that particular part of the universe long ago.

Earth's Atmosphere

The protective blanket of air that covers the Earth is called the atmosphere. The Earth's atmosphere not only prevents too much heat from entering the planet, but also protects us from asteroids and meteors. The Earth's gravity helps hold the atmosphere in place.

Quick Q's:

1. What is a barometer?

A barometer is used to measure the pressure in the atmosphere. When the pressure is high, the weather will be fine, sunny and still. When it is low, the weather will be stormy. When the pressure increases the liquid in the barometer is squeezed and when the pressure decreases it is released. This change is recorded.

2. What is the exosphere?

The exosphere is the final layer of the Earth's atmosphere. It extends way into outer space. The air in the exosphere is very thin, but the temperature is very high, because the Sun's rays shine directly on it.

3. Why is the ozone layer important?

The ozone layer is important because it stops harmful ultraviolet rays from the Sun from reaching the Earth. If the rays are allowed through the atmosphere, they can cause severe health problems like skin cancer. Chemicals called CFCs have made a hole in the ozone layer above the North and South Poles.

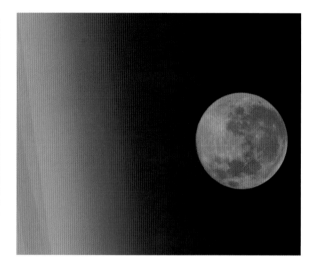

Q How many layers does the Earth's atmosphere have?

A The Earth's atmosphere is composed of several layers. These include the troposphere and the stratosphere. Each layer is divided according to the temperature and density of air in that layer.

Q What are the gases that make up the Earth's atmosphere?

A The Earth's atmosphere is composed of many gases. Nitrogen is the main gas found in the atmosphere. It accounts for about 78 per cent and oxygen makes up 21 per cent. The remaining one per cent is a combination of carbon dioxide and water vapour. There are also very small amounts of trace gases like neon and helium that go to make up the Earth's atmosphere.

◀ **Long way out**
The outer layers of the atmosphere extend far into space.

Q What is the significance of the troposphere in the weather pattern?

A The troposphere is the layer closest to the Earth's surface, and it is here that weather is created. Air in the troposphere rises and falls, helping to form clouds, rain and snow. This layer stretches about 8–14.5 kilometres (5–9 miles) above sea level.

▼ **A warm blanket**
The Earth is protected by layers of gases. SOHO sends information about these layers back to Earth.

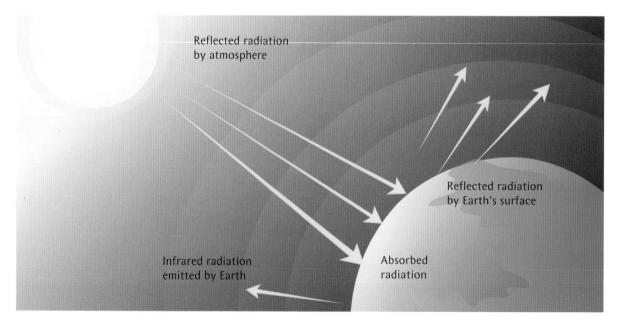

Reflected radiation by atmosphere

Reflected radiation by Earth's surface

Infrared radiation emitted by Earth

Absorbed radiation

▲ Dangerous additions
The pollution of the atmosphere by factories and vehicles is creating a dangerous hole in the protective ozone layer above the Earth and increasing the Earth's temperature. It also makes people fall ill more often.

Q **How does the stratosphere help us?**

A The stratosphere is the layer just above the troposphere. It extends upwards from the troposphere to about 50 kilometres (31 miles) above the Earth's surface. Compared to the troposphere which is full of moisture, the stratosphere is dry. The stratosphere contains the ozone layer. Ozone absorbs harmful ultraviolet rays from the sun.

Q **Is the temperature the same in the different layers of the atmosphere?**

A The temperature in the troposphere is between -52 and 17 °C (-62 to 62 °F). The temperature in the stratosphere is about -3 °C (26 °F). The next layer up, called the mesosphere, is very cold. The temperature here is as low as -93 °C (-135 °F). In the outer layers of the atmosphere the temperature starts to rise again, because there is more heat from the Sun. Temperatures in the outer layer can be as high as 1,727 °C (3,140 °F).

When the Earth gets hotter

The atmosphere protects us from the Sun's heat by reflecting a lot of it back into space. However, some gases in the atmosphere trap some of this heat, keeping the Earth warm even at night. This process is called the greenhouse effect and the gases that cause it are known as greenhouse gases. These gases include water vapour, carbon dioxide, and CFCs. Humans are adding carbon dioxide and CFCs to the atmosphere all the time. Too much heat is being trapped, and the Earth is getting warmer. Global warming is leading to the melting of glaciers and polar ice caps and an alarming rise in sea levels. It will change the Earth as we know it.

South Pole

Expanding hole

Try these too...

Seasons and Climate (28-29), Origin of Life (88-89), The Poles – The Arctic and Antarctica (122-123), Light (180-181), Communication and Satellites (192-193)

◄ A hole above our heads
For over 20 years, scientists have noticed an expanding hole (seen here in pink over the South Pole) in the ozone layer above each of the poles. This is due to the increasing use of chemicals that go into our refrigerators and aerosol cans. The hole means we have less protection from the ultraviolet rays of the Sun. These harmful rays can cause skin cancer.

Seasons and Climate

The Earth not only orbits the Sun, but also rotates on its own axis as it does so. The Earth's axis is in fact tilted – meaning that neither of the Earth's poles faces the Sun directly. This tilted axis is responsible for weather and different climates.

Quick Q's:

1. What causes day and night?

The Earth turning on its axis is responsible for day and night. At any time, half the Earth faces the Sun, where it is day, and half faces away, where it is night.

2. Does the Sun really rise in the east?

The Earth spins in an eastward direction. This makes the Sun appear as if it is rising in the east and setting in the west.

3. Why are days longer in summer and shorter in winter?

The angle at which sunlight falls on a particular area determines the length of day and night in that region. During summer the Sun stays above the horizon longer, making the days longer.

4. What is the Coriolis effect?

The wind moves to the right in the northern hemisphere and to the left in the southern hemisphere. This is called the Coriolis effect. It is caused by the Earth's rotation. It is mainly responsible for thunderstorms and hurricanes.

Q How is weather different from climate?

A Sunlight falls at varying angles onto the Earth's surface, heating up each of its regions differently. The difference in temperature eventually leads to different types of weather. A climate is when particular weather conditions prevail in a place for an extended period of time. So we can talk about the weather tomorrow or this month, but when we talk of climate we are talking of much longer time periods – decades or even centuries.

Q What is a season?

A Each season is a period within a year defined by distinct weather. The tilt in the Earth's axis is responsible for seasons. In temperate and polar regions four seasons are recognized – spring, summer, autumn and winter. Some tropical and subtropical regions have a rainy season (sometimes called a monsoon season) and a dry season, while others have hot, rainy and cool seasons.

Q What are the factors that influence weather on the Earth?

A Temperature, rainfall, wind, cloud and atmospheric pressure are the main factors that influence weather patterns across the world. Wind is caused by the unequal heating of the Earth's surface. When the air above a certain region becomes warm and light, it rises and the heavier cool air sweeps across from another area to take its place. This movement of air is called wind. Atmospheric pressure also affects the movement of wind, which always flows from a region of high pressure to that of low pressure. The difference in pressure between the two areas determines the speed with which the wind blows. If there is a small difference, we feel a breeze. If the difference is large, it leads to a storm. If the wind is flowing over a large water body such as a sea, it can pick up moisture and carry clouds and rain with it. Low pressure usually means stormy weather and rain, while high pressure usually means lots of sun and not much wind. There are other factors, such as the ocean currents created by the Earth's rotation, which also influence weather.

▼ The blowing wind
The wind always blows from an area of high pressure to an area of low pressure.

Q How are clouds formed?

A The Sun's heat causes water in the oceans, rivers and lakes to evaporate and form water vapour. The warm water vapour rises upwards, and as it rises, it cools down. As a result, the water vapour in the air condenses to form clouds containing tiny droplets of water. These droplets grow larger in size and finally fall down as rain. Sometimes, the temperature is so low that these droplets freeze into ice crystals and fall down as snow.

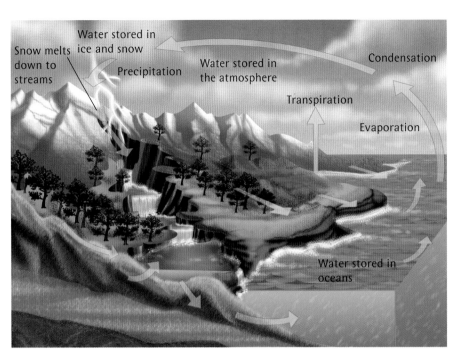

▸ **The water cycle**
All the water in the Earth's atmosphere, both on its surface and underground, is a part of the water cycle. The water is recycled again and again.

▾ **Cold places**
The closer you are to the North or South Pole, the colder it is. Some animals have adapted so they can survive in the freezing temperatures.

Q Which is the place on the Earth that has the coldest climate?

A The climate of Antarctica is the coldest on Earth. Nearly all of Antarctica is covered with an ice sheet about 2.5 kilometres thick. The lowest temperature recorded on this continent is -89.6 °C (-128.56 °F) at Vostok research station at the centre of the East Antarctic Ice Sheet.

Solstices and equinoxes

In the northern hemisphere the longest day falls during the summer, on 21 June, when the northern half of the Earth is tipped towards the Sun. This is known as the summer solstice. In the extreme north the Sun does not set at all during this period. During the winter solstice (22 December), the northern part of the Earth is tipped away from the Sun, resulting in the longest night of the year. On 23 September and 21 March the Earth is positioned in such a way that the length of day and night is equal (12 hours each). These days are known as the autumnal and spring equinoxes respectively.

Try these too...

Earth's Atmosphere (26–27), Plant Life (96–97), South America (112–113), Australia and Oceania (114–115), Africa (118–119), Asia (120–121), The Poles – The Arctic and Antarctica (122–123), Scientific Revolution (150–151)

Mountains, Valleys and Caves

Mountains are formed when two of the continental plates that make up the Earth's crust collide. The force caused by the collision pushes both plates (also called tectonic plates) upwards, creating a mountain. Valleys and caves are also natural features created by erosion and the movement of the Earth's crust.

▲ **Climbing mountains**
Scientists climb mountains to study them.

Quick Q's:

1. Which is the highest mountain peak in the world?

At a height of about 8,848 metres (29,028 feet) above sea level, Mount Everest is the highest peak in the world. It is a part of the Himalayan mountain range that was formed about 10–15 million years ago.

2. How big is the Grand Canyon?

The Grand Canyon is about 446 kilometres (277 miles) long and roughly 1.6 kilometres (1 mile) deep. It is made up of several layers of rock, each one older than the one above it.

3. How are glacial valleys formed?

When glaciers slowly flow downhill, they collect many pieces of rock on the way. These pieces scrape against the valley floor, digging deeper into it, until a U-shaped valley is formed.

Q Can we live on mountains?

A It is not easy to live on high mountains. The weather is extremely cold and not suitable for farming. At very high altitudes, oxygen levels are so low that it becomes difficult to breathe without an oxygen tank and mask.

Q How are mountains different from plateaus?

A Like a mountain, a plateau is higher than its surrounding area. However, plateaus have a flat top, while mountains have peaks. Like mountains, plateaus are formed when two continental plates collide, but erosion due to wind and water flattens the top. Plateaus are not as tall as mountains. In fact, some plateaus, such as the Tibetan Plateau, lie between two mountain ranges.

Q How is a valley formed?

A A valley is a low-lying area of land that is usually found at the foot of mountains or hills. The most common way valleys are formed is by the erosion of land from running water. River valleys are formed by the action of the river. As a river flows downhill, it cuts through the land like a knife. Over thousands of years the river erodes the land to form a valley, usually in the shape of a V. In contrast, valleys formed by glaciers are often U-shaped, because they are formed by rocks carried in the glacier that erode the soil.

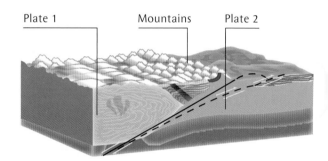

Plate 1   Mountains   Plate 2

▲ **Forming a mountain**
Mountains are formed when two of the Earth's tectonic plates collide. The crust is forced up between the two plates, giving birth to the mountain range.

◄ **U-shaped valley**
Glaciers carry stones that scour out the soil, forming U-shaped valleys. Rivers, in contrast, usually form V-shaped valleys.

Q What is a canyon?

A A deep valley with cliffs on both sides is called a canyon. Sometimes a large river may run through a canyon. The Grand Canyon in Arizona, USA is the world's largest canyon. It was formed by the Colorado River. Millions of years ago, this region was covered by sea. Slowly, a part of the sea floor was pushed up to form a plateau. Over the years, rainwater collected to form a river. This river cut into the rocks on the plateau to form the canyon.

Caves of lava

When volcanoes erupt, lava flows down the side of the volcano. The surface of the lava cools and becomes solid, while hot lava continues to flow underneath it. Once the eruption is over, there is a hollow tube, or cave, left behind underneath the hard crust of lava.

Q. What are caves?

A. Caves are huge holes under the ground, in cliffs or under the sea. Caves can be formed in many ways. Most rock caves, especially limestone caves, are formed by rainwater that seeps into tiny cracks in the rocks. The rainwater contains minerals and chemicals that slowly causes the rock to dissolve, leaving behind a large hole. This process may take several thousand, or even a few million years.

Q. How are sea caves formed?

A. Sea caves are formed by waves that wear away the rocks at the base of a cliff. These rocks are usually very weak and have tiny cracks in them. The continuous pounding of the waves causes the tiny cracks to widen and soon the rocks begin to crumble and form small hollows. These hollows keep expanding as sand, gravel and rocks brought by the waves erode their inner walls. Some sea caves are submerged during high tide and can only be seen when the water goes down at low tide.

▲ **Sea cave**
Sea caves are most common in areas where the rocks on the coast are soft.

Try these too...

Other Landforms (32–33), Volcanoes (36–37), Earthquakes and Tsunamis (38–39), South America (112–113), Australia and Oceania (114–115), Africa (118–119), Asia (120–121)

Q. What is a rift valley?

A. A rift valley is created when two tectonic plates pull away from each other, leaving a low space in the middle. The Great Rift Valley is the best known rift valley in the world. It covers a distance of over 6,000 kilometres (3,700 miles), stretching from northern Syria in West Asia to central Mozambique in East Africa. It began to form about 35 million years ago, when the African and Arabian tectonic plates began to pull apart. Even today it is still growing, as East Africa slowly separates from the rest of Africa.

▼ **Rift in the Earth**
When two of the Earth's plates move away from each other, the soil covering them falls down and forms a rift valley. The rift valleys in East Africa now form a series of lakes.

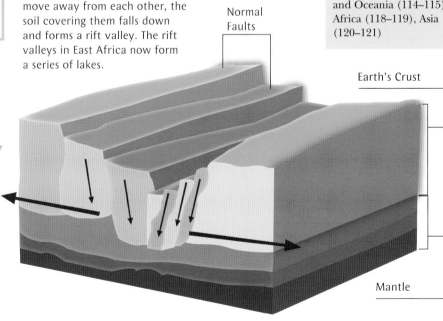

Normal Faults

Earth's Crust

Mantle

Other Landforms

Rivers, lakes and streams are natural bodies of water that are found across the world. When it rains or when snow on mountains melts, the water flows down the slopes, forming streams. Several streams join together to form a river. Small rivers drain into larger rivers. The water in rivers keeps flowing until it reaches the sea, though a few rivers hit very dry desert land and dry up.

Quick Q's:

1. Which is the largest freshwater lake in the world?

Lake Superior, one of the Great Lakes of North America, is the largest freshwater lake in the world. This lake is over 560 kilometres (350 miles) long and about 257 kilometres (160 miles) wide.

2. What is the Sahara known for?

The Sahara is the largest hot desert in the world. Located in Africa, it spreads across Mauritania, Morocco, Mali, Algeria, Tunisia, Niger, Libya, Chad, Egypt, Sudan and Eritrea.

3. Which is the longest river?

The Nile is the longest river on Earth. It flows for 6,695 kilometres (4,184 miles).

4. Why is Lake Baikal special?

Lake Baikal in southern Siberia is the deepest lake in the world, with a maximum depth of 1,637 metres (5,371 feet). It has been around for almost 30 million years.

▲ **Largest freshwater lake**
Lake Superior in North America is the largest freshwater lake in the world by area and the third largest by volume.

Q How are lakes formed?

A Sometimes, rainwater collects in big hollows in the ground to form lakes. These hollows can be formed by the movement of the plates that make up the Earth's crust, or by moving glaciers. Lakes are also formed by landslides that leave huge depressions in the ground. Most lakes and rivers contain freshwater. In places containing a large amount of salt, lake water can be salty.

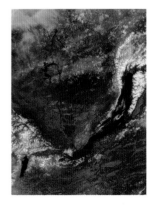

◀ **View from space**
This photograph, taken from an artificial satellite, shows Lake Baikal in southern Siberia. The size of the lake has been reduced in recent years, as more and more of its water is taken away for irrigation. It is considered to be one of the most serious problems in the region.

Q What are waterfalls?

A Sometimes the surface over which a river flows drops suddenly. Then the water flows over to form a waterfall. There are different kinds of waterfalls. A cascade waterfall flows down a series of natural rock steps. There are no steps in a free-falling waterfall. In a fan waterfall, the water spreads out as it falls down. Angel Falls in Venezuela is the highest free-falling waterfall in the world. The water falls 807 metres (2,648 feet) without any interruption. Often, the sunlight falling over a waterfall creates a rainbow.

Q Do rivers flood?

A Yes, they do. Rivers often overflow their banks and flood the land around them. This can happen when there has been a lot of rain or a lot of snow has melted in the mountain where the river starts its journey. Floods are often very destructive. They can damage crops and houses and kill people. But in the long run they can also do some good. They bring fresh soil down the river and spread it on the flooded land. Egyptian farmers have been dependent on the annual flooding of the Nile for thousands of years. The Amazon and the Ganges rivers regularly bring fertile soil to the agricultural areas downstream.

▼ **Longest river**
The ancient civilization of Egypt started along the banks of the Nile.

Try these too...

North America
(110–111), South
America (112–113),
Australia and Oceania
(114–115), Europe
(116–117)

◀ **Largest desert**
The Sahara is the world's
largest hot desert. It
spreads right across
northern Africa from
the Atlantic Ocean in
the west to the Red Sea
in the east. Sand and
rock cover most of the
dry Sahara, but there are
oases where people have
lived for centuries.

What is a desert?

A desert is a dry region with very little
rainfall. During the day, temperatures can rise
above 50 °C (122 °F). However, nights in a
desert can be extremely cold. Most deserts
are covered with sand and rocks. Animals and
plants that live in this habitat are specially
adapted to life with little water and extreme
changes in temperature.

What are montane deserts?

Some deserts, located at very high
altitudes, are known as montane deserts. They
are common in the Himalayas. Some, like the
Tibetan Plateau, are relatively flat. Very few
animals can survive the extreme cold and
dryness, but the yak lives in Tibet.

What is an oasis?

For most part deserts are dry and have
no water bodies. However, small springs with
trees and plants growing around them can
be found in certain places. These isolated
regions are called oases. An oasis is vital for
all forms of life in the desert.

Cold desert

**Most deserts are hot during the day, but some deserts
are in the coldest parts of the Earth. Some cold deserts are
covered in ice throughout the year, allowing very few plants to
grow. Cold deserts are also not very suitable for animals. Few
species can survive such extreme cold for long periods
of time. Antarctica is the largest cold desert in the world.
Patagonia in the southernmost part of South America and
Gobi in Mongolia are also cold deserts.**

Oceans

Oceans occupy about 70 per cent of the Earth's surface. There are five oceans in the world. They are the Atlantic, Pacific, Indian, Arctic and Antarctic oceans. The surface under the oceans is called the ocean floor. Like land, the ocean floor also has natural features like plains, valleys and mountains.

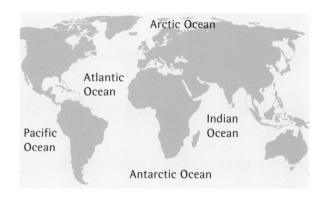

▲ Oceans of the world
The five oceans of the world cover over 70 per cent of the surface of the Earth.

Q Which ocean is also known as the Southern Ocean?

A The Antarctic Ocean is also called the Southern Ocean. Until recently, the Antarctic Ocean was considered to be a part of the other main oceans, as it was actually formed from parts of the Pacific, Atlantic and Indian oceans. In the year 2000, however, it was officially named the 'Southern Ocean'.

Q What is the ocean floor like?

A The ocean floor is far from flat. The edges of islands and continents gently slope into the surrounding water to form an area called a continental shelf that is higher than rest of the ocean floor. A continental shelf usually extends about 75 kilometres (47 miles) out to sea but some, like the Siberian shelf in the Arctic Ocean, can extend up to 1,500 kilometres (932 miles). The continental shelf contains large deposits of petroleum, natural gas and minerals. It also receives the most sunlight, so marine life thrives here. The point where the continental shelf starts to plunge steeply towards the deep ocean floor is called the continental slope. It is here that the deep canyons of the ocean are found.

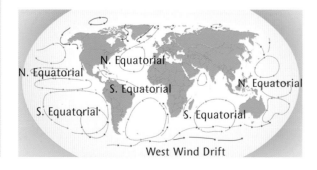

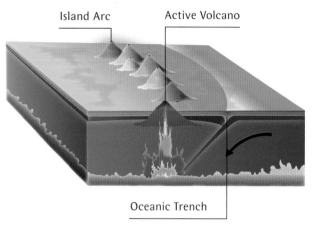

▲ Not a flat floor
The ocean floor has mountains and valleys. Some of the mountains are tall enough to rise above the surface and form islands.

Q What causes the formation of mountains and valleys on the ocean floor?

A Like the rest of the Earth, the ocean floor is divided into tectonic plates. The movement of these plates is responsible for features like ridges, trenches, and valleys. Ridges are formed when two plates drift apart. Boiling rock from inside the Earth, called magma, oozes out through the cracks between the plates and cools to form a ridge. Trenches are formed when a heavier plate sinks down under a lighter one.

◄ Ocean currents
The water in the oceans and seas is always in motion, due to the rotation of the Earth, the gravitational pull of the Sun and Moon, and the difference in temperature and salt content of the water. These movements form strong currents in the oceans, both at the surface and deep down.

Q What is a mid-ocean ridge?

A The ridges on the ocean floor are connected to form a single chain called a mid-ocean ridge. The mid-ocean ridge is over 80,000 kilometres (50,000 miles) long and is the longest mountain chain on Earth. On average, these mountains lie about 2,500 metres (8,200 feet) below the ocean surface, with their peaks sometimes breaking above.

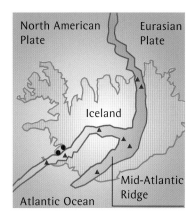

◀ Mountains down there
The mid-ocean ridge exists on the floor of all the oceans in the world. The diagram shows a part of the mid-Atlantic ridge, which extends below Iceland. Many volcanoes lie along the ridge.

North American Plate
Eurasian Plate
Iceland
Mid-Atlantic Ridge
Atlantic Ocean

Q How are volcanic islands formed?

A Volcanoes under the sea are responsible for the formation of volcanic islands. As magma keeps oozing out of a volcano, it can collect, causing the volcano to grow and rise above the ocean surface as an island.

Q What is special about the Hawaiian group of islands?

A Volcanic activity does not always take place near plate boundaries. There are some places deep inside the Earth that are much hotter than others. As a result, there is constant volcanic activity above these spots, known as hot spots. This activity leads to the formation of underwater volcanoes. The constant movement of tectonic plates eventually shifts the volcano away from the hot spot. Soon, another volcano is created in the area near the hot spot. This often leads to the formation of a chain of islands, such as the Hawaiian Islands.

Q How are waves different from tides?

A Waves are caused by wind, while tides are the regular rise and fall of the ocean's surface caused by the gravitational pull of the Sun and the Moon on the water that is in the ocean. Waves are formed when winds blow over the surface of the ocean. Stronger winds create larger waves. The water in a wave normally moves in circles. As a wave approaches the land it is slowed down by the rising slope of the seabed. But it is the bottom portion of the wave that is slowed down. The top part of the wave keeps moving and crashes on to the shore as a breaker.

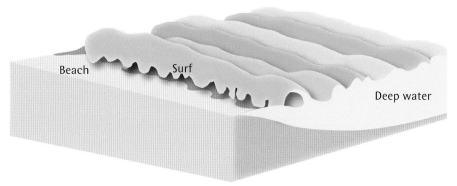

Beach   Surf   Deep water

Try these too...

Volcanoes (36–37), Earthquakes and Tsunamis (38–39), Hurricanes and Tornadoes (40–41), Whales (56–57), Seabirds (60), Sharks and Rays (68–69), Life of a Fish (70–71), Electricity (186–187)

▼ The breaker
Breakers are higher when the seabed slopes down quickly from the shore. The beaches of Hawaii and Australia are famous for their high breakers.

Feeling the heat

The temperature of the water from an underwater hot spring can be as high as 400 °C (752 °F). However, this water is rich in minerals, helping some unusual creatures like giant tubeworms and eyeless shrimps survive in an environment where nothing else can live.

Volcanoes

A volcano is a mountain through which molten rock and gases erupt from the Earth's crust. Volcanoes are named after the Roman god of fire, Vulcan.

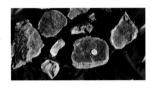

▲ **Volcanic rocks**
Hardened lava from volcanoes forms new rocks.

Quick Q's:

1. Which is the highest volcano on Earth?

Mauna Loa in Hawaii is the highest volcano on Earth. It rises about 4 kilometres above sea level; below that, it extends to 5 kilometres down before it reaches the seabed. Its massive weight has pushed the volcano down a further 8 kilometres below the seabed! So Mauna Loa is 17 kilometres (56,000 feet) from its base to its summit.

2. Which is the most active volcano?

Mount St Helens in Washington State of USA is the most active volcano. It last erupted in 1980.

3. What are geysers?

Geysers are jets of hot water that erupt from the Earth. When water trickles down into the hot molten rock under the Earth's crust, it is heated up. As the water becomes hotter, the pressure builds up, finally causing it to spurt out.

Q How are volcanoes formed?

A Volcanoes are formed by tectonic plates colliding with each other. The heavier plate is usually forced down below the lighter one, where part of it is melted by the heat of the crash. The melting plate forms magma or molten rock that collects below the surface of the Earth in magma chambers. As the amount of magma increases, the pressure inside the chamber rises. This creates a mountain, or volcano. The volcano has a cone, from which gases and lava may trickle out. When the pressure gets too high, the whole chamber explodes, ejecting the magma. This is a volcanic eruption.

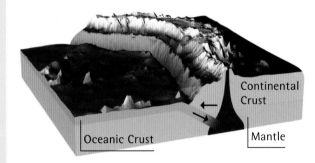

Continental Crust

Oceanic Crust

Mantle

▲ **Movements of the Earth**
The tectonic plates that cover the Earth can move in various ways, and are constantly rubbing against one another, sometimes violently.

Q What are the various things that happen during a volcanic eruption?

A Magma, or molten rock, erupts through the surface of Earth during an eruption. Magma that comes out is called lava. It can be thick and slow moving or thin and fast. Pieces of rocks and ash also erupt from the volcano. Pumice stone, a light rock full of air bubbles, is formed in an explosive volcanic eruption. These volcanic materials are called pyroclasts.

▲ **Hot water**
Old Faithful is a geyser of hot water in the Yellowstone National Park, USA. It erupts from the Earth every 90 minutes, on average.

Q Do volcanoes erupt regularly?

A Volcanoes may be active, intermittent, dormant or extinct depending on how often they erupt. Active volcanoes erupt often. Intermittent volcanoes erupt at regular intervals. Dormant volcanoes have been inactive for a long time. They are the most dangerous because they are merely 'sleeping' and can erupt without warning. Extinct volcanoes have not erupted for thousands of years. It is difficult to distinguish between dormant and extinct volcanoes because some volcanoes may remain quiet for a long time before suddenly becoming active again.

▼ **Active volcano**
Mount St Helens is the most active volcano in the world. It last erupted in 1980.

Q What are the different types of volcanoes on the Earth?

A Volcanoes are classified according to their shapes and the type of material they are composed of. A shield volcano is a gentle sloping volcano that has long-lasting, gentle eruptions. Most of the volcanoes in the Hawaiian islands are shield volcanoes. A strato volcano is a steep volcano shaped like a cone. When it erupts, it emits gases, ash, pumice and lava. These volcanic eruptions are accompanied by deadly mudflows, making strato volcanoes the most dangerous among the volcanoes on Earth. Famous strato volcanoes include Mount Vesuvius in Italy and Mount Fuji in Japan.

▲ The cone shape
The cone-shaped volcano, known as a strato volcano, may be the most famous, but is only one of many types of volcanoes.

Q Are there volcanoes under the sea?

A Volcanoes form under the sea in the same way as on land. When two oceanic plates collide, one may get pushed under the other. The heat generated by the crash causes one plate to melt and form magma. The hot magma rises and forms an underwater volcano, just as it does on land. The Vailulu volcano in Ta'u Island in the Pacific Ocean is an underwater volcano.

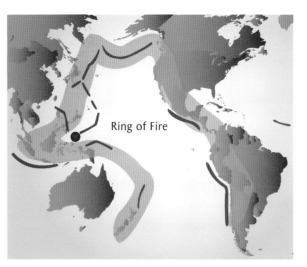

Ring of Fire

Q What is the 'ring of fire'?

A The area encircling the Pacific Ocean is called the ring of fire because most of the Earth's active volcanoes are located in a ring around it. The massive Pacific plate is expanding continuously at the edges of the ocean and hitting the other smaller plates next to it. The collisions cause frequent volcanic activity and earthquakes. The ring of fire stretches from New Zealand, along the eastern coastline of Asia and along the western coast of North and South America.

◄ Ring of fire
The ring of fire around the Pacific Ocean has been responsible for some of the most destructive volcanic eruptions and earthquakes in human history, including the 1906 San Francisco earthquake and the 1995 earthquake in Kobe, Japan. The biggest earthquake ever recorded was also in the ring of fire – the Great Chilean earthquake of 1960, 9.5 on the Richter scale.

Try these too...

The Hot Planet (14), The Red Planet (16), Oceans (34–35), Origin of Life (88–89), Dinosaurs (90), North America (110–111), South America (112–113), Australia and Oceania (114–115), Europe (116–117), Africa (118–119), Asia (120–121), The Poles – The Arctic and Antarctica (122–123), Ancient Americas (132)

An island disappears

One of the largest volcanic eruptions recorded in recent history occurred on the island of Krakatau in Indonesia in 1883. The eruption was so massive that most of the island disappeared into the sea (pale blue area between the two small islands). Over much of the world, the sky was dark with ash for days.

Earthquakes and Tsunamis

The Earth is made up of a boiling hot, liquid centre covered by a crust. This crust is broken into pieces called tectonic plates, which move around, sometimes colliding into each other. These collisions lead to earthquakes, some so small that they are hardly felt. But some earthquakes are so massive that they cause the ground to shake violently, destroying houses and killing people.

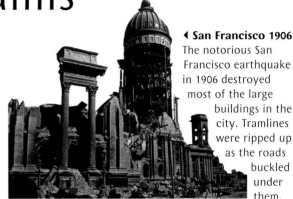

◀ **San Francisco 1906**
The notorious San Francisco earthquake in 1906 destroyed most of the large buildings in the city. Tramlines were ripped up as the roads buckled under them.

Quick Q's:

1. Which is the worst earthquake in history?

In 1556, an earthquake struck three provinces in China. About 830,000 people were killed in the disaster. It was the worst earthquake in history.

2. Can we predict earthquakes?

No, we cannot. The movements of the Earth are too complex for us to be able to predict earthquakes. But we do know the lines along which the Earth's plates meet, so we know the areas that are more likely to have earthquakes.

3. What is liquefaction?

Liquefaction is caused by the violent shaking of the ground during an earthquake. Moist soil or sand turns into slurry, like quicksand. This liquid can suck in entire buildings.

4. Is a tsunami the same as a tidal wave?

A tsunami is differeent from a tidal wave. A tidal wave is generated by high winds, but a tsunami is caused by underwater earthquakes, landslides or volcanic eruptions.

Q Do earthquakes occur everywhere?

A Earthquakes usually occur along a region called a fault, where broken rocks under the Earth's surface rub against each other and cause tremors. Faults are marked by cracks on the Earth's surface, caused by the movement of tectonic plates. Most faults are located near the edges of the plates, but small faults can be found far away from the boundaries.

Q How do faults produce earthquakes?

A Faults allow the rock fragments that form the Earth's crust to move about. Over a period of time, plate movement builds up pressure, causing rocks along a fault to bend or break with a jolt. This sudden movement releases energy that moves through the surface of the Earth in the form of waves. This is an earthquake. The energy moves out in a circle from the point where the movement occurs.

▶ **Fault in the Earth**
The San Andreas Fault in California, USA, is one of the few faults in the Earth's surface that can actually be seen by any observer on the ground. Most of the other faults are covered by soil or water. These faults mark the lines on the Earth's surface where two tectonic plates of the Earth meet. As a result, areas around these faults are the ones most prone to volcanic activity and earthquakes.

Q Where is an earthquake most dangerous?

A The point inside the Earth where the rocks first begin to break is the focus of the earthquake. The point on the Earth's surface that lies directly above the focus is called the 'epicentre'. This is where the earthquake is strongest. In a major earthquake, the maximum damage takes place at the epicentre, and there is less damage as you get further away from it. The epicentre is directly above the hypocentre, the actual location of the energy released inside the Earth. Seismic waves ripple out from the hypocentre. After an earthquake, scientists can find the centre by looking at the seismic wave data from three separate locations. The extent of the damage caused by an earthquake may also depend on the nature of the soil.

Q Do earthquakes occur only on land?

A Earthquakes also occur under the ocean. Sometimes, massive earthquakes that start on the ocean floor can create giant, destructive waves called tsunamis. These waves move at great speeds (up to about 800 kilometres or 500 miles per hour) and can travel thousands of kilometres across the ocean. In deep water, the waves are not very high. They gain strength and height as they approach the shore. Tsunamis can be about 30 metres (98 feet) high. These huge waves break on to the shore with a great deal of force, bringing down trees and large buildings.

When disaster strikes

On 26 December 2004, a tsunami spread across the Indian Ocean, killing over 250,000 people. The tsunami was caused by an underwater earthquake that occurred near the island of Sumatra, Indonesia. The tsunami hit the coasts of about 15 countries. Its effect was felt even in the southern tip of Africa, about 8,500 kilometres (5,300 miles) away from the epicentre of the earthquake!

Before

After

Q Do earthquakes cause destruction every time they occur?

A Some earthquakes are extremely destructive. A strong quake can topple buildings and bridges, trapping people underneath them. If gas pipes and electrical wires break, they can start fires that rage for several days. Earthquakes can also cause landslides and avalanches. The violent shaking of the Earth sometimes loosens chunks of snow or mud that slide down the slopes of mountains and hills, burying houses and people under them.

Q Can an earthquake be measured?

A Earthquakes are measured using the Richter scale. It was developed in 1935 by Charles Richter and Beno Gutenberg at the California Institute of Technology. This scale uses numbers from 1 to 10 to measure the intensity of an earthquake. Each increase of one point on the scale means a ten-fold increase in the strength of the earthquake. So a level 5.0 earthquake is ten times stronger than a level 4.0 earthquake. The Richter scale works by measuring vibrations around the epicentre of an earthquake.

▲ **Earthquake effect**
An earthquake can lead to a deadly avalanche or a landslide that can cause more damage than the original earthquake.

▲ **Old instrument**
The ancient Chinese invented an instrument that reacted to tremors in the Earth – a ball dropped from the mouth of the dragon into the mouth of a frog, warning people about a possible earthquake.

Try these too...

Hurricanes and Tornadoes

Sometimes the weather becomes wild. Blizzards, thunderstorms, hurricanes and heatwaves are some examples of extreme weather conditions. Such severe weather often causes a great deal of damage to both life and property. Hurricanes and tornadoes especially are very destructive.

Quick Q's:

1. Can hurricane winds be measured?

Hurricanes are divided into five categories depending on their wind speeds. Category 5 hurricanes are the worst, causing maximum damage. Winds of a category 5 hurricane can reach speeds of about 250 kilometres per hour (155 miles per hour). Category 1 hurricanes are much weaker, and only travel at 119–153 kilometres per hour (74–95 miles per hour).

2. What is a storm surge?

Sometimes the strong winds of a hurricane can cause the water level in the ocean to rise. Huge waves hit the coast along with the storm, causing severe flooding. This is called a storm surge.

3. What is the Fujita scale?

The Fujita scale is used to measure the intensity of a tornado. It ranks tornadoes by the damage caused to man-made structures.

4. How did tornadoes get their name?

The word tornado is from the Spanish *tomear*, meaning 'to turn'.

Q What is a hurricane?

A Hurricanes are large, violent storms that form over the ocean near the equator. These storms are accompanied by winds that travel at an average speed of about 119 kilometres per hour (74 miles per hour). Hurricanes usually occur between June and November.

▲ **Eye of the hurricane**
This satellite image clearly shows the eye of the hurricane, an area of calm in the middle of the storm.

Q How does a hurricane form?

A When the air above the sea is heated it rises, creating an area of low pressure. Cooler wind moves in to take place of the warm air. The Earth's rotation causes the rising hot air to twist and form a cylinder. As the warm air rises higher, it cools down and forms huge thunderclouds and finally becomes a hurricane. Meanwhile, the cooler air at the bottom also becomes warm, adding more energy to the storm.

Q What is the eye of a hurricane?

A The centre of a hurricane is called the eye. The eye is an area of clear skies, light winds and no rain. It is also the warmest part of the storm and is surrounded by a wall of heavy rain and strong winds. People faced with a hurricane usually experience the heavy rain and strong winds first, then there is a period of calm as the eye passes over the area, followed by more stormy weather.

▼ **Huge destroyer**
In 2005, Hurricane Katrina, seen here in a satellite image, destroyed large parts of the city of New Orleans in the USA.

Q · What is the worst hurricane on record?

A The hurricane that ripped through the Caribbean islands of Martinique, St. Eustatius and Barbados in October 1780 is the worst on record so far. It killed nearly 22,000 people. However, this hurricane does not have a name, because the practice of giving human names to major hurricanes started during World War II.

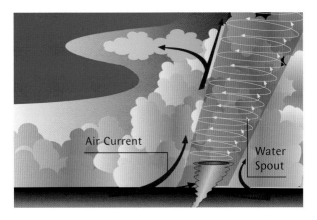

▲ **The making of a storm**
Warm air rises from the sea, taking water with it in the form of a funnel, and starting a storm.

Q · What is a tornado?

A A tornado is a black, funnel-shaped storm that is highly destructive. These storms usually form where cold polar winds mix with warm, moist tropical winds. They start as rotating thunderstorms called supercells. Gradually the spinning wind in the supercell forms the funnel of a tornado. The wind in the funnel spins so fast that it sucks objects into it like a vacuum cleaner.

Q · What is Tornado Alley?

A Tornado Alley is an area that extends across the Great Plains of the USA, from central Texas in the south to the border of Canada in the north. The conditions in this region are most suitable for the formation of severe tornadoes, which occur during spring and early summer.

Chasing the storm

Most of us would prefer to stay as far away as possible from all violent storms, especially hurricanes and tornadoes. Some people however, chase hurricanes and tornadoes. For these people, confronting a storm is exciting. Storm chasers use special equipment to locate and follow storms. They usually have a well-equipped vehicle fitted with the latest technology, including cameras, radios, scanners and first-aid kits. The videos, photographs and all other data collected by storm chasers have helped scientists understand hurricanes and tornadoes better.

Q · What is a waterspout?

A Tornadoes usually travel across land. However, occasionally, tornadoes pass over water. In these cases, the high-speed winds suck in water, creating tall columns of spinning water called waterspouts. These waterspouts are weaker than land tornadoes and occur in warm tropical oceans. However, they are still strong enough to cause huge damage to any boat or ship caught in them.

▲ **Waterspout**
When tornadoes pass over water, they suck the water up into tall spinning columns called waterspouts.

Try these too...

Seasons and Climate (28–29), Communication and Satellites (192–193), Water Transport (196–197)

Monkeys

Monkeys belong to the group of mammals called primates, which also includes apes and humans. All three species share certain characteristics, such as narrow noses and five fingers and toes. However, unlike apes and humans, many monkeys have tails. Monkeys from Asia and Africa have noses that point downwards, while monkeys from Central and South America have broad noses and nostrils that open sideways.

Quick Q's:

1. Why is the Japanese macaque also known as the snow monkey?

The Japanese macaque, commonly known as the snow monkey, is one of the few primate species that live in cold regions. They are found in the mountains of Honshu in Japan. When it is very cold, these monkeys move near hot springs to keep themselves warm.

2. What is grooming?

Monkeys and apes groom each other's fur using their hands. This helps not only to get rid of parasites and dirt but is also an important part of socializing.

3. Why are monkeys called social animals?

Most species of monkeys live in groups. The size of a group depends on how much food is available and if there are predators around.

4. Do howler monkeys howl?

Howler monkeys make a peculiar barking sound. They can be heard up to 3 kilometres (1.9 miles) away.

Q **What are the common characteristics of primates?**

A All primates have a large brain, and their eyes face forwards, allowing binocular vision. Most of them have thumbs on both hands and feet that can be used for grasping. Their highly developed brain helps them to remember things, and to understand others.

Q **How many primate species are there in the world?**

A There are more than 350 species of primates in the world, divided into two groups. Small to medium-sized primates, such as lemurs and lorises, have long whiskers and well-developed senses of smell and hearing. The rest of the primates, including humans, apes and other monkeys, are part of the 'humanlike' category. This group consists of about 175 species. Most of these primates have flat faces and a poor sense of smell.

▲ **Top of the forest**
Colobus monkeys are usually found at the top layer of branches in African rainforests.

Q **What does a monkey eat?**

A Most monkeys will eat whatever they come across, including birds' eggs, fruit and the sap from plants. Several species of monkey will even attack and eat other monkeys. Howler monkeys of South America and colobus monkeys of Africa eat the leaves of any type of tree. The digestive system of leaf-eating monkeys is similar to that of other herbivores, like deer and cows.

◀ **Big hug**
Snow monkeys are often found huddling near hot springs to keep warm.

◀ **Ringed tail**
Lemurs are easily identified by their ringed tails.

Q Why are spider monkeys so called?

A A spider monkey is a species of New World monkey (from the American continent) that has long, slender, spidery limbs. It displays great acrobatic skills, using its hands and strong tail to grip branches as it swings through the trees. Spider monkeys only travel on particular routes through trees, marking the branches with their own individual scent as they go.

Q What is a tarsier?

A Tarsiers are very different from other monkeys. They have enormous eyes, long feet and are active at night. Tarsiers eat insects, but also prey on small birds, lizards and snakes. They use their long back legs to leap on to prey. Holding the prey with their hands, they kill it with their sharp, pointed teeth.

▲ **Five hands?**
The spider monkey of central and South America has a tail whose tip is so well developed it can almost be considered a fifth hand. Each tip even has its own unique 'fingerprint'.

◀ **Night hunter**
Tarsiers have huge eyes that help them to find prey in the dark.

Try these too…

Apes (44-45), Venomous Snakes (76-77), Other Prehistoric Animals (94-95), South America (112-113), Africa (118-119), Ancient India and China (126-127)

Alarm calls

Monkeys use several methods of communication. A few species of monkey that live alone use scent to communicate. Urine, faeces or special scent glands are used to mark territory or to let other monkeys know they are ready to mate. Monkeys that live in groups communicate using signs and calls. Some species, like the African vervet monkeys, use different alarm calls for each of their main predators – eagles, leopards and snakes. The monkeys react differently to each call. When they hear the eagle alarm call, the monkeys hide among dense vegetation. At the sound of the leopard call they climb as high as possible.

Apes

Apes are primates with long arms, a broad chest, and no tail. Early apes evolved several million years ago, long before humans. Only six species of ape survive today. Gibbons, siamangs and orangutans live in Asia, while gorillas, chimpanzees and bonobos are African apes.

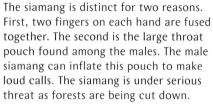

▼ In danger

The siamang is distinct for two reasons. First, two fingers on each hand are fused together. The second is the large throat pouch found among the males. The male siamang can inflate this pouch to make loud calls. The siamang is under serious threat as forests are being cut down.

Quick Q's:

1. Which species is known as the crying ape?

Chimpanzees are crying apes. They bark and produce loud calls to warn the rest of the group about approaching danger.

2. Is a siamang also an ape?

The siamang is a black-coloured gibbon found in Malaysia and Sumatra. The siamang is one of the three species that form the group of lesser apes. It is the largest of the lesser apes, growing to a height of about 1 metre (3 feet).

3. What are bonobos?

Bonobos are a species of chimpanzee, discovered in 1928 by American scientist Harold Coolidge. They are the closest relatives to humans. They walk on two feet longer than any other apes feet. Some bonobos in captivity have learnt to speak a human language. Unlike other apes, a bonobo society is controlled by a female. Today, bonobos are found only in the forests of central Congo in Africa. There are so few of them that they are in danger of becoming extinct.

Q **Which is the largest of all apes?**

A Gorillas are the largest apes. Adult males are about 1.8 metres (6 feet) tall and weigh up to 170 kilograms (375 pounds). They have huge heads, a bulging forehead and a crest with thick muscles on top of the head. Although they are portrayed as aggressive and dangerous killers, gorillas are in reality shy, peaceful vegetarians. They are extremely intelligent and can learn complex tasks. Each evening, gorillas make nests using leaves and twigs in which they curl up and sleep.

▶ Gentle giant

Gorillas do not attack anyone unless provoked.

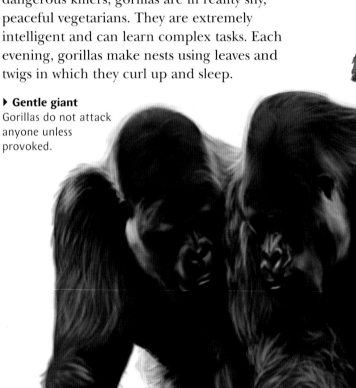

Q Where can you find orangutans?

A Orangutans are the largest Asian apes, found in the islands of Sumatra and Borneo. The word orangutan means 'man of the forest' in the Malay language. They have large, bulky bodies, thick necks and long arms. They move by swinging from one branch to another. But because they are so heavy, they frequently have to climb down and walk on their four limbs. Orangutans are omnivores, which means they eat both meat and plants. They are extremely intelligent and often use objects as tools, such as the big, broad leaves that they use as umbrellas. Unfortunately, despite being officially protected, they are in danger of extinction because of deforestation and hunting.

▶ **People of the forest**
Orangutans are so close to humans that they can imitate many of our actions.

Try these too...

Monkeys (42–43), Other Prehistoric Animals (94–95), Africa (118–119), Asia (120–121), Ancient India and China (126–127), Discovery of New Lands (144–145), The Industrial Revolution (148-149)

Q Why are gibbons known as lesser apes?

A Gibbons are smaller than the other apes. They live in pairs rather than large groups. They do not make nests and from a distance they look more like monkeys than apes. But their skulls and teeth are more like those of the great apes.

Q What is brachiation?

A Brachiation is a method by which gibbons and spider monkeys move about. In this type of movement, they swing through tree branches with their arms. They can swing distances of about 15 metres (50 feet) at speeds of 56 kilometres (35 miles) per hour.

▼ **Long hands**
Gibbons are lesser apes found in China, India and parts of Southeast Asia. These apes can swing across large distances from one branch to the other using their long arms. Gibbons can also leap across distances of up to 8 metres (27 feet).

Fatal bushmeat

Many species of apes are killed for their meat. The meat of these wild animals is known as bushmeat. In some parts of Africa, chimpanzees in particular are hunted for food,

though this is illegal in most countries. Apes can also be carriers of HIV, the virus that causes AIDS. Ape hunters often come into contact with the infected blood, and this is one of the ways that humans are suspected to have contracted AIDS.

Big cats

A big cat is a cat that can roar! This group includes the lion, tiger, jaguar and leopard. They have large eyes, sharp teeth, excellent hearing and powerful limbs with sharp claws. Most have long tails and coats that are either striped or spotted. Big cats are found in all continents except Australia and Antarctica.

Quick Q's:

1. What do cats use their tongues for?

A cat's tongue is rough and covered with sharp, hook-like projections called papillae. Cats use their tongues to clean the flesh from the bones of their prey and to groom themselves.

2. How does a jaguar kill its prey?

The jaguar uses its powerful jaws and sharp teeth to pierce the skull of its prey between the ears. Its strong teeth can even break open turtle shells.

3. Are white tigers albinos?

White tigers are not albinos. A true albino would not have stripes, but white tigers have prominent stripes. They are not a separate species, but differently-coloured members of the same species. Their colour is caused by a mutation in their genes, which rarely occurs naturally. In recent times, the first pair of white tigers was found in a forest in central India. Since then, most white tigers we know of have been bred in captivity and so can usually be seen only in zoos.

Q How are big cats different from other cats?

A Big cats are similar to our pet cats in many ways. However, only big cats can roar. This is because of a difference in the structure of a bone that is present in the mouth of all cats. This bone, called the hyoid bone, connects the tongue to the roof of the mouth. In small cats, the hyoid is hard, while in big cats the hyoid is flexible, helping them open their mouths really wide and roar aloud.

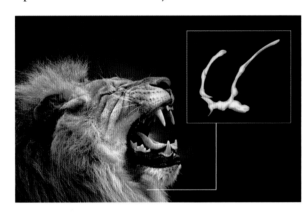

▲ **Roaring apparatus**
The flexible hyoid bone of the big cats allows them to roar.

▼ **Living in a pride**
Lions are the only big cats that live in prides. Each pride has one adult male with three or four lionesses and their cubs. Male cubs are thrown out of the pride as soon as they become semi-adults.

Q Is the cheetah a big cat?

A The cheetah is not actually a big cat as it cannot roar, but purrs like our domestic cat. However, it has many other characteristics of a big cat, and is sometimes regarded as the smallest member of the big cat family. It is the fastest of all land animals, and can run at a speed of up to 110 kilometres per hour (70 miles per hour) over a short distance.

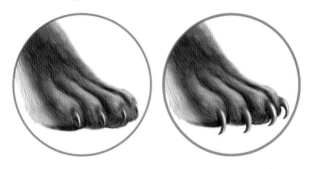

▲ **Hidden weapons**
Big cats usually draw their claws into the paw (left) and extend the claws (right) when about to jump on their prey.

Q What is special about the claws of a big cat?

A All big cats – except the cheetah – have retractable claws. These claws can be drawn into the paw when the cat is not using them. This prevents the cat from getting hurt while grooming. The cheetah has short claws. It uses them to get a good grip on the ground while chasing its prey at high speeds.

Q Why do the eyes of a big cat glow in the night?

A The eyes of a big cat – or any other cat, for that matter – have a mirror-like tissue in them that gather even the faintest light and focus it on an object, making it clearly visible to the cat. It is this mirror-like structure that causes the cat's eyes to glow in the dark.

Q Are black panthers also big cats?

A Black panthers are actually black leopards or jaguars. They are the result of a condition called melanism that is common among jaguars and leopards. This is when the black pigment called melanin in the root of the fur is produced in large quantities. It is this condition that gives black panthers their colour. A few leopards and jaguars have less melanin than average. This gives them a greyish colour, and they are often known as white leopards or white jaguars.

Q Are teeth important to big cats?

A Big cats rely on their teeth to kill prey. They have strong jaws, with three pairs of incisor teeth, one pair of canines, two or three pairs of premolars, and one pair of molars. Apart from jaguars, all the other big cats drive their large powerful canines into the neck of their prey, between the gaps in the backbone. The teeth cut through the spinal cord, often killing the prey instantly. The small but sharp incisor teeth located between the canines help the cat scrape meat off the bones. The molars help to crack the bones open when the cat is feeding. Jaguars usually attack their prey on top of the skull, piercing it in between the ears. They can do this because they have wider jaws than those of other big cats.

▶ **Black panthers**
Black panthers are actually leopards or jaguars with more than the usual amount of melanin.

Q How do big cats mark their territory?

A All big cats are highly territorial – each individual has a particular territory that includes hunting grounds, dens and water holes. Big cats do not like to share their territories, even with members of their own species. They warn other cats off by marking these territories, usually by spraying urine or scratching trees. Sometimes, big cats rub their cheeks against rocks, trees or any other object. Other cats usually leave the area once they smell or see the signs.

Try these too...

Other Prehistoric Animals (94–95), South America (112–113), Europe (116–117), Africa (118–119), Asia (120-121)

◀ **Solitary hunter**
Adult leopards usually live by themselves except during the mating season. But they require a smaller territory than a tiger or a pride of lions.

Mixing breeds

A 'liger' is born to a male lion and a female tiger. This hybrid big cat looks like a lion with stripes. Some ligers have manes, while all ligers love to swim – just like tigers. Ligers can grow to be giants. Some of them even reach a height of about 4 metres (12 feet) and weigh over 400 kilograms (900 pounds). 'Tigons', which are born to a male tiger and a lioness, do not grow as big.

Bears

Bears can be found in a wide range of habitats, including mountains and Arctic regions. There are eight species of bear – the spectacled bear, the sun bear, the giant panda, the Asiatic black bear, the American black bear, the brown bear, the sloth bear and the polar bear.

Quick Q's:

1. How do you know when a bear is angry?

When threatened or agitated, bears stand up on their hind legs. They probably do this to appear larger to their enemies. They also use their clawed paws to slash at an attacker.

2. How does the giant panda spend most of its day?

The giant panda bear eats about 18 kilograms (40 pounds) of bamboo leaves and stems or about 40 kilograms (85 pounds) of bamboo shoots each day. It spends up to 14 hours just eating.

3. What is special about the Kermode bear?

The Kermode bear is a type of American black bear. It inhabits the rainforests of British Columbia, Canada. The Kermode bear is the only black bear to have a white coat.

4. Which is the smallest bear in the world?

Sun bears are the smallest of all bear species. Even so, they grow up to 1.5 metres (5 feet) in length and weigh up to 66 kilograms (146 pounds).

Q Do the eight species of bear have any common features?

A All species are fairly similar, although there are slight differences in size and diet. Bears have stocky bodies, powerful limbs, thick fur and a short tail. They have elongated heads, rounded ears and long snouts. They have a keen sense of hearing and smell. All bears, except the polar bear, are omnivorous. Their varied diet includes roots, nuts, fruit, berries, honey, caterpillars and ants. Bear teeth are small, and are mainly used for defence or as tools. The molar teeth are broad and flat, suitable for shredding and grinding fruit, nuts and berries.

Q Do bears have claws like cats?

A Bears have four limbs with paws. Each paw has five long, sharp claws. Unlike cats, bears cannot retract their claws. They use them to climb trees, open termite nests and beehives, dig for roots, and catch prey. All bears have long, shaggy fur. The colour of fur varies from species to species.

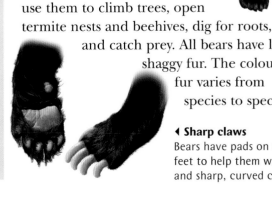

◀ Sharp claws
Bears have pads on their feet to help them walk and sharp, curved claws.

◀ Great swimmers
Polar bears are excellent swimmers and spend almost as much time in water as they do on land.

◀ Ferocious grizzly
The brown bear, known as the grizzly bear in North America, is a ferocious predator. When threatened or during a fight for a mate, grizzlies stand up on their hind legs and use their long-clawed forepaws to fight.

Q Which is the largest of all bear species?

A The polar bear is not only the largest of all bears, but also the largest carnivore on land. Found in the Arctic regions, polar bears can grow to a length of 2 metres (7 feet) and can weigh up to a massive 800 kilograms (1,760 pounds). They have creamy white fur that blends in with the ice. Polar bears are excellent swimmers and move quickly on land and in water. They prefer to eat meat, and their diet mainly consists of seals and young walruses. During the summer when ice floes (sheets of ice) melt and food is scarce, polar bears feed on berries and bird eggs.

Q Where can you find black bears?

A There are two kinds of black bear – Asiatic and American. The Asiatic black bear inhabits the temperate and subtropical forests of Asia, while the American black bear is native to North America. The Asiatic black bear is also known as the moon bear because of the white, crescent-shaped mark on its chest. Its coat is mostly black in colour, although bears with brown coats are not uncommon. The American black bear is the smallest of all North American bear species, but it can still grow up to 1.8 metres (6 feet) in length and weighs about 40–300 kilograms (90–660 pounds). Most of these bears have a glossy black coat, although some are honey-coloured.

▶ **Moon bear**
The Asiatic black bear is common in many parts of Asia, such as Siberia and Japan. In some places it has been domesticated and taught to do tricks, though this practice involves cruelty to the bear and is now illegal.

Q How do sloth bears eat?

A The sloth bear has a flexible white snout that is very useful for digging food out of the ground. The sloth bear uses its long claws to rip open the nests of ants and termites. It then uses its snout and hairless lips to form a kind of suction tube that sucks in its prey.

▶ **Good climber**
Bears climb well and can judge which branches will take their weight. They often climb high to reach a beehive that has their favourite food, honey. Bees cannot sting them through their thick fur.

Try these too...

North America (110–111), South America (112–113), Europe (116–117), Asia (120–121), The Poles – The Arctic and Antarctica (122–123)

Sleeping the winter away

Some bears, like brown bears, black bears and polar bears live in places that have very cold winters. Since food is scarce in the winter, these bears spend the time sleeping in warm, cosy dens. Pregnant bears usually give birth during the winter in these dens. Before they go into their winter sleep, bears fatten themselves up during the summer and autumn when food is readily available. This winter sleep is not the same as hibernation as the bear can easily wake up. Also, a bear's body temperature does not drop as drastically during the winter as that of hibernating animals.

Canines

The canine family includes dogs, wolves, foxes, coyotes, dingoes and jackals. Though dogs were probably the first animals to be domesticated by humans, wild canines can still be found in every part of the world. Wolves and wild dogs live in large packs, while the other canines are solitary or live in small groups.

▲ **Fierce hunters**
Wild African hunting dogs are feared by other animals because they do not give up the chase.

Quick Q's:

1. Which is the fastest canine in the world?

Greyhounds are the fastest canines in the world. They have been known to run at speeds of up to 70 kilometres per hour (44 miles per hour). African hunting dogs are also very fast and can maintain speeds of 50–60 kilometres per hour (31–37 miles per hour) for very long distances while chasing prey.

2. What is unique about fennecs?

Fennecs are the smallest canines. These tiny foxes are only 65 centimetres (2 feet) long from the top of their ears to the tips of their tails, and weigh less than 1.5 kilograms (3.3 pounds). These desert-dwellers have huge ears that help them to dispel excess heat from their body.

Q. What makes canines good hunters?

A. All canines have a keen sense of hearing and smell. As a result, they can locate prey a long way off. Wild canines are very determined hunters, willing to chase prey over long distances. They also have several sharp teeth used for killing, feeding and defence. Canines use their chisel-like incisors for cutting food and grooming. These are located in the front of the mouth. Next to them is a pair of dagger-shaped canine teeth used for fighting and hunting.

Q. Can canines run fast?

A. Canines can run extremely fast and have a lot of stamina. This ability is due to their long legs and ankle bones. Canines have a highly flexible backbone that can be arched as they run. Their feet are small, and all their toes have strong but blunt claws. Their small, light feet and limbs help them to run more efficiently than other animals with larger legs. Wolf packs and hunting dogs are known to chase their prey for hours. They finally overtake animals that may be faster than them over short distances.

Q. What is the structure of a wolf pack?

A. Wolf packs have a breeding male, called the alpha, which rules over the others in the pack. He asserts his authority by using dominant body posture, facial displays, growls, barks, scent marking and at times, even fighting. The alpha's mate, called beta, is the second in command.

Q. Do foxes live in groups like wolves?

A. Some species of fox, like the red fox, live in small groups, but foxes usually hunt alone. A male and female fox pair defends the territory in which they hunt and raise their young. Sometimes several female foxes, usually a mother and her daughters, live in a group with a single male. The younger adults in a red fox group act as helpers, assisting the breeding pair in defending their territory and caring for the young.

◀ **Desert fox**
Fennecs live in the hot Sahara desert. Their coats can repel sunlight in the day and conserve heat at night.

◀ Wolf pack
Wolf packs are closely knit and usually all members are related to one another, though distantly. The pack hunts and feeds together, though smaller family groups may sleep separately in dens that are close to one another.

Coyote legends

Coyotes are of very major cultural significance to Native Americans. Most Native American tribes have a character called Coyote in their legends. According to various stories, this character can be a trickster or a hero. The coyote also appears in creation myths of many tribes. In fact, the Navajo tribe regards the coyote as God's dog.

Q How do canines hunt larger animals?

A Canine packs hunt larger animals using a technique called relay hunting. In this method, one member of the pack chases the prey for a while, then another takes over. Each member of the pack takes a turn in chasing until the prey becomes exhausted. The canines then immediately surround the prey and move in for the kill, often attacking from behind and injuring their victim. In this way, canines are able to take on very large animals, such as bison.

Q Why do wolves howl?

A Howling is a popular method of communication among wolves. It helps pack members communicate with each other, even when moving through thick forests. Howling can be used to gather pack members at a specific location. It can also help a wolf lay claim to its territory and warn off rivals.

◀ Howling wolf
There are many myths surrounding the howling of wolves. Wolves were believed to howl at the full moon. However, this is because they are more likely to hunt on a bright night and they howl to bring the pack together.

Try these too...

North America (110–111), South America (112–113), Europe (116–117), Africa (118–119), Asia (120–121), Native Americans (133–135)

Elephants

Elephants are the world's largest land animals. They are divided into three different species – savannah, forest and Asian elephants. Savannah and forest elephants are together known as African elephants.

Quick Q's:

1. Do the members of a herd stick together?

The members of a herd feed, bathe and migrate together. They usually stay very close to the leader. They also protect one another from predators. The young, sick and old are especially well-defended by the healthier members. When faced with danger, the head of the herd leads the rest away. When the leader dies, the next oldest female takes over.

2. Do elephants eat a lot?

The elephant's digestive system is very weak. It can digest only 40 per cent of the food it eats. It has to make up by eating a great deal. An adult eats about 140–270 kilograms (300–600 pounds) of leaves and grass every day.

3. How big are the tusks of an African elephant?

An African elephant's tusks are between 1.8–2.4 metres (6–8 feet) in length and weigh about 20–45 kilograms (50–100 pounds). Those of an Asian male are only about 1.5 metres (5 feet) in length and weigh about 30 kilograms (70 pounds).

Q How are African elephants different from Asian elephants?

A African elephants are larger and have less hair. They have bigger, fan-shaped ears. Both male and female African elephants have tusks. In contrast, Asian elephants have lower-hanging ears and only the male members have tusks. The savannah elephant is light grey, while forest and Asian elephants have dark grey skin.

▶ **Big pet**
Asian elephants have been domesticated by people for centuries.

Q Are the elephant's tusks really teeth?

A The tusks of an elephant are simply elongated incisor teeth. A calf is born with a pair of incisors that are replaced within 6 to 12 months. The second set grows into tusks.

▶ **Tragic tusks**
Elephants have often been hunted for their precious ivory tusks.

Q How do elephants use their trunks?

A The elephant's trunk is a combination of its nose and upper lip. The elephant uses its long, flexible trunk to grasp objects, pluck leaves, break off branches and carry heavy objects like logs. While strong, the trunk is also very sensitive. Small, finger-like projections at the end help elephants to pick up small objects. The trunk is also used to suck in water for drinking or to spray water over the body for bathing. Elephants pick up dust with their trunks in the same way when they want to have a dust bath. When lying in water, the elephant sticks its trunk out to breathe. Elephants use the nostrils at the tip of the trunk to capture the scent in the air. The trunk is then placed in their mouth, where special organs identify the scent.

▼ **Moving in a herd**
A herd of African elephants moves towards a watering hole. Note how the young members of the herd are surrounded by older and stronger members for protection. Elephant herds are led by the oldest female.

Hoofed Animals

The nails of some mammals are large and hard enough for them to walk on. These nails are called hooves and such animals are called hoofed animals, or ungulates. This group includes pigs, hippopotamuses, camels, giraffes, goats and cattle.

▶ **Camel's cousin**
The llama is found in the Andes mountains.

Q How did the hippopotamus get its name?

A The word hippopotamus means river horse in Greek. The hippopotamus spends a large part of its day in shallow water and usually comes out only at night.

Q Do hippopotamuses sweat blood?

A Common hippos do not have sweat glands, but their pores secrete a reddish-pink fluid which is often mistaken for blood. This fluid gives their skin a shiny appearance and prevents it from cracking in the heat.

Q How many species of camels are there in the world?

A There are two species of camels. They are the Bactrian and the Arabian camel. The Bactrian camel has two humps on its back, while the Arabian camel has one. The humps contain fat that provides the animal with nutrients when food is not available.

Q How are llamas different from camels?

A Llamas are found in South America. Although they are in the same family as camels and even look a lot like them, llamas do not have humps. They are usually white, with black and brown patches. Alpacas are similar to llamas but much smaller.

Q Is there any difference between antelope and deer?

A All species of antelope have pointed, hollow horns that are permanent. Deer have branched antlers that they shed every year. Deer antlers are solid and bony. Only male deer grow antlers, while both male and female antelope have horns.

Try these too...

North America (110–111), South America (112–113), Africa (118–119), Asia (120–121), Ancient Americas (132)

▼ **Hollow weapon**
Antelope horns are hollow and light. But they are still formidable weapons.

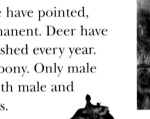

Living tall

The giraffe is the tallest living mammal. An adult male giraffe can grow to a height of about 6 metres (20 feet). In contrast, the giraffe's body is not as long as that of most other hoofed animals. Its front legs are slightly longer than its hind legs. Giraffes' necks can be over 1.5 metres (5 feet) in length, but only have seven vertebrae (neck bones). Its long neck and extraordinary height help the giraffe to pluck leaves that are beyond the reach of other animals. Giraffes also have tongues that can be extended as far as 45 centimetres (18 inches)!

▲ **Two humps**
The Bactrian camel (above) is found in the Gobi desert of Mongolia. The Arabian camel is found in Asia and Africa.

Odd-toed Mammals

Some mammals have an odd number of toes or hooves. This group includes animals like horses, zebras, rhinoceros and tapirs. Horses, zebras and donkeys have only one toe in each foot, which is in the form of a hoof. A rhinoceros has three toes. Tapirs have four toes in their front feet, three in their hind feet.

Quick Q's:

1. Where did the horse come from?

The earliest ancestor of the horse lived in North America about 55 million years ago. It was the size of a small dog, and did not look anything like today's horse. But its teeth were like any horse we know today. This animal went through many changes over millions of years before the modern horse evolved.

2. Where are tapirs found?

There are five species of tapirs in the world. Three of these are found in the rainforests of South America, while the other two inhabit parts of southeast Asia and Iran. All tapirs prefer water to land and spend a great deal of time in lakes and streams.

Q How can you tell the different types of zebra apart?

A There are three main kinds of zebra – the plains, mountain and Grevy's zebra. The plains zebra, found in the African grasslands, is the most common of all three species. It is striped all over and its stripes are wider than those of the other two species. Mountain zebras are native to the mountainous regions of southwest Africa. They have a white belly. Grevy's zebra is the largest of the zebra species. It has a mane that stands up straight, large ears and narrow, closely set stripes that extend all the way down to its hooves.

Q How many species of rhinoceros are there?

A There are five species of rhinoceros in the world today. They are the Sumatran, Javan, Indian, white and black rhinoceros. The white and black rhinoceros are found in Africa, while the others live in Asia. All rhinos have thick skin with folds. They have short, thick legs and a tiny tail. They are solitary animals that come together only during the mating season.

Q Does the tapir belong to the same family as zebras and rhinos?

A Although it looks a lot like a pig, the tapir is in fact closely related to zebras and rhinos. This animal has a short, muscular trunk and is about 1 metre (3.2 feet) tall. It has splayed hooves, which help it to get a firm grip on soft, muddy ground.

◀ **Staying in a herd**
Plains zebras are among the most common animals seen in the African savannah. They usually do not go very far from watering holes.

▼ **Mother and child**
Baby tapirs are various shades of pink and have prominent stripes. Their colour changes to grey and white and the stripes fade as they grow older.

▼ **Under threat**
Indian rhinos have one horn, while African rhinos have two. The horns are supposed to have healing properties and are used in various forms of traditional medicine. As a result, rhinos have been hunted and now their numbers have grown alarmingly small. There are so few Javan and Sumatran rhinos left that the species is under threat of extinction.

Odd Mammals

Most mammals share certain characteristics. The majority of mammals give birth to live young and look after them, and most of them (apart from some sea mammals) have four limbs and live on land. But there are some exceptions, such as platypuses, anteaters and bats.

Q Do any mammals lay eggs?

A The duck-billed platypus and the spiny anteater lay eggs. They are found in Australia, Tasmania and New Guinea. They were among the first mammals on Earth. Apart from laying eggs, they are similar to other mammals. They are warm-blooded, have hair and produce milk to feed their young. But neither anteaters nor platypuses have any teeth. They have snouts that look like beaks.

Q Why do some mammals like kangaroos carry their babies in a pouch on their bellies?

A Kangaroo babies are born early, before they have finished developing. When the baby is born, it climbs into its mother's pouch where it remains for several weeks until it is strong enough to move about on its own. The baby may remain in the pouch for more than a year, climbing out to play more and more often. Apart from kangaroos, koalas, possum and wombats also carry their babies in a pouch. All the mammals that do this are known as marsupials.

Q How are bats able to fly?

A The front legs of bats act as wings. Each leg has four long fingers to support the wing. The wings have a double layer of skin stretched between the finger bones and attached to the side of the body and to the hind legs. Bats have three pairs of flight muscles, attached to the upper arms and chest, that give them the power to fly.

▶ It's a mammal
The platypus lives in and around rivers in eastern Australia and Tasmania. The male has a spur on the hind foot that can secrete poison.

Following its echo

Bats use a special sense of vibration, called echolocation, to find food and to navigate. They emit sounds that bounce back as echoes after striking an object. Bats can identify the direction, distance, speed, and sometimes, even the size of an object by listening to this echo. This special technique helps them to find food and avoid obstacles in the dark.

◀ Big jumper
The kangaroo can jump so far that it is difficult to catch one. Their numbers have grown many times in the absence of predators in Australia, where they live.

Try these too...

South America (112–113), Australia and Oceania (114–115), Europe (116–117), Africa (118–119), Asia (120–121)

Whales

Whales might live in the oceans and might even look like very large fish, but they are mammals. Like most other mammals, whales give birth to live young and breathe with their lungs. Whales belong to a group of animals called marine mammals. They are among the largest animals on the planet.

Quick Q's:

1. What is blubber?

Blubber is a layer of fat found between the skin and flesh of all whales. It preserves body heat and stores energy as well as keeping whales afloat.

2. Do whales live as a family?

Most whales are social creatures. They travel and feed in groups called pods. Many of them migrate long distances in groups between their feeding and breeding grounds.

3. What do whales use their tails for?

The tail of a whale is divided into two parts, called flukes. While fish move their tails sideways to swim, whales swim by moving their flukes up and down in the water.

4. Which is the largest whale in the world?

Blue whales are not only the largest whales, but also the largest animals ever to live on Earth. They can be as long as 34 metres (112 feet). They are also the loudest animals on Earth – 1.5 times as loud as a pneumatic drill. But they use such a low frequency that we cannot hear them.

Q Why do whales have holes on their heads?

A Whales do not have gills like fish. Instead they take in air through nostrils like all the other mammals. The nostrils of whales, called blowholes, are located on top of their heads. Every once in a while, whales come to the surface of the water and open their blowholes to breathe.

▲ **There she blows**
Whale hunters and whale watchers spot whales by the fountain of water coming out of their blowholes.

Q Is that a fountain of water coming out of the blowhole?

A The whale opens its blowhole to breathe out stale air. When this air comes in contact with the colder air outside, the water vapour in the atmosphere condenses. This looks like a fountain or spout.

▲ **Killer whale**
The killer whale or orca is the most common member of the family of marine mammals that includes whales and dolphins. They can be found in all the oceans of the world. They are highly social animals and travel in stable groups, led by the oldest female member of the group.

▶ The baleen comb
A humpback whale and its comb of baleen (inset). There was a time when baleen was used in women's clothing, and many whales were hunted for it.

Long way home

Every year the California grey whales migrate for about 20,000 kilometres (12,427 miles). They migrate all the way from the Arctic Ocean to the Mexican coast and back. This is the longest migration undertaken by any mammal. In total, the California grey whale spends about one-third of its life migrating.

Q Are whales vegetarian?

A Whales are divided into two main groups – toothed whales who hunt for prey and baleen whales, who feed on krill, plankton and other tiny marine creatures in the water. Toothed whales, including killer whales, sperm whales and beluga whales, have small, sharp teeth in their jaws. These teeth are used to kill prey. Baleen whales, including grey whales, humpback whales, bowhead whales and blue whales, are toothless. Instead, they have sieve-like structures, called baleen, that hang from their upper jaws. The whales swim with their mouths open, taking in lots of water rich in tiny animals such as krill and plankton. The prey gets trapped in the comb-like edges of the baleen plates and the whale licks the food off the plate.

Q Do whales like to play?

A Although they are very big, whales can be playful. Sometimes they pop their heads above the surface and float motionless. This behaviour is known as 'logging'. Some whales, like humpback whales and orcas, leap right out of the water, which is known as 'breaching'. Whales also stick their tails out and splash them around. This is called 'lob-tailing'.

Try these too...

Oceans (34–35), Other Marine Mammals (58–59), Origin of Life (88–89), North America (110–111), Australia and Oceania (114–115), The Poles – The Arctic and Antarctica (122–123), Native Americans (133–135), Discovery of New Lands (144–145)

◀ The giant
Only a small part of this blue whale is seen above the surface of the ocean. Unlike other baleen whales, blue whales do not live in large groups. These huge animals need a lot of space in which they can get enough food to support themselves. In autumn, which is the mating season, they can sometimes be seen in pairs. Female blue whales give birth once every two or three years.

Other Marine Mammals

Seals, walruses and sea lions fall in the group of 'fin-footed' mammals who can move across land using their fins. All species in this group take to the water almost every day, and get their food underwater. There are 18 species of seals today, making them the largest group of fin-footed mammals.

▲ **Large colony**
Seals live in large colonies on remote islands. The colonies are divided into nurseries, an area for half-grown seals, and an area for adult seals, which is nearest to the sea.

Quick Q's:

1. Which seal dives the deepest?

Weddell seals are not only good swimmers, but also great divers. They have been known to dive to depths of over 500 metres (1,600 feet), and stay there for more than an hour.

2. Which are the largest and smallest seals in the world?

Seals range in size from 1 metre (3 feet) to over 5 metres (16 feet). Galapagos fur seals and ringed seals are the smallest, while the male southern elephant seal is the largest in the world.

3. Why was the sea otter hunted so extensively?

The sea otter has the densest and most luxurious fur among all mammals. The brown fur has up to 394,000 hairs per square centimetre! This fur was sought after by the richest people in the eighteenth and nineteenth centuries. So the sea otter was hunted all over the North Pacific, until it was almost extinct. The animal has been protected from hunters in recent decades and it is showing signs of recovery.

Q **Why are seals good swimmers?**

A Seals have a torpedo-shaped body that makes it easy to move through water. They also have strong limbs shaped like paddles that help to propel them forward.

Q **Why do seals appear clumsy while walking on land?**

A Most seals are very clumsy on land. Their front limbs are of no use for walking, and they slide on ice with great difficulty. Some types of seals have longer, more mobile flippers, so they are better adapted for moving on land. When on land, seals are most vulnerable to hunters.

▲ **Sleek predator**
A seal becomes a sleek, fast predator the moment it is in water. Most seal species are able to stay submerged and chase their prey for many minutes without breathing.

▶ Fast asleep
Walruses can be found sleeping on rocky beaches most of the time. Occasionally, one of them will slip into the water, hunt for a while, then return to the beach and go to sleep once more.

Q How are walruses different from seals?

A Walruses are much bigger than seals. They inhabit the Arctic regions at the edge of the polar ice sheet. The most unique feature of the walrus is its tusks, which are actually a pair of elongated upper canine teeth. Walruses use these tusks not only to defend themselves, but also as hooks to climb out of the water on to the ice. Male walruses have bigger tusks, which they use during courtship fights. Like all marine mammals, walruses have a layer of blubber that protects them from the cold.

The siren

Dugongs and manatees are the sirens of Greek mythology. Ancient sailors probably mistook these animals for creatures that were half-fish and half-human, giving rise to the legends of beautiful half-women-half-fish who lured sailors to their death. In reality, however, dugongs and manatees are very different from the sirens of legends. They are heavy animals, like a huge, thick sausage, tapering a bit towards the tail. They swim slowly near the shore, eating sea grass and other underwater vegetation. They are better described by their other name – sea cows.

Q What do sea lions eat?

A Sea lions are the largest member of the eared seal family. An average male Steller's sea lion weighs 907 kilograms (2,000 pounds). These animals eat only small fish, squids and octopus most of the time, though they have been known to prey on other seal species from time to time.

◀ Star performer
Sea lions are highly intelligent. They are popular at aquarium shows, where they catch and throw balls with ease.

Try these too...

Whales (56–57), North America (110–111), South America (112–113), Australia and Oceania (114–115), The Poles – The Arctic and Antarctica (122–123)

Seabirds

Birds that spend most of their time at sea are called seabirds. These include skuas, gulls, terns, auks, penguins, pelicans, petrels, gannets and cormorants. The earliest seabirds had teeth and lived in the Cretaceous period, which began 146 million years ago. Modern seabirds have been around since the Palaeogene period that began 65 million years ago.

▲ Drying up
After fishing, cormorants have to spread out their wings to dry as they do not have waterproof feathers.

Quick Q's:

1. Are most seabirds white?

Seabirds are white, grey or black. These colours help them hide from enemies and also from prey. Their legs and beaks are sometimes brightly coloured.

2. How do seabirds catch their food?

The albatross feeds on fish and krill that are found on the surface of the water. Gannets and boobies dive to pick up prey. Some, like the chinstrap penguin, dive and chase their prey. Skuas and frigate birds are known to steal food from others.

3. Is so much salt good for birds?

Seabirds have salt glands on their face that excrete some of the salt they take in. But the salt does not seem to harm the birds – seabirds live longer than other types of birds. In fact, the albatross can live for up to 60 years.

Q. Do seabirds ever live on land?

A. Seabirds come on to land to lay their eggs. The snow petrel nests 483 kilometres (300 miles) away from the sea on the Antarctic continent. Although seabirds usually fly and fish alone, most of them nest in colonies on land. The colonies house anything from a few dozen to more than a million birds. Murres build their nests close to each other for protection, while albatrosses prefer to leave space between their nests.

▶ Good divers
Murres dive beneath the surface to feed on fish.

Q. How are seabirds different from other kinds of birds?

A. Seabirds have adapted to life around saltwater. Birds like the albatross that fly long distances over the open ocean have long, strong wings to help them glide, while birds that dive for fish have shorter wings. All seabirds have webbed feet so that they can skim the water's surface or dive down in to the water with ease. Seabirds have lots of feathers that are packed densely, to keep out the water. A thick layer of down keeps them warm.

◀ Strange nest
Petrels make their nests with pebbles. They move to land only to breed.

▶ Good dads
Unlike most birds, the male phalarope guards his eggs until they hatch.

Q. How far does a seabird migrate?

A. Seabirds migrate a long way to lay eggs. The Arctic tern holds the record for flying longer distances than any other bird. When it is summer in the northern hemisphere, it flies up to the Arctic. And when it is summer in the southern hemisphere, it flies all the way to Antarctica. The terns travel 20,000 kilometres (12,000 miles) each way! Other long distance flyers include sooty shearwaters, albatrosses and phalaropes. While many seabirds fly over the open sea, many are happy to keep close to the shore.

Q. What kind of parents do seabirds make?

A. Seabirds make good parents. They nest at safe spots and are careful with their eggs. Both the mother and father care for their young. Some seabirds care for their young for six months, while some, like frigate birds, watch their young for fourteen months.

Birds of Prey

Birds of prey (raptors) are meat-eating birds that use their beaks and claws to hunt. There are about 500 species of birds of prey. The largest of them is the male Andean condor, and the elf owl is the smallest.

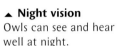 large, forward-facing eyes

soft, round wing edges for slow flying

▲ **Night vision**
Owls can see and hear well at night.

▲ **Majestic birds**
Eagles are larger than most other raptors, and they are more powerfully built. Their large pupils give them good night vision.

Q Which birds are raptors?

A Vultures, hawks, eagles, kites, falcons, harriers, buzzards, owls, secretary birds and ospreys are all types of birds of prey. Of these, only owls hunt at night. Female raptors that feed on live prey are often larger than the males, although male and female vultures are the same size. Vultures feed on carrion, or dead animals, instead of live prey.

Q What makes raptors such good hunters?

A Raptors have larger eyes than most other birds and have excellent colour vision. They have a sharp, curved beak and strong feet with powerful claws (talons). Raptors' sharp ears can hear prey moving and detect how far away it is.

That's really high!

Did you know that a Ruppell's griffon vulture can fly as high as 11,000 metres (37,000 feet)? On 29 November 1973, one of these birds crashed into an aircraft over the Ivory Coast!

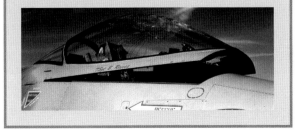

Q Do birds of prey have special wings?

A Falcons have thin, pointed wings. These help them to fly fast, and to change their direction while chasing their prey. Their wings also enable the falcons to dive suddenly to catch their prey. Hawks and eagles have rounded wings that help them soar, without flapping their wings, high up on air currents. They are able to mark their prey even from high up in the air.

Q What do raptors eat?

A All raptors are meat-eaters. Some, like eagles, feed on rodents, snakes, lizards and fish. Most vultures feed on carrion. Vultures have a sensitive sense of taste, so they are able to detect if food is poisonous. Some vultures, like the palm nut vulture, eat the fruit and husks of certain palm trees as well as shellfish and carrion. Bat hawks, unsurprisingly, exist on a diet of bats.

Q What is a raptor's gizzard?

A A gizzard is a specially adapted stomach that helps a bird to grind food. Birds often have stones inside their gizzards. Birds of prey have a special gizzard, which makes pellets out of whatever the bird cannot digest, like hair, bones and feathers. When it has finished eating, the bird spits the pellets out.

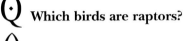

▲ **Bald and beautiful**
Vultures do not have feathers on their heads and necks. This ensures that they do not get too dirty when they stick their heads into carcasses, which helps to prevent infection.

Try these too...

North America (110-111), South America (112-113), Africa (118-119), Asia (120-121), The Poles – The Arctic and Antarctica (122-123)

Songbirds

The crow and the nightingale have something in common — they are both songbirds. There are about 4,500 species of songbirds. These include crows, finches, larks, mockingbirds, nightingales, ravens, robins, sparrows, thrushes, weaverbirds and warblers.

Quick Q's:

1. When did the first songbirds sing?

The first songbirds appeared about 50 million years ago. They were found in the lands now known as Australia, New Zealand and Antarctica in the southern hemisphere.

2. Which is the largest songbird?

The raven, which is part of the crow family, is the largest songbird, measuring about 60 centimetres (24 inches) in length. All members of the crow family are songbirds, though it may not seem so to us.

3. Do songbirds only live on land?

Most songbirds are found on land. The five species of dipper are the only aquatic songbirds.

Q What makes songbirds special?

A Songbirds have specially developed vocal cords (syringes) which they use to produce sounds or 'songs'. Some songbirds, like the wood thrush, can control both syringes independently and therefore sing two songs at the same time. Unlike other birds, songbirds have a special section in their brains that helps them to learn their songs.

Q Why do songbirds sing?

A Most male songbirds sing to catch the attention of a female songbird. Female songbirds are attracted to males that are good singers. So, males try to sing loud and for as long as they can.

Q Do songbirds have to learn from their parents how to sing?

A Scientists have found that a young songbird that has not learnt to sing from its parents can only sing a short song. Songbirds learn their songs when they are very young, by listening to their parents.

Q Where do songbirds live?

A Most songbirds live in trees and often feed on fruit, berries and insects. In most places, you just have to look out of the window to find a songbird – eight out of every ten perching birds are songbirds!

▲ **Tree life**
Most songbirds have toes arranged in a way that helps them to perch on trees.

Q How long do songbirds usually live?

A Songbirds live for about five years. They lay their first clutch of eggs when they are less than one year old. The eggs often hatch after just ten days. The hatchlings are born blind and have no feathers. In contrast, the egg of an albatross, which is not a songbird, takes 80 days to hatch, so the hatchlings are much more developed.

▲ **Wood thrush**
The wood thrush sings a melodious flute-like song.

▲ **Copy cat**
Starlings are strange birds. They copy the songs of other songbirds when they run out of their own songs.

Waterfowl

The waterfowl family is made up of ducks, geese and swans. Waterfowl can swim, float and even dive. Many waterfowl migrate long distances every year.

Q How have waterfowl adapted to life in the water?

A Waterfowl have webbed feet that help them paddle. They have flat bills, and their feathers have a coating of oil that works like waterproofing. The feathers of ducks, eider (sea ducks) and geese are soft and warm. They are used to stuff pillows, quilts and sleeping bags.

Q What makes a goose a goose?

A Geese live in the northern hemisphere. They are long-necked migratory birds that love the water. The Canada goose is the biggest goose in the world, while the rare lesser white-fronted goose is the smallest goose in the world. The Abyssinian blue-winged gander (male goose) tries very hard to win the female's attention. It struts around with its head bent over its back, showing off its blue wing patch. The nene, the official bird of Hawaii, is a land goose.

Is that a quack?

Different waterfowl have different calls. Female mallards honk loudly, but the male mallard's sound is softer. The tundra whistling swan has a sharp whistle that can be heard up to 6 kilometres (3.7 miles) away. Geese make a sound like a 'honk', while ducks quack.

▶ **Grace in feathers**
Black swans are found in Australia. They are excellent swimmers. They are also the fastest flyers among waterfowl.

Q Why do waterfowl migrate?

A Most waterfowl are migratory. They migrate to avoid the heavy rains and hot summers in the south and the bitter winters in the north. Waterfowl often travel long distances in search of pleasant weather. Snow geese nest in the Arctic tundra in the summer and fly south to spend the winter in Mexico. In winter, bar-headed geese migrate from India to Tibet. They fly 1,600 kilometres (1,000 miles) a day over the Himalayas, the highest mountains in the world. Flying at 3,600–4,300 metres (12,000–14,000 feet), they survive winds that blow at more than 322 kilometres per hour (200 miles per hour) and freezing temperatures. Although oxygen is low at such heights, waterfowl are able to absorb more oxygen with each breath while flying.

Q What makes ducks different from other waterfowl?

A Ducks are smaller than swans and geese. They have squat bodies, and are found in both freshwater and saltwater. They have big, flat bills that help them to scoop food off the water's surface or from just below it. Small, freshwater ducks are called teals. Another group of ducks, called wigeons, have lovely blue-grey bills. Dabblers are ducks that stand and fish in shallow water. The eider is a large sea duck prized for its soft feathers. Most of the common domestic ducks are mallards.

Try these too...

Oceans (34–35), North America (110–111), South America (112–113), Africa (118–119), Asia (120–121)

▲ **Big goose**
The Canada goose has a wide wingspan of 160 centimetres (5 feet).

▲ **Tough customer**
Geese can be very aggressive if they feel threatened.

Flightless Birds

Not all birds can fly. Some, like the ostrich and penguin, have such short, weak wings that they just cannot take to the air. Most flightless birds are believed to have occupied islands where there were no predators. In the absence of real danger, these birds did not really need to fly.

▸ Kiwi
The kiwi is a small, shy, nocturnal bird. It has nostrils at the end of its long bill and a keen sense of smell. The kiwi is the national symbol of New Zealand.

▲ Kakapo
The kakapo's green colour helps it blend in with its leafy surroundings.

Quick Q's:

1. Which is the smallest flightless bird?

The Inaccessible Island rail, of the South Atlantic is the world's smallest flightless bird. It is no more than 17 centimetres (7 inches) and weighs less than 30 grams (1 ounce).

2. Was there ever a flightless bird that was larger than the ostrich?

The aepyornis that lived on the island of Madagascar was the largest bird ever to live on this planet. It was more than 3 metres (10 feet) tall and weighed about 500 kilograms (1,100 pounds).

3. What do kiwis use their beaks for?

Kiwis have nostrils at the end of their long beaks. They thrust their beaks into the ground in search of food.

Q Where are flightless birds found?

A Most flightless birds are found on small islands. New Zealand has the largest number of flightless birds, from kiwis and penguins, to the now extinct moa. This country is also home to the kakapo – the world's only flightless parrot.

Q Why can't flightless birds fly?

A All flying birds have a keel, or breastbone, to which powerful muscles that aid flying are attached. In flightless birds this keel is either very small or completely absent. This makes their wings weak, so they cannot fly.

Q Which is the world's largest flightless bird?

A The ostrich is not only the largest flightless bird, but is also the biggest of all living birds. It can grow to a height of about 2.5 metres (8 feet) and can weigh up to 150 kilograms (330 pounds). Ostriches may not be able to fly, but they run at speeds of about 65 kilometres per hour (40 miles per hour).

Q How do flightless birds defend themselves from predators?

A Many flightless birds became extinct because of their inability to fly. However, others have unique adaptations that protect them from a similar fate. For example, ostriches can outrun most of their predators and can also deliver a fatal kick with their clawed feet. Others, like penguins, are excellent swimmers. Most flightless birds have colours that help them blend in to their surroundings.

long featherless neck

short tail

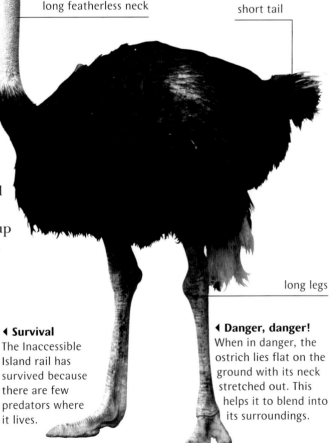

long legs

◂ Survival
The Inaccessible Island rail has survived because there are few predators where it lives.

◂ Danger, danger!
When in danger, the ostrich lies flat on the ground with its neck stretched out. This helps it to blend into its surroundings.

Penguins

Penguins are the most common flightless birds. There are about 17 different kinds of penguin in the world, most of which are found in the Antarctic region. Underwater, the wings of penguins act like flippers, helping these birds to swim at speeds of about 24 kilometres per hour (15 miles per hour).

◀ Royal looks
The emperor penguins look majestic with their big heads, smart black hoods and patches of bright colour on their bodies and faces.

▲ Tough life
The Antarctic region remains frozen most of the year. Creatures living here have a layer of blubber and other adaptations that help them survive the cold.

Q How can penguins live in places as cold as Antarctica?

A Like whales, penguins have a thick layer of fat (blubber) that protects them from freezing temperatures. Their feathers are stiff and tightly packed together. A special structure near penguins' tails produces oil that coats their feathers and makes them waterproof.

Q Can penguins walk?

A Penguins are very clumsy on land. Their feet are paddle-shaped and are better equipped for swimming than walking. When on land, penguins waddle about slowly. Sometimes they even slide across the ice on their bellies.

Q What do penguins eat?

A Most penguins feed on krill, fish and squid. They catch and swallow their prey as they swim. Penguins can dive almost 500 metres (1,640 feet) in search of food.

Q Which is the world's largest penguin?

A The emperor penguin is the tallest and the heaviest of all penguins. This species can grow to a maximum height of about 1.1 metres (3.7 feet) and can weigh about 41 kilograms (90 pounds). The smallest penguin is the fairy penguin which is barely 41 centimetres (16 inches) tall and weighs about 1 kilogram (2.2 pounds).

Try these too...

The Poles – The Arctic and Antarctica (122–123)

Model dad

Male emperor penguins make one of the best fathers in the animal kingdom. After laying a single egg the female penguin goes out to the sea in search of food. The male holds the egg on his feet under a warm layer of skin called the 'brood pouch' to hatch it. The egg takes about 60 days to hatch, and the male continues to guard the chick through the winter. He goes hungry until the female returns.

Fish

Fish are cold-blooded vertebrates (animals with a backbone), that live in water and mainly breathe through gills. Some, like the lungfish, have lungs to breathe with. Most fish have scales for protection and fins to help them swim. Fish were one of the earliest creatures to inhabit the Earth. They appeared about 500 to 475 million years ago.

Quick Q's:

1. Do fish look after their eggs?

Most fish lay their eggs and then swim away. But not the seahorse. Seahorses make very caring parents. The female seahorse lays eggs in a pouch on the male's stomach, and the male then carries these eggs for three weeks until they hatch. The male stickleback fish builds a nest of algae and other aquatic plants for its eggs. It also releases a sticky glue-like substance to hold the nest together.

2. Do fish go to sleep?

Some fish enjoy a nap. All members of the parrotfish family sleep at night. They make a bed out of their own saliva that covers them fully. Then they go to sleep on the sea floor. But most other types of fish continue to swim slowly even when they are resting, so it's difficult to tell if they have gone to sleep.

3. What are fins?

Fins are thin skin stretched over fan-like bones. A fish usually has pectoral, dorsal and caudal (tail) fins that help it to swim.

Q What were the earliest fish like?

A The first fish were jawless and finless. There is one such fish, the lamprey, that still exists. It looks like an eel, with a mouth like a sucker, sharp teeth and no fins. The hagfish is another early fish that can still be seen today. It lives in saltwater and feeds off the insides of dead fish. It defends itself by secreting slime. Today, most other fish have jaws and fins.

Q Do all fish have bones?

A Most fish do have bony skeletons. There are two groups of bony fish – lobe-finned and ray-finned fish. Their fins have different shapes. Lobe-finned fish include lungfish and the prehistoric coelacanth. Other commonly known fish, including herring, tuna, salmon, sunfish and flatfish, are ray-finned fish.

Q What about the boneless fish?

A Sharks, rays and skates are all fish that have no bones at all. Their skeletons are made of cartilage, which is a rubbery tissue softer than bone. These fish have strong jaws and sharp teeth. Their mouths are on the lower part of their heads, while their eyes are on top. This means they can't see what they are eating.

eye
dorsal fin
long blade - like snout
mouth

▶ **Smart moves**
Do you know how the male seahorses win over females? They display their pouch, where they will carry eggs. They open and close the pouch and even fill it with water to show off. Male seahorses also have tail pulling competitions to impress the females and also snap at and wrestle with one another.

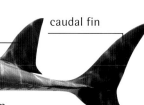

pouch to carry eggs

tail

Q How many species of fish are there?

A There are over 40,000 species of fish. Most fish live either in freshwater or in saltwater, but not both. Some fish which live in the sea, like salmon, move into rivers to breed. Some freshwater eels do the opposite and breed in the sea.

▲ **Bones and all**
This is a ray-finned fish. Its fins are adapted for swimming.

▼ **Killing saw**
The sawshark belongs to the family of fish without bones. It has a unique blade-like snout that is edged with teeth. It uses this to kill its prey.

second dorsal fin
caudal fin
pectoral fin

Friends and Enemies at Sea

Symbiosis means 'living together'. In a symbiotic relationship, two creatures can help each other to survive. This help can be with finding food, protection, cleaning or transportation. The larger creature is often the host, with the smaller creature living on it. Sometimes, both creatures live independently and still help each other.

▲ Marine parasite
The pearlfish – found in tropical and subtropical waters around the world – is responsible for more sea cucumber deaths than any of the cucumbers' other predators.

Q Can fish live in symbiosis with other water creatures?

A The clownfish lives among the stinging tentacles of sea anemones. This keeps it safe from its enemies. When other fish come to eat the sea anemone, the aggressive clownfish drives them away. It also cleans algae off the anemone. The clownfish is not harmed by the stinging tentacles of the anemone because it has a protective mucous layer surrounding it. This relationship is called mutual symbiosis because both members benefit from it.

Line up for a scrub!

There are a number of fish and invertebrates, like shrimp, that act as cleaners. These animals clean their hosts of parasites and dead skin. They clean the teeth, skin, gills and mouth of the hosts. Different types of fish and even sharks and stingrays come to the cleaners for their services. In exchange, the cleaners, some of which even enter the mouth of the host, are not attacked, and get a good feed!

Q Can a host be harmed?

A The pearl fish is a parasite which enters a sea cucumber to feed on it. The sea cucumber gets irritated by this and tries to rid itself of the pearl fish by expelling it with its digestive waste. Sometimes, the sea cucumber expels most of its digestive tract with the effort. This can seriously affect its health. This relationship is called parasitism – one member benefits at the expense of the other.

Q Do hosts and guests share their food?

A Sometimes, two animals share a home and food. Crabs dig holes in the seabed and the arrow goby fish burrows inside these holes. The fish plays housekeeper by feeding off the crabs' waste. Another example is the hermit crab, which picks up and places a tiny sea anemone on its back. The anemone, with its stinging tentacles, protects the crab from other animals. In return, the anemone gets free food when the crab eats.

Try these too...

Oceans (34–35), Whales (56–57), Other Marine Mammals (58–59), Fish (66), Sharks and Rays (68–69), Life of a Fish (70–71), Origin of Life (88–89), North America (110–111), South America (112–113), Australia and Oceania (114–115), Europe (116–117), Africa (118–119), Asia (120–121), The Poles – The Arctic and Antarctica (122–123)

▼ Another housekeeper
The spotted goby also has a symbiotic relationship with crabs.

Sharks and Rays

Sharks, skates and rays all have the same ancestors and are among the oldest fish on Earth. They were here even before the dinosaurs! These fish have cartilage or tough tissue instead of bones, and they breathe through gill slits. They don't have scales; instead their skin is covered with small tooth-shaped growths called denticles. The denticles give these fish a rough, sandpapery texture if rubbed the wrong way.

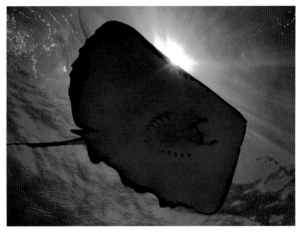

▲ **Ouch, what a stinger!**
The sting ray has a sharp stinger on its tail. When attacked it lifts its tail and stings its enemy.

Quick Q's:

1. Which is the earliest shark we know of?

The cladoselache is the earliest shark-like fish we know of. It grew to over 2 metres (6.5 feet) in length. It lived during the Devonian period, well before the age of the dinosaurs.

2. Are all sharks aggressive?

No. The horn shark, which is 1.2 metres (4 feet) long, hides under rocks during the day and comes out at night. It is a timid shark that eats only small fish and crustaceans.

3. Do sharks ever attack whales?

The cookie-cutter shark attaches itself to a whale and then bites out a bit of its flesh with its razor-sharp teeth. However, because cookie-cutter sharks are small, the whale is only slightly wounded by this.

4. How long do sharks normally live?

Sharks can live for many years. The great white shark can live up to one hundred years.

Q How big are sharks?

A There are over 350 species of shark in the ocean, and not all are large killers. Of these, less than 50 species grow longer than 2 metres (6 feet). One of the biggest sharks is the gentle whale shark, which is 15 metres (50 feet) long and eats plants and small shellfish. The smallest shark is the pygmy ribbontail catshark at just 24 centimetres (9.5 inches) long.

Q How does a shark find its prey?

A Sharks and rays have a strong sense of smell and can sense blood in the water hundreds of metres away. They usually find their prey through their sense of smell. They have a sharp sense of hearing. They also move very fast through the water. While attacking, an average shark can reach a speed of 19 kilometres per hour (12 miles per hour).

▶ **Size matters**
The great white shark is 3.7–3.75 metres (12–16 feet) long. The biggest great white shark on record was 7 metres (23 feet) long. These huge creatures are ferocious predators. They eat fish, rays and other sharks, as well as feeding on carrion (decaying bodies of fish and animals).

Q What is a ray?

A There are thousands of species of rays, which belong to the same family as sharks. Rays look like sharks that have been flattened out. They have flat, kite-like bodies that help them to glide through the ocean.

Q Can rays be dangerous?

A Rays come in all different sizes, and some are dangerous. The giant manta is enormous, but harmless. Other rays can sting or produce an electric shock to stun their prey and enemies. The lesser electric ray can transmit a powerful electric shock between 14 and 37 volts.

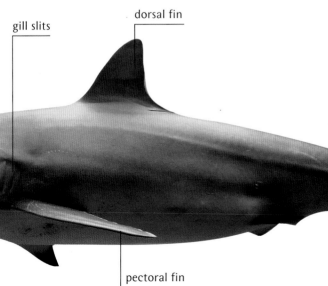

gill slits

dorsal fin

eye

mouth

pectoral fin

Q What is a ghost shark?

A The chimaera or ghost shark belongs to the same family as sharks, and its skeleton is also made of cartilage. Chimaeras have long tails, which they use to prod the muddy seabed for shellfish and other small prey. Most chimaeras have a poisonous spine on the upper part of their body that they use to defend themselves. They have three pairs of tooth plates: two pairs in their upper jaw and one pair in their lower jaw.

Q What is the difference between a chimaera and a shark?

A The chimaera is similar to the shark, but it has a bit of skin covering its gill slits called an operculum, whereas sharks do not. Most chimaeras have a poison-filled spine in front of their dorsal fins. The upper jaws of chimaeras are fused to their skulls, while those of sharks are not. Sharks have replaceable teeth, but chimaeras have permanent tooth plates. Chimaeras always hatch from eggs. The female chimaera lays large eggs in a leathery egg case, and the case lies at the bottom of the ocean for anywhere between six months and one year before the eggs hatch. Some sharks lay eggs and others give birth to live young. Sharks can lay up to 100 eggs, while those that give birth to live young have one or two young at a time.

▲ **Deadly teeth**
Sharks may have up to 3,000 teeth at one time. Various species of sharks have teeth of different shapes and sizes. This great white shark has sharp, wide, wedge-shaped and serrated teeth that allows it to catch and tear its prey.

Try these too…

Oceans (34–35), Whales (56–57), Other Marine Mammals (58–59), Fish (66), Friends and Enemies at Sea (67), Life of a Fish (70–71), Origin of Life (88–89)

Not quite a devil

The manta ray is the largest type of ray. It can grow to more than 5 metres (15 feet) wide. It is sometimes called the devil ray because of the horny cartilage on its head, but it has no sting and does not attack humans. These horns are actually fins that guide plankton and small fish into the mouth of the manta ray.

▼ **On the floor**
Chimaeras live on temperate ocean floors. They are related to sharks and rays.

Life of a Fish

A fish might have a nervous system and a brain, but it does not have a cerebrum – the part of the brain that guides thought. Most fish cannot see very far but they can distinguish between colours. Flatfish have both eyes on the same side of their head. The four-eyed fish has a piece of tissue separating each eye in to two which helps it to spot its enemies better.

Quick Q's:

1. How do pufferfish get their name?

Pufferfish defend themselves by puffing their bodies up with water until they are round and look much bigger and more scary than they actually are.

2. Is size enough to scare an enemy off?

If that doesn't scare their enemies, the pufferfish poison them. The poison, tetrodotoxin, is also found in the blue-ringed octopus and is 1,200 times stronger than cyanide. A pufferfish's poison can kill 30 people!

3. How can deep-sea fish see in the dark?

Fish that live in the deepest part of the oceans are bioluminescent, meaning they glow in the dark. Certain chemicals in the body of these fish produce a glowing light that helps them find their way through the dark waters. They also have large eyes and feelers, which help them to locate prey. In fact, it is because of these glowing fish that the deepest part of the ocean is known as the 'twilight zone'.

Q. Do fish have senses?

A. Fish can smell and feel. They can taste with their mouths and tongues. They also have an extra sense called electroreception that allows them to sense light, chemicals and vibrations. Fish do not have ears outside their body, but sound vibrations travel to their inner ears so they do have a sense of hearing.

Q. Can fish fly?

A. Some fish use large fins to help them leap across the water, so that they look like they're flying. Flying fish can cover 30–50 metres (98–164 feet) in one glide, travelling through the air at up to 60 kilometres per hour (37 miles per hour). Hatchetfish, which live in the Amazon, have wing-like pectoral fins which they beat as they fly short distances.

Q. Can fish perform tricks?

A. Some fish can fool their enemies with their appearance. The sabre-toothed blenny looks like the wrasse, which is trusted by sharks and other fish because it cleans them of parasites. The blenny imitates the wrasse to trick sharks and larger fish. It swims up close to them and then it bites off a piece of flesh.

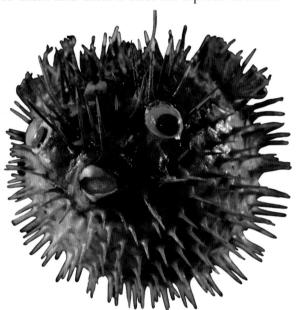

▲ All blown up
The pufferfish, also known as a blowfish, has an elastic stomach which it fills up with water in order to inflate itself.

wing-like pectoral fin

upward pointing eyes

dorsal fin

caudal fin

◀ Hatchetfish
Hatchetfish are found in seas worldwide but are most commonly seen in the western Pacific. They are small and have large tubular eyes. Their eyes point upwards allowing them to see fish in the lighter waters above. Hatchetfish live at great depths, between 200 and 600 metres (660 and 1960 feet). Their bodies are compressed and covered in delicate silvery scales. The large eyes gather the faintest traces of light that is available.

Q Can fish change colour?

A Some fish use camouflage to stay safe. The cuttlefish has yellow, red, black and brown pigment sacs under its skin. When it feels threatened, it sends a signal to the colour sacs and they spread the colour of the rock or sand the fish is next to through its body. The fish blends into its background, so that threatening predators cannot see it.

Q Do fish defend their young?

A Most fish are happy to eat any fish eggs and young they can find, even their own. But in the case of some fish, like the bubblenest builders, the male looks after the eggs and the young, defending the nest from other fish. With cichlids, both parents guard their young and take it in turns to fan and blow fresh water onto the eggs. They protect their eggs and young from other fish and kill any predators that come too close. Some cichlids keep the young from one batch of eggs close by to guard their siblings from the next batch.

▶ Big mouth
The shape of a fish's mouth is a good clue to what the fish eats. The larger the mouth, the bigger the prey it can consume. Fish have a sense of taste and are known to taste something before swallowing it if it is not an obvious prey item.

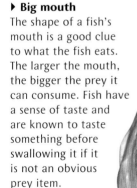

That's some red herring!

Herring have a strange way of keeping in touch with each other at night, when they can't see each other because of the dark – they break wind. The noise, called 'fast repetitive tick', is the herrings' way of finding each other without their enemies catching on. The herring gulps air at the surface of the water, and then lets it out through a hole in its rear end.

Q How do fish survive in freezing water?

A Fish that live in the freezing seas of Antarctica have an anti-freeze chemical (glyco protein) in their blood that prevents it from freezing. This allows them to live in icy water. This is the ice fish and cod's survival trick. Other Antarctic fish like barracuda, skates, krill and lantern fish have blood that circulates very slowly. This means that they can save their energy and use it to stay alive.

Try these too...
Oceans (34–35), Whales (56–57), Other Marine Mammals (58–59), Fish (66), Sharks and Rays (68–69), Origin of Life (88–89), Australia and Oceania (114–115), Europe (116–117), Africa (118–119), Asia (120–121), The Poles – The Arctic and Antarctica (122–123)

▲ Colour me up
Cuttlefish are also known as chameleons of the sea because they can change their colour at will.

Reptiles

The word reptile means 'to creep'. Reptiles are cold-blooded vertebrates (animals with a backbone). Most reptiles are covered with scales or plates to keep their skin moist. They breathe through lungs.

Q Why do reptiles like the sunshine?

A Reptiles are cold-blooded animals. This means that they need to bask in the sun and warm up to get energy. Although reptiles love the sun, they can overheat, and then they have to move in to the shade and cool down. If it gets too cold out, reptiles become slow and need to sleep or hibernate until the weather is warmer. Even in sub-tropical areas, many snakes hibernate right through the winter. The population of reptiles falls off as one moves to colder regions.

◀ **Lizard of the Americas**
The green iguana is between 1.2–1.8 metres (4–6 feet) long.

Q Where are baby reptiles born?

A Some lizards and snakes give birth to live young, but most reptiles build nests and lay eggs in them. Most reptiles are not caring parents, and they leave the nest once they have laid the eggs, though the eggs contain sufficient food for the baby reptile. Fortunately, their hatchlings are born with the ability to look after themselves, and when they hatch, they already look like adults. Some reptiles, however, do make good parents. Alligators guard their eggs and help the hatchlings when they come out.

▲ **Egg talk**
Snakes search for a moist, warm and safe spot to lay their eggs. Snake egg shells are soft and leathery, not hard and brittle like birds' eggs. Baby snakes are born with a tooth, which they use to break out of the eggs. They make a slit in the leathery shell with their tooth to slither out.

Q Fish are scaly. Are they reptiles?

A A reptile's scales are different to those on a fish. A reptile's scales are attached to each other, and they are actually thick skin. Fish scales, in contrast, are stuck to the top of the skin. Blood vessels run through the lower layer of a reptile's skin, but not a fish's. As they grow, reptiles regularly moult, or shed their outer layer of skin. Snakes and worm lizards shed this layer of skin in one piece. Other reptiles shed it in several smaller pieces.

Q Which was the first reptile?

A The oldest known reptile was hylonomus. It was around 25 centimetres (10 inches) long. Reptiles developed from amphibians, and the first true reptiles had a solid skull with holes only for nose, eyes and a spinal cord. These early reptiles gave rise to another line called synapsids, which had another pair of holes in their skulls behind the eyes. Synapsids developed into mammals.

Q I'm feeling cold! Am I a reptile?

A Reptiles include crocodiles, alligators, caimans, lizards, snakes, worm lizards and turtles; but not humans!

Lizards

Lizards make up the largest group of reptiles. There are over 4,300 species of lizards. They have four legs, a long tail and movable eyelids. A lizard's lower jaw is fixed to its upper jaw, while a snake's jaws are separate.

Open frill

Q How do I know a lizard if I meet one?

A Lizards have dry, scaly skin and clawed feet. When they are in danger, many types of lizards can shed their tail to distract an enemy. A new tail grows back.

Q What do lizards eat?

A Most lizards eat insects. Some, like the green iguana, are vegetarians. Bigger lizards, like the gila monster, eat eggs and small animals. The biggest lizards of all, the monitors, eat small animals.

Q Are lizards poisonous?

A The gila monster of North America and the beaded lizard of Mexico and Guatemala are poisonous. Some of the other larger lizards can bite, but they are not poisonous. The komodo dragon's bite poisons the victim's blood. Most lizards are not dangerous to humans. In fact, they help us by eating insects.

▲ **Scary frill**
The opened frill of the lizard makes it look much larger.

Q Is that lizard wearing a bib?

A The frilled lizard of Australia has two large frilly pieces of skin on both sides of its neck. When in danger, its frill fans out around its head and measures about 30 centimetres (12 inches) in diameter.

Q Which is the biggest monitor lizard?

A The fierce komodo dragon is the biggest monitor in the world. It weighs about 135 kg (300 pounds). Its mouth is full of poisonous bacteria, and when it bites, the bacteria poisons the blood of its prey, killing it.

Colourful character

Chameleons have an amazing ability – they can flush their skin with coloured pigment. This helps them to take on the colour of their background so they can hide from their enemies. Some chameleons can move each eye separately, so they can see two things at one time.

▲ **Multipurpose tongue**
Lizards use their tongue to catch insects for food. They also use their tongue to wipe clean their mouths and eyes.

Try these too...

Origin of Life (88–89), Dinosaurs (90), North America (110–111), South America (112–113), Australia and Oceania (114–115), Africa (118–119), Turtles (74), Snakes (75)

▼ **Child eater**
Komodo dragons are huge and fierce. They have even been known to eat small children.

▶ **Poisonous**
The beaded lizard found in Mexico is a venomous lizard.

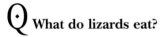

Turtles

Turtles and tortoises form another group of reptiles which includes terrapins. Turtles usually live in the sea, and although tortoises belong to the same family, they prefer to live on land. Freshwater turtles are often called terrapins. The back of a turtle is covered with a bony shell, and they have beaks but no teeth.

Quick Q's:

1. How large can a turtle become?

The leatherback turtle can grow up to 2.4 metres (8 feet) and weigh up to 870 kilograms (1,900 pounds).

2. How long does a turtle live?

The common snapping turtle lives for about 40 years, whereas the giant tortoise would need a huge birthday cake to fit about 170 candles!

3. Can I be friends with a turtle?

Most turtles are harmless. But the common snapping turtle that lives in ponds and rivers can attack people. Their bites, however, are rarely fatal.

Q Why do tortoises have a shell?

A A turtle's upper shell or carapace is like armour. The flat lower shell is called the plastron. A turtle can draw its head, legs and tail in to its shell whenever threatened. Other animals cannot break open the shell and get to the turtle.

Q Can a tortoise swim?

A Tortoises have stubby, strong feet and a heavy shell, which is why they move about slowly. They live entirely on land. Although a few species of tortoise can swim, most of them cannot. Turtles, however, are advanced swimmers, with webbed feet that help them to paddle through water. Smaller turtles do the most swimming. Larger turtles, like snapping turtles, prefer to walk along the floor of the river.

Q What does a turtle eat?

A Most sea turtles eat fish, crabs, shrimps and jellyfish. The adult green turtle eats only seaweed and algae, grazing in the sea like cows do on a field.

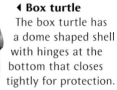

◀ Protective shells
Some tortoises and turtles can fold their necks under their spine. But those living in the southern hemisphere fold their necks to one side.

Q How does a turtle breathe?

A Turtles breathe using lungs like humans, but they can survive for hours without oxygen. When they are swimming, they need to come up to the surface to breathe periodically. Some, like the Fitzroy River turtle, have a pair of air sacs near their rear end, in which they store air when they are underwater.

◀ Box turtle
The box turtle has a dome shaped shell with hinges at the bottom that closes tightly for protection.

Snakes

Snakes are reptiles that developed from lizard-like ancestors. However, unlike most lizards, snakes do not have legs. They have transparent scales that cover their eyes to protect them. They breathe with only one lung located on the right side of their body. In most snakes, the left lung does not develop or is absent.

▲ **New clothes**
Look at the snake shedding its skin starting from the mouth. Snakes shed their skin when they have grown too large for their old skin. Just as you buy new clothes when your old ones are too tight, snakes too grow a new, larger skin.

Q How do snakes eat if they do not have teeth?

A Snakes have a flexible lower jaw. They can open their mouths very wide and swallow prey that is bigger than they are. After a big meal, a snake moves very slowly, so that the prey can be digested. Digestion needs so much energy that some snakes, like the Mexican rattlesnake, increase their temperature by 14 °C (57 °F). Once digestion is complete, a snake excretes the hair and claws of its prey. Snakes cannot digest plants.

Q How does a snake hear a snake charmer?

A If you were a snake you would not have any ear ache or trouble with cleaning ear wax. This is because snakes don't have external ears, so they cannot hear like we do. However, they have an inner ear that can feel vibrations on the ground and in the air. When the snake sways to a snake charmer's instrument, it is actually reacting to the vibrations of the charmer's movement, not to the sound the instrument is making. A sleeping snake might not wake up if you called it, but it would be sure to feel the vibration in the ground if you walked close by.

Q Do snakes shed their skin?

A As they grow, snakes shed all of their skin. The skin comes off like a sock, beginning at the mouth. Snakes can only shed their skin when the air is moist. If the air is dry, the skin does not come off. This is dangerous for the snake, since the old skin can get infected. Skin left attached to the tail can cut off the supply of blood to the tip which can cause it to drop off.

Try these too...

Reptiles (72), Lizards (73), Venomous Snakes (76–77), Constrictors (78–79), North America (110–111), South America (112–113), Australia and Oceania (114–115), Africa (118–119), Asia (120–121)

One giant leap

Some snakes, like the Singapore paradise tree snake, can glide as far as 137 metres (449 feet) through the air. These snakes jump off branches and can even turn 90 degrees in the air to chase their prey or to move from tree to tree. This has led to the legend that snakes can fly.

▲ **Snake charming**
Snake charmers usually remove the snake's fangs before trying out their tricks with them.

Venomous Snakes

There are over 2,500 types of snakes in the world. Of these, only about 450 varieties are venomous, or poisonous. These include vipers, cobras, mambas and sea snakes. Even poisonous snakes will only attack if they feel threatened.

Fang

Quick Q's:

1. Which snake has the longest fangs?

The gaboon viper has the longest fangs, which can grow to lengths of about 5 centimetres (2 inches).

2. Which is the most venomous snake in the world?

The inland taipan, a venomous snake found in Australia, is the most venomous snake in the world. Its venom is 400 times more powerful than the venom of a rattlesnake. Cobras, however, kill more people, because they live near populated areas.

3. Which snake is the fastest in the world?

The black mamba found in Africa can travel at speeds of 19 kilometres per hour (11.8 miles per hour. This makes it the fastest snake in the world.

4. How does the spitting cobra get its name?

When threatened, spitting cobras spray venom into the eyes of the enemy, causing temporary blindness. This gives the snake enough time to escape. Spitting cobras are known to spit venom to distances of about 2.5 metres (8 feet)!

Q Are fangs important to snakes?

A Venomous snakes inject poison into their victims through their fangs. All venomous snakes have a venom sac that is connected to their fangs. When they strike the prey, the venom sac is squeezed to release the venom, which then travels through a hollow passage in the fangs into the victim.

Q Why are the fangs of the cobra shorter than those of the viper?

A Cobras and all the other snakes in their family have short fangs. Unlike vipers, these snakes cannot fold their fangs out of the way when they are not being used. If the fangs were too long, a cobra would injure itself when it closed its mouth.

▲ **Poison teeth**
Vipers, one of the most poisonous snakes, have only one pair of fangs. Their fangs are longer than those of other snakes.

▼ **Spitting snake**
Notice (left) the cobra's most recognizable feature – its hood or flap of skin muscle that it can extend to scare its enemies. The image on the right shows a cobra spitting venom. The cobra produces neurotoxic venom to kill its victims.

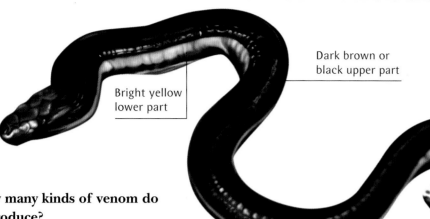

Bright yellow lower part

Dark brown or black upper part

Oar-like tail that helps it to paddle in water

◀ **Marine reptile**
Sea snakes are found in warm waters, mainly around the coasts of Asia and South America. They have flatter heads than other snakes, which help them to swim.

Q How many kinds of venom do snakes produce?

A There are two types of snake venom. Snakes like the cobras produce neurotoxic venom. This affects the nervous system, paralyzing the victim and leading to a quick death. Vipers produce hemotoxic venom that affects the blood and organs but does not kill immediately. As a result, doctors sometimes have a chance to treat the victim.

Q How is a pit viper different from a true viper?

A Both true and pit vipers belong to the same family. However, pit vipers have specialized heat-detecting organs, or 'pits' that are located between their eyes and nostrils. These sensors help pit vipers identify the differences in the temperature between their prey and the surroundings, thereby allowing the snake to hunt even in the dark.

Q Is the rattlesnake poisonous?

A The rattlesnake is a highly poisonous pit viper found in parts of North America and Mexico. Most species of rattlesnakes produce the hemotoxic kind of venom, which is extremely poisonous. The snake usually warns its enemies and victims that it is going to attack by shaking the rattle at the end of its tail. The rattle is made up of a series of hard, ring-like scales that are connected. Every time the snake shakes its 'rattle', these scales move across each other to produce a loud rattling sound that scares most animals away.

Q How are sea snakes able to live in water?

A Sea snakes have paddle-like tails that help them to swim in water. They also have a large lung that is almost as long as their body. This enables them to stay underwater for long periods. Sea snakes eat fish and other small marine animals.

▼ **Rattle**
The rattle is made up of hard scales from the tip of the tail. Each time a rattlesnake sheds its skin a new rattle segment is added.

Try these too…

Reptiles (72), Lizards (73), Snakes (75), Constrictors (78–79), North America (110–111), South America (112–113), Australia and Oceania (114–115), Africa (118–119), Asia (120–121)

Venom to the rescue

Snake venom is rich in proteins, so it is used to make different kinds of medicines, including painkillers. Most medicines used to treat snake bites are actually made from snake venom.

Constrictors

Some non-venomous snakes, like boas and pythons, have a unique way of killing their prey. They coil their bodies around the prey and squeeze it until the prey suffocates to death. The snake then opens its jaws wide and swallows the prey whole. Snakes that kill their prey in this manner are known as constrictors.

Quick Q's:

1. Are there diffeerent kinds of python?

There are 25 different species of pythons in the world. They are found in Africa, Asia and Australia. All species of pythons are constrictors, and none of them is poisonous. Some pythons have patterns on their scales.

2. Is it true that boas and pythons can go without food for several days?

After a big meal, boas and pythons do not eat for several days. This is because the digestive juices in the snake's stomach take a long time to digest the food.

3. Which is the longest snake in the world?

The reticulated python is the longest snake in the world. An adult reticulated python can grow up to 10 metres (33 feet) in length.

4. Why are royal pythons also called ball pythons?

The royal python is a type of python found in Africa. When in danger the royal python coils itself tightly into a ball. This ability has earned it a second name – ball python.

Q Is the anaconda a constrictor?

A The anaconda is a type of boa. In fact, it is the only boa that lives in water. For this reason, the anaconda is also known as the water boa. Like all boas, the anaconda also kills its prey by suffocating it. It usually lies still in streams or swamps waiting for its prey to come near. The snake then grabs the unsuspecting victim with its powerful jaws and pulls it underwater to drown it.

▼ Heavy
Green anacondas are found in the rainforests of the Amazon and Orinoco basins, and also in Trinidad.

▲ Deadly coils
It is almost impossible for prey to escape once a python has coiled around it.

Q What is special about the green anaconda?

A The green anaconda is the heaviest snake in the world. An average green anaconda that is about 6 metres (20 feet) long, usually weighs a hefty 250 kilograms (551 pounds). Some green anacondas are believed to weigh more than 500 kilograms (1,100 pounds)!

Q How are constrictors able to swallow prey as big as monkeys and deer?

A The jaws of constrictor snakes are like rubber bands. They might look small but they can be stretched to a large extent. This is because the upper and lower jaws are attached to ligaments instead of the skull. This helps the snake to open its mouth wide enough to swallow a monkey or a deer whole.

Q Do all pythons have red eyes?

A Albino pythons have red eyes and tongues. This is due to a condition called albinism, when the snake lacks melanin – a pigment that gives the snake its natural colour. Albino pythons can be white, yellow, orange or brown, but they all have red eyes.

▲ **All the colours**
Different species of the rainbow boa come in a wide range of colours. They live on the ground in the forests of South America. The name is also used for the slender boa, which has colourful markings on its body and is kept as a pet in some countries.

Q Why are newborn emerald tree boas red or orange in colour, while the adults are green?

A When they are growing, emerald tree boas change colour several times. They are usually born red or orange. Within a year, the young emerald tree boa turns golden yellow, before finally becoming green. As the snake grows older the green colour gets darker. Adult emerald tree boas spend most of their lives draped around branches during the day, and hanging down from the branches at night to hunt their food. This snake spends its entire life in trees. Their dark green colour helps to camouflage them. Emerald tree boas are among the few snake species that do not lay eggs but carry their young inside their bodies until the time of birth.

▲ **Patient killer**
Green tree pythons spend hours or even days perched on a branch and hardly making a single movement. But when any potential prey is within reach, this snake can move very quickly and coil itself around the victim.

Try these too…

Reptiles (72), Lizards (73), Snakes (75), Venomous Snakes (76–77), North America (110–111), South America (112–113), Australia and Oceania (114–115), Africa (118–119), Asia (120–121), Ancient Americas (132), Incas and Aztecs (141)

Snakes with legs?

Scientists believe that snakes evolved from lizard-like creatures. Over millions of years, these creatures lost their legs until they began to slither on their bellies like snakes. Pythons are living proof of this theory. All pythons have two tiny spurs (claws) towards the back of their long bodies. These spurs are thought to be the remains of hind feet.

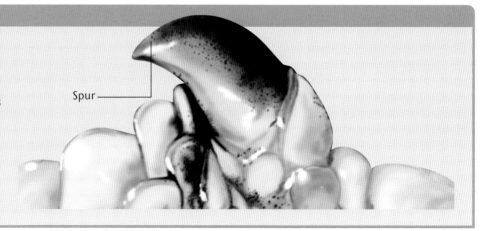

Spur

Crocodilians

Crocodiles and their relatives are together known as crocodilians. This group of reptiles includes alligators, caimans and gharials. Crocodiles, alligators and caimans are found in the rainforests.

Quick Q's:

1. What is crocodillin?

Crocodillin is a substance that is found in crocodilian blood. Scientists believe that this substance could cure some diseases that cannot be treated with antibiotics.

2. Which is the largest crocodile species?

The saltwater crocodile is not only the largest of all crocodiles, but also the largest reptile in the world. This huge reptile can be more than 6 metres (20 feet) in length and weigh over 1,500 kilograms (3,307 pounds).

3. Which is the smallest crocodile?

The dwarf crocodile is exceptionally small. Adult dwarf crocodiles do not grow more than 2 metres (6.5 feet) in length.

4. How many kinds of caiman are there?

There are six types of caiman. The largest is the black caiman of the Amazon, which can grow up to a length of 6 metres (20 feet). The commonest is the spectacled caiman, which grows to an average length of 2.1 metres (7 feet) and can be found all over Latin America.

Q Is that a crocodile or an alligator?

A Crocodiles and alligators might look a lot like each other, but they are in fact very different. The snout of a crocodile is longer and V-shaped, while the alligator has a broader, U-shaped snout. Another way to tell the two reptiles apart is to look at their teeth. The crocodile's lower teeth are visible even when the animal's mouth is closed. Crocodiles also have special glands that help them live in saltwater, while alligators can survive only in fresh water.

▾ Narrow-jawed crocodilian
The gharial is the second-longest of all crocodilians – a large adult can be 7 metres (23 feet) long. Their long narrow jaws are adapted to a diet of small fish.

▾ It's an alligator
There are two species of alligators – American and Chinese. The longest alligator ever measured was 5.8 metres (19 feet) long. It was found in Marsh Island, Louisiana, in the USA. The Chinese alligator is an endangered species and lives only in the Yangtze River valley.

Q Why do crocodilians have eyes on top of their heads?

A All crocodilians spend a great deal of time in water. They usually lie submerged so that their prey cannot spot them. But they can keep a lookout for prey as they cruise through rivers and streams, since their eyes are placed on top of their heads. Incidentally, crocodiles do shed crocodile tears, as the saying goes. They do this to clean their eyes, and not because they feel sad for their victims.

Q Do crocodilians chew?

A Crocodilians cannot chew their food. They usually tear off huge chunks of flesh or swallow their prey whole, if it is small. Once they have killed their prey with their vicious jaws, crocodilians toss their heads back so that the food falls in to their throats.

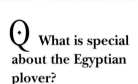

Q What is special about the Egyptian plover?

A The Egyptian plover is a bird that is believed to share a special bond with the crocodile. The plover feeds on parasites that live in the crocodile's mouth. The reptile is said to open its mouth and allow the bird to clean its teeth without harming the plover in any way.

▲ **Latin American cousin**
The caiman is the major crocodilian found in Central and South America, especially in the Amazon rainforests.

Try these too...

Reptiles (72), North America (110–111), South America (112–113), Australia and Oceania (114–115), Africa (118–119), Asia (120–121)

▲ **It's a crocodile**
The Nile crocodile is one of three crocodile species found in Africa. For centuries, it has been both feared as a man-eater and worshiped for its strength. Recently, a notorious crocodile named Gustav, was living in the rivers near Lake Tanganyika in Burundi, Africa. This crocodile, held responsible for killing hundreds of people, was last seen in 2005.

Q Do crocodilians make good parents?

A Crocodilian mothers are extremely protective. They build nests to lay their eggs. Unlike other reptiles, the female crocodilian does not abandon her eggs. Instead, she settles nearby her nest to keep predators away. After the eggs hatch, the mother takes her young along for a swim. Nearly all crocodilians carry their young about in their mouths. The mother looks after her babies for about a year. Crocodile mothers can be very aggressive if their babies are in danger.

Sunbathing

Crocodilians are cold-blooded creatures, so they can often be spotted basking in the sun. This helps them to raise their body temperature and get energy. Most crocodilians bask more after a meal as heat helps them to digest the food faster.

Amphibians

Amphibians live on land and in water. Of the 6,000 species of amphibians, most begin their life in water. The skin of an amphibian is thin and moist and helps the amphibian to breathe, so they need to live in moist, damp places.

Quick Q's:

1. What do frogs and toads eat?

Frogs catch live prey (mostly insects) by darting out their long, sticky tongues. The marine toad eats plants as well as other dead animals.

2. Do toads have long tongues like frogs?

Toads have shorter tongues than frogs and have to use their wide mouths to catch their prey.

3. Why do some frogs and almost all toads secrete poison?

Frogs and toads secrete poison for safety. Most poison-arrow frogs and mantella frogs are brightly coloured to warn their enemies. Some harmless frogs copy this colouring to protect themselves from predators who mistake them as poisonous!

4. Can toads help out in the garden?

Frogs and toads help to keep insects in the garden under control. They eat snails and slugs, which destroy plants. They are also an important part of the food chain. Rats, foxes, crows and hedgehogs eat them.

Q How do amphibians give birth?

A Most amphibians are born in water, where the eggs are laid. Although some frogs, toads and caecilians give birth to live young that look like adults, most frogs lay eggs in a blob of jelly and most toads lay eggs in long strips of gel. Some caecilians lay eggs in burrows. Male frogs call loudly to attract females to suitable water bodies such as ponds At the start of the mating season, male frogs eggs are a favourite food of other animals in the water. So frogs lay enough eggs to ensure that some survive.

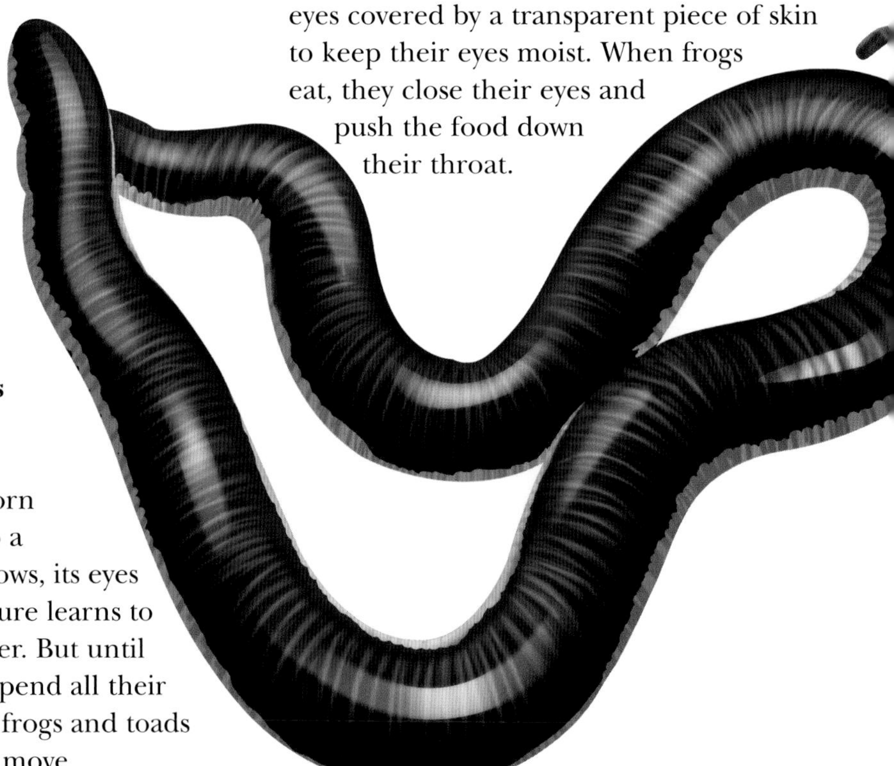

▶ Worm lookalike
Caecilians are amphibians that look like giant earthworms or small snakes. They live hidden in the ground most of the time. Most species have smooth, dark skin. Their eyes are covered by skin for protection underground. They have two tentacles on their heads. There are 171 species of caecilians. Most of them live in hot and moist places around the world.

Q What are the changes that happen to amphibians as they grow?

A All amphibians are born from an egg and grow into a tadpole. As the tadpole grows, its eyes grow eyelids and the creature learns to see both in and out of water. But until they become adults, they spend all their time in water. Tadpoles of frogs and toads lose their tails before they move on to land and become adults.

▲ Long tongue
Frogs have a long tongue hinged at the front of the mouth. They flick this tongue out quickly to catch food.

Q Is it a frog or a toad?

A Frogs have longer legs than most toads, which help them to take long leaps. The hind feet of a frog are webbed, to help it swim. Toads hop around and have dry, thick, warty skin. Unlike most amphibians, toads like to live in dry places. Both frogs and toads have bulging eyes covered by a transparent piece of skin to keep their eyes moist. When frogs eat, they close their eyes and push the food down their throat.

Q Are amphibians safe to touch?

A Most toads and some salamanders secrete a poison through their skin to defend themselves against predators. Most frogs are not poisonous, although rainforest frogs like the poison-arrow frog are so poisonous that some people tip arrows with its poison to use for hunting.

Q How big are amphibians?

A Amphibians range in size from the tiny 9.8 millimetre (0.38 inch) Brazilian gold frog to the Japanese giant salamander, which is 1.5 metres (60 inches) long and weighs 25 kilograms (55 pounds). Amphibians are found almost everywhere on Earth, even in the Arctic.

▲ **Highly poisonous**
Most of the 220 species of the poison-arrow frog of Central and South America are brightly coloured to scare away potential predators.

Try these too...

Reptiles (72), Lizards (73), Turtles (74), Dinosaurs (90), North America (110–111), South America (112–113), Australia and Oceania (114–115), Europe (116–117), Africa (118–119), Asia (120–121)

▲ **The familiar frog**
With over 5,000 species, frogs are among the most common animals in the world. They are found from the warm tropics to the cold sub-arctic regions, but most species are found in the tropical rainforests. Adult frogs are equally comfortable in land and water.

Sing a song for her

Male frogs and toads have a special pouch in their throat that helps them to croak. The sound is amplified by one or more vocal sacs, which are membranes of skin under the throat or on the corner of the mouth. Croaking loudly is a good way to attract females in the mating season. Some frogs and toads croak loudly to scare other males away and can even puff themselves out to look bigger.

Insects

Insects make up the largest group of creatures on Earth. Eight out of every ten animals are insects. There are about 925,000 species of insects. Of these, there are about 5,000 species of dragonflies, 110,000 species of bees and ants and 3,500 species of cockroaches.

Quick Q's:

1. How many insects am I standing on?

If you are in a field, there could be dozens of insects under your feet. One acre can be home to more than 400,000,000 insects. 100,000,000 collembola (springtails) can live in a square metre!

2. Can I eat an insect?

Some insects can be poisonous. However, in certain parts of the world, people do eat non-harmful insects, such as ants, crickets and grasshoppers, since they are a cheap source of protein. But they have to be cooked in a certain way before they are safe to be eaten.

3. How long have insects been around?

One insect fossil, found in Russia, dates back to more than 100 million years before the first dinosaurs. Cockroaches are also older than dinosaurs.

4. How many babies can one pair of houseflies have?

In five months, one pair of houseflies can grow into a family of 191×10^{18} if all their young live and multiply. That is 191 followed by 18 zeros!

Q What is an insect?

A Insects are arthropods – animals that have a protective cover or an exoskeleton (a skeleton outside the body). The exoskeleton supports the body and keeps the soft inner organs safe. Since the skeleton can't grow with the insect, the insect has to shed or moult the skeleton regularly, and a new one grows back. Insects are the only invertebrates (animals without backbone) that can fly. Some insects such as cockroaches and some types of ants grow wings when they are adults. All insects have six legs. Scorpions, spiders and centipedes are not insects, since they do not have six legs. True insects also have external mouths and 11 abdominal segments.

▼ Digging up the soil

Many insects, such as ants, make their homes by digging up the soil. In the process, they move the soil around and allow air to pass underground, which improves the fertility of the soil. Using chemical insecticides doesn't only kill pests, it kills these beneficial insects as well.

▼ Long jump champion
There are more than 11,000 species of grasshoppers. Some can jump 20 times the length of their own body!

Q What is an insect's body like?

A In Latin, the word insect means 'cut in sections'. An insect's body has three parts: a head, a thorax, and an abdomen. The head has a pair of antennae, eyes and a mouth. The head is used for eating, to feel around and to gather information. Some insects have simple eyes like ours, but most have complex eyes made up of six-sided lenses. The second part of the body, the thorax, supports the six legs and wings. The last part, the abdomen, digests the food and helps the insect breathe, since insects do not have separate noses like we do.

▶ Lady on a leaf
There are over 4,500 species of ladybirds, which are also known as ladybugs and lady beetles. They help us by eating pests.

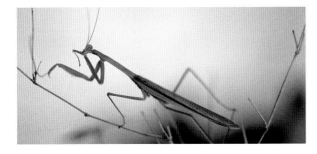

Try these too...

Amphibians (82–83),
Insect Life (86–87),
Origin of Life (88–89),
Plant Life (96–97),
North America
(110–111), South
America (112–113),
Australia and Oceania
(114–115), Europe
(116–117), Africa
(118–119), Asia
(120–121)

◀ Not at prayer
The praying mantis is
easily recognized by
its resemblance to a leaf
and the way it holds its
antennae together, as if
it has its hands joined
in prayer.

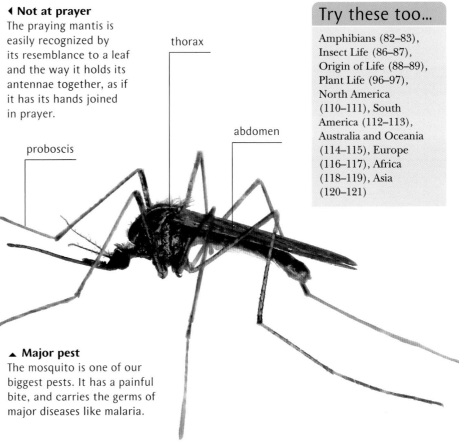

proboscis

thorax

abdomen

▲ Major pest
The mosquito is one of our
biggest pests. It has a painful
bite, and carries the germs of
major diseases like malaria.

Q How do insects breathe?

A Insects have spiracles (little holes)
on the sides of the thorax and abdomen.
Air enters through these spiracles and then
breathing tubes carry the oxygen all over
the body. The spiracles close when the insect
is in water, ensuring that the insect doesn't
drown. However, insects have to come up
for air regularly when they are underwater.

Q Why do we need insects?

A There are many insects that help us.
Butterflies, ants, bees and wasps pollinate
flowers and help to grow new plants,
including fruit trees. Insects give us honey,
medicines, silk, lacquer and wax. Some
beetles eat dead animals. Some insects eat
other insects. Grasshoppers lay so many eggs
that if all of them were to hatch, they could
eat up most of our crops and plants. This
does not happen because there are other
insects that eat up most of the grasshopper
eggs. Agricultural scientists have been
breeding insects to keep pest populations
under control. This is better than using
chemical insecticides, which are poisonous
not only for insects but also for humans.
Scientists have also been using insects as an
ingredient for vaccines, for example in a new
trial vaccine against cervical cancer. However,
there are many insects that are undoubtedly
pests. Mosquitoes, bedbugs and lice drink our
blood and spread diseases. Others, like the
housefly and the tsetse fly, can make us ill.
Locusts chew up our crops. Termites and
borers eat up wooden homes and furniture.

Long and short

**One of the longest insects is the stick insect, which is about
36 centimetres (14 inches) long. It belongs to the orthoptera
insect family, which includes crickets, grasshoppers, praying
mantids, leaf insects and cockroaches. Most stick insects are
females and they can lay fertile eggs without the help of a male.
When the eggs hatch, out come more females. The smallest insect
of all is the fairy fly, which is 0.17 millimetres
(0.007 inches) long and can fly
through the eye of a needle.**

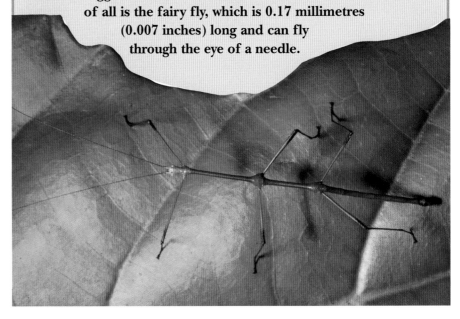

Insect Life

Most insects go through various stages of life. They are born from eggs, and grow into a nymph or larva. The larva then becomes an adult insect, also called an imago. Sometimes there is a fourth stage in which the larva becomes a pupa before finally becoming an adult. The changes an insect goes through are known as metamorphosis.

▲ Short life
For most insects, the adult stage of life is the shortest.

Quick Q's:

1. How does a bee become queen of the colony?

Worker bees produce royal jelly. When a bee larva is fed a diet of royal jelly, it grows into a queen bee. All the others in the colony are fed royal jelly only for about two days. Then, they are given pollen and nectar or honey instead.

2. Why are dung beetles so called?

Dung beetles use the dung from plant-eating animals by rolling it into balls. This is where these beetles lay their eggs. The larvae feed on the dung. The beetles bury each ball.

3. Are all insect eggs round and smooth?

Some species of assassin bugs lay eggs that have spines. These eggs hatch into larvae, which are almost like adults, but do not have wings.

Q Do all larvae snooze in a cocoon?

A The butterfly larva is one of the few that makes a chrysalis or cocoon around itself to rest in, while it grows into an adult. Most other insects move straight from the larva to the adult stage.

Q Do insects lay their eggs in a nest?

A Some insects lay their eggs inside plant stems. Walking stick insects scatter their eggs about on the ground, while certain beetles lay their eggs on dead animals so that their larvae have food when they hatch. A tarantula wasp lays one egg on a tarantula spider.

▼ Laying eggs
Insects such as butterflies lay their eggs on the underside of leaves.

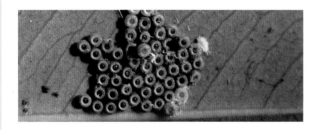

▼ Growing up fast
The life cycle of a mosquito usually lasts for about two weeks.

▶Deep sleep
The larva stops feeding and undergoes drastic physical changes during the pupal stage. This stage occurs only in insects like butterflies that undergo complete metamorphosis.

Q What is the life cycle of a mosquito?

A Mosquitoes lay their eggs in water. The larva is born in water and feeds on tiny organisms just below the surface of the water. It comes up periodically for a breath of air. Mosquito pupae do not feed but are more active than other insect pupae. After a few days, an adult mosquito emerges from the pupa, and spends the rest of its life on land.

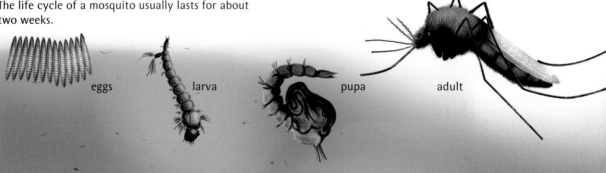

eggs   larva   pupa   adult

Q **Do insects live with their parents?**

A Most insects lay their eggs in batches and then fly away. The young, when they hatch, live close to each other and feed together. They find safety in numbers even though their parents are not around to protect them. Some adult insects meet up only when it is time to breed, and move on after that.

Q **How many insects live together?**

A Many insects live in groups, swarms, colonies or nests. A colony of ants can have just 50 ants. One big nest in Japan had 1,080,000 queen ants and 306,000,000 workers in 45,000 smaller nests, each of which was connected with the others. Some insects, like locusts, live in swarms. One swarm can hold 28,000,000,000 locusts. When a locust swarm attacks a field, it's bad news for the farmer. Each locust weighs only about 2.5 grams (0.09 ounce). But an average swarm has a weight of 70,000 tons!

Click and roll

Most beetles struggle to roll over when they are upside down on their backs. But not the click beetle. When it is upside down or needs to get out of a jam, it bends itself until a special spine on its thorax snaps into place. Then the beetle shoots into the air with a 'click' sound. This usually does the trick, since when it falls back down, it lands the right way up!

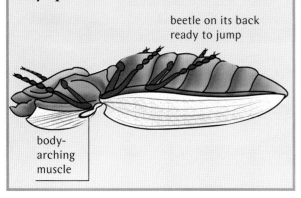

beetle on its back ready to jump

body-arching muscle

Try these too...

Amphibians (82–83), Insects (84–85), Plant Life (96–97), South America (112–113), Africa (118–119), Asia (120–121)

▲ **Food for the young**
Ladybirds mate in spring or summer. Adult females then lay several eggs near a colony of plant-eating pests like aphids, or greenfly. When the larvae hatch, they feed on these insect pests.

Q **Why do social insects have such large families?**

A Insects that live in colonies are known as social insects. Like with bees, the members of ant and termite colonies also have different functions. With these insects, the queen lays eggs. Other members of the colony are known as workers. They go out to gather food, while the soldiers protect the colony. Laying eggs is important work in a termite colony – one queen termite can produce almost 30,000 eggs every day. A queen bee can lay more than 1,000 eggs a day.

▶ **Leading the way**
Worker ants usually hunt for food and then leave a trail of scent leading the other ants in the colony to the food source.

Origin of Life

The Earth was formed about 4.5 billion years ago. But the earliest fossils found show that life on Earth only began about 3.5 billion years ago.

Quick Q's:

1. Why is the coelacanth called a living fossil?

The coelacanth is one of the earliest known fish that has survived until today. It grows to a length of 2 metres (6.5 feeet). Until a coelacanth was caught by a fisherman off the east coast of South Africa in 1938, it was thought to be extinct.

2. What are the different ages in which life formed?

Life began in the Precambrian age. Then came the Palaeozoic age, which saw the first plants, most invertebrates, the first vertebrates, fish, amphibians, and reptiles. The Mesozoic age or the Age of Reptiles was when dinosaurs ruled the Earth. This was also when flowering plants, birds, and some mammals developed. Humans only appeared much later, in the Cenozoic period.

3. Is there any new clue on how life began?

Scientists have found some animals among the mixture of gases that come out of volcanoes. Much of Earth was like this when life began. So any animal that can live here may hold a clue to the origin of life on Earth.

▼ Early Earth
Artist's impression of how the Earth looked in the early days — mostly water, a few volcanic islands, and dinosaurs roaming the land, seas and sky.

Q What was the Earth like in the early days?

A When the earth began, it was hot, dry and dusty. There was no oxygen. According to some scientists, the blue-green algae were the first living things to appear. They produced their own food and oxygen using sunlight – a process called photosynthesis that plants use today. Slowly, the oxygen in the atmosphere increased, and larger organisms were able to develop.

Q Did life definitely start on Earth?

A Some scientists believe life didn't begin on Earth, but came from outer space. They believe that a comet hit the Earth, carrying the proteins from which living things are formed. There are a number of theories regarding the origin of life on Earth (or in space), but none of them have been proven yet.

Q When did the first animals appear?

A Between about 600 million years ago and 517 million years ago, the first animals appeared in the oceans. They had soft bodies. These flat creatures were the ancestors of sea anemones, sea urchins, jellyfish and worms. They were all invertebrates – animals without a spine.

▶ First spine
Artist's impression of how the Pikaia probably looked. This seahorse lookalike is important as it was the very first vertebrate.

Q What was the first animal with a spine?

A The first animal with a spine was called the pikaia. It looked like a flat worm and was about 5 centimetres (2 inches) long. It swam close to the sea floor, by twisting its body back and forth and using its tail fin to steer. The pikaia is now extinct.

Q When did the first fish appear?

A The pikaia was followed by fish without jaws, so their mouths had to remain open to catch plants and animals as they swam by. Then, about 475 million years ago, the coelacanth developed jaws and teeth. Since they could eat more effectively, these fish with jaws grew faster. Amazingly, coelacanths are still around today!

Studying those that died ages ago

Scientists called palaeontologists study the lives of prehistoric plants and animals by looking at fossils. When these animals and plants died, soil settled on top of them. Over time, this soil gradually hardened into rock. This happened again and again till there were several layers of rock, with the oldest layer at the bottom. The print of the dead animal or plant that died during a certain period can be seen clearly on the rocks. These prints are called fossils. Fossils have helped us to discover what life was like before humans were around.

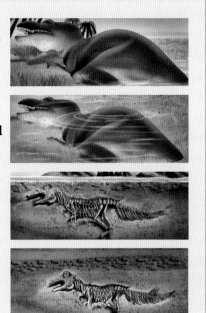

Q When did the first land creatures appear?

A As the seas filled with more animals feeding on one another, some marine creatures (including some fish) began to move to land to escape their predators and to get food more easily. Some of these creatures developed into insects like mayflies and dragonflies. They grew lungs and their fins changed to legs. These were the very first amphibians – animals that could live either on land or in water. A typical animal of this period was the acanthostega. It had four stubby feet and looked like a lizard. It spent most of its time on the shores of lagoons.

▼ Ancestor of amphibians
This armoured fish may have been the ancestor of amphibians who first left the sea and started to move on to land. Fins below the body may be the precursor to legs.

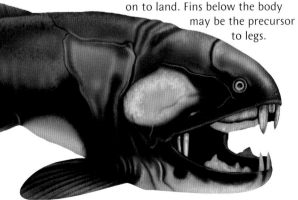

▼ Clues to early forms of life
Stromatolites are stone structures that may have been formed by organisms such as the blue-green algae, when they cemented the sediments at the bottom of the sea. Scientists have found fossilized remains of some very early life inside stromatolites.

Try these too...

Oceans (34–35), Fish (66), Amphibians (82–83), Insects (84–85), Plant Life (96–97)

Dinosaurs

Dinosaurs get their name from the Greek words deinos, which means large and scary, and sauros or lizard. These fearsome reptiles ruled the Earth during the Mesozoic era, which lasted from 248 to 65 million years ago.

Quick Q's:

1. What did the dinosaurs eat?

Despite their reputation as violent monsters, 65 per cent of the dinosaurs were vegetarian. They lived around the same time as the first flowering plants were developing on the Earth. But most of the plants around them were like ferns. Some types of dinosaurs, such as the turanoceratops, had special parrot-like beaks with which they could bite off the needles from ferns.

2. Were the meat-eating dinosaurs special?

Most meat-eating dinosaurs were smaller than their prey! But they were faster, with bigger and stronger jaws, sharp teeth and deadly claws that could kill and then tear apart the thick skin of another dinosaur.

3. Why is the tyrannosaurus rex so famous?

Tyrannosaurus rex, also known as T-rex, was one of the largest meat-eating dinosaurs. It could stand up to a height of 12 metres (40 feet). It weighed between 5 and 7 tons; that is five to seven times the weight of an average elephant.

Q How did the first reptiles evolve on Earth?

A About 300 million years ago, amphibians evolved into reptiles. These reptiles continued to adapt to their environment. They developed a better way of breathing than amphibians – amphibians breathe by moving their throat muscles, but the dinosaurs moved the muscles below the rib cage and abdomen, just like us. As a result, they could take in more air.

Q Did the Earth look the same as it does today?

A At the time of the reptiles, the Earth was hot and dry. There was just one landmass since the continents had not yet formed, and there was no polar ice since it was too hot. Reptiles – some of them as long as 6 metres (20 feet) – roamed the land. These primitive reptiles evolved into dinosaurs, about 210 million years ago, towards the end of the first part of the Mesozoic era.

Q Aren't dinosaurs from the Jurassic period in time?

A The Mesozoic era was so long that it is divided into three periods. The first is called the Triassic period. It occurred 248–208 million years ago. Then came the Jurassic period, 208–146 million years ago, when huge meat-eating dinosaurs were in charge. Finally came the Cretaceous period, 146–65 million years ago, which saw the end of the dinosaurs.

Q Were dinosaurs always large?

A Early dinosaurs of the Triassic age were not very large. Even the biggest did not grow larger than 4 metres (13 feet) long. During the Jurassic period, dinosaurs grew much larger. The giant plant-eating dinosaurs of this time, called sauropods, were 30–45 metres (98–150 feet) long.

▼ Flying reptile
The pteranodon was one of the largest flying reptiles, with a wingspan of up to 9 metres (30 feet). Its sharp beak was toothless.

Q What happened to the dinosaurs?

A Nobody is sure. But many scientists think volcanic eruptions led to such a thick cover of dust over the Earth that sunlight could not get through. This meant that plants could not make food, so the dinosaurs had nothing to eat, and they died.

▼ Age of dinosaurs
The age of dinosaurs was so long that it is divided into three periods by scientists.

MESOZOIC ERA		
TRIASSIC	JURASSIC	CRETACEOUS
248-175 million years ago	175-130 million years ago	130-65 million years ago

Armoured Dinosaurs

Some dinosaurs had armour-like plates on their bodies that protected them from predators and harsh weather. Dinosaurs like the stegosaurus also had a double row of plates on their back. The plates were mainly used to keep dinosaurs cool, although they were also useful for scaring off predators. Some other dinosaurs had spines sticking out of their bodies to scare other animals away, or to help during a fight.

Q What was unique about the ankylosaurus?

A The ankylosaurus family were plant-eating armoured dinosaurs that existed during the Cretaceous period. But although these animals did not eat meat, they could still be vicious. They had club-shaped tails with spikes at the end, which they used to defend themselves. By swinging their heavy tails, an ankylosaurus could seriously injure any enemy that tried to attack it.

Q Which was the spiniest armoured dinosaur?

A Kentrosaurus, which means spiked lizard, had plates and spines sticking out of its back. Instead of jaws, it had a spiky beak. Kentrosaurus grew up to 5 metres (16 feet) long and weighed about 2 tons, but its brain was as small as a walnut.

Q Why was the pachycephalosaurus special?

A The plant-eating pachycephalosaurus, which means the thick-headed lizard, gets its long name from its strange head. The pachycephalosaurus had a dome-shaped head that made it look as if it was wearing a tight cap. Its skull was about 25 centimetres (10 inches) thick and housed a tiny brain. The pachycephalosaurus probably used its thick head as a weapon when defending itself from other dinosaurs.

Q Were there any other armoured dinosaurs around?

A The ceratops family were plant-eating dinosaurs with beaks, one or more horns and muscular frills around their necks. The frills may have been useful in supporting the neck in earlier species, but later might have been used to defend the neck while fighting. The triceratops and protoceratops were the best-known ceratops. From our point of view, the funniest thing about the ceratops was that these huge dinosaurs had beaks like the parrots of today.

▲ **Three horns**
This fossil of the skull and ribcage clearly shows two of the three horns with which triceratops used to defend themselves.

Try these too…

Origin of Life (88–89), Plant-eating dinosaurs (92), Meat-eating Dinosaurs (93), North America (110–111), South America (112–113)

Protected to the eyelids

Euoplocephalus was a dinosaur that lived during the late Cretaceous period, whose name means well-armoured head. It even had heavy spiky armour on top of its eyelids. In case of an attack, it could shut its eyes, and they would be protected by the armour. This was not so helpful when attacking an enemy, since the euoplocephalus could not see with its eyes shut!

Plant-eating Dinosaurs

Meat-eating dinosaurs like tyrannosaurus rex may be the best-known dinosaurs. But plant-eating dinosaurs were more numerous and included some of the biggest dinosaurs that ever lived. The most gigantic of these, known as sauropods, were very tall with long necks.

Quick Q's:

1. When did sauropods live?

Sauropods were plentiful during the Triassic and Jurassic periods. Very few of these gigantic creatures survived into the Cretaceous period.

2. What did the stegosaurus use the plates on its back for?

The stegosaurus probably used its plates to scare away its enemies. Many scientists think these plates also helped the dinosaur to regulate its body temperature.

3. How big were the plates on the stegosaurus?

The largest plates on the back of the stegosaurus were at least 60 centimetres (2 feet) tall and wide.

4. What was unique about the maiasaura?

Maiasauras were duck-billed, plant-eating dinosaurs that lived in herds of 10,000 or more. Unlike all the other dinosaurs, maiasauras were believed to have looked after their offspring, just like modern mammals.

Q Which was the largest plant-eating dinosaur?

A Argentinosaurus, a sauropod, was not only the largest plant-eating dinosaur, it was probably the largest dinosaur to have ever roamed the Earth. This dinosaur is believed to have grown to a length of about 40 metres (130 feet). It might have weighed about 80–100 tons. It had a long neck and tail, and a small head.

Q What unique features did sauropods have?

A All sauropods were plant-eaters. They had huge bodies, small heads, long necks and strong legs. Sauropods had chisel-shaped teeth that helped them to grind leaves and other plants. Sauropods were most noted for their size. Even the smallest of sauropods were 6 metres (20 feet) long.

Q Which is the most famous sauropod?

A Brachiosaurus is the best-known member of the sauropod group. Until recently this gentle giant was considered to be the largest dinosaur ever. This record has now been broken by the discovery of the argentinosaurus fossil in South America.

Q Were sauropods the only plant-eating dinosaurs?

A Apart from sauropods, there were several other groups of plant-eaters. Orbithopods had bird-like feet, beaks and long, stiff tails. Ceratops had beaks, one or more horns and muscular frills around their necks. Stegosaurs had armoured bodies with thick scaly skin and spikes or plates along the back. Ankylosaurus had hard armour-like skin and a club-shaped tail, which was used to drive its enemies away.

◀ **Largest land animal ever?**
Argentinosaurus may be the largest land animal ever, but there are others that may have been even bigger. No one knows for sure.

Meat-eating Dinosaurs

All carnivorous dinosaurs fell into the group called Theropods. Some theropods were omnivorous, meaning they ate both meat and plants. The theropods walked upright on their hind legs and had short front limbs with sharp claws. Of all the theropods, tyrannosaurus rex is the most famous.

Q Which was the largest meat-eating dinosaur we know of?

A Theropods were not as large as their plant-eating cousins. However, some, like tyrannosaurus rex and giganotosaurus, grew to a length of about 12.5 metres (41 feet). Scientists have recently discovered the remains of what is now considered to be the largest meat-eating dinosaur to have ever lived – mapusaurus. This dinosaur is believed to have been over 13 metres (42 feet) long.

Q Did T-rex really hunt down its prey?

A T-rex was built like a true predator. It walked upright on two powerful legs, and had a narrow snout that gave it a good view of its surroundings. Like most predators, T-rex had small eyes that faced forwards giving the dinosaur a sharp view of its prey. It also had a good sense of smell. Despite these features, many scientists believe that T-rex was mainly a scavenger that hunted only when it was necessary.

Q What made the velociraptor a good hunter?

A Velociraptor grew to a height of about 1 metre (3 feet) and was 2 metres (6 feet) long. Its small frame made velociraptor fast and agile. This dinosaur could chase its victims at speeds of about 60 kilometres per hour (40 miles per hour). Velociraptor may also have hunted in groups, helping it to take down even the largest dinosaurs of the time.

Try these too...

Dinosaurs (90), Armoured Dinosaurs (91), North America (110–111), South America (112–113), Africa (118–119), Asia (120–121)

▲ **Deadly claws**
Velociraptors had a sharp, hook-shaped claw on each foot. This claw was drawn into the toe when not in use.

Pricey fossil

In 1990, Susan Hendrickson, a fossil hunter, discovered the largest fossil of a T-rex near Faith in South Dakota, United States. The fossil was named 'Sue' after the person who discovered it. Soon after its discovery, Sue was at the centre of a legal battle. The bones were found on land that was owned by a private rancher. The land was held in trust by the United States government. The rancher claimed that the fossil belonged to him since he owned the land on which it was found. This started a dispute over the ownership of Sue. After a five-year-long legal battle, a judge ruled in favour of the rancher, who later sold the fossil at a Sotheby's auction for a whopping 8.4 million dollars (about 4.6 million pounds) – the largest amount ever paid for a fossil.

▲ **Big bite!**
T-rex had 60 razor-sharp teeth that could grow up to 23 centimetres (9 inches) long! Its huge jaws could break the backbone of its prey.

Other Prehistoric Animals

Prehistoric animals are those that existed in the prehistoric age, the time before recorded history began. Several animals, including the woolly mammoth and the woolly rhinoceros, roamed the Earth during these times. Some of these prehistoric animals lived at the same time as the dinosaurs. Most of what we know about them is from the study of their fossils.

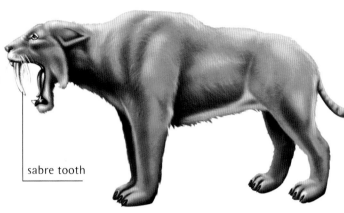

sabre tooth

Q What animals other than dinosaurs lived during the Jurassic period?

A The sabre-toothed cat, or smilodon, was about the same size as an African lion. Bones of almost 2,000 of these animals were found near Los Angeles in the United States. The smilodon had strong front legs and a short tail. Its long teeth, from which it gets its name, came in handy for hunting. The sabre-toothed cat became extinct about 11,000 years ago.

▲ Teeth as sharp as knives
The smilodon was a sabre-toothed cat with protruding canines. There were six species of this extinct killer. They could weigh up to 200 kilograms (450 pounds), about the size of an average lioness. Smilodon fossils have been found in North and South America. The fossils of other sabre-toothed cats have been found in other parts of the world. The earliest of these fossils have been dated to 33.7 million years ago, while the most recent sabre-toothed cat became extinct about 9,000 years ago.

▶ Father of elephants
There were many types of mammoths, some larger and some smaller than the modern elephant. Most mammoths had curving tusks. The fossils of many woolly mammoths have been found in the Arctic regions.

Q What is a mammoth?

A A mammoth is an ancestor of the Asian elephant. Scientists think the first mammoths developed in northern Africa around 4.8 million years ago. They had long, curved tusks and some types were covered with long hair during the last Ice Age. Mammoths migrated from Africa to Europe, Asia and even as far as North America.

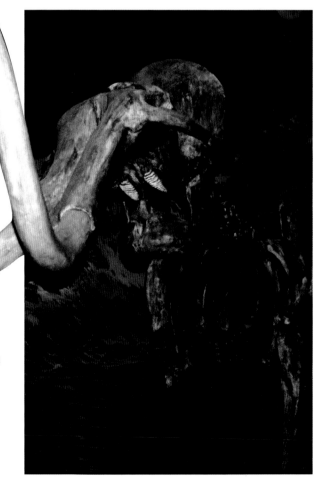

◄ Half bird half dinosaur
The mysterious archaeopteryx lived in the late Jurassic period, about 155-150 million years ago. The fossil of this animal, which may have been the first ever animal capable of true flight, has been found in Germany. It was the same size as the magpie.

Q Could archaeopteryx fly?

A No one knows for sure if archaeopteryx could fly. Some scientists argue that the fossil of archaeopteryx, first described in 1862, is a fake. They believe that someone added the impression of feathers to a small reptile skeleton. But recent research has supported the theory that archaeopteryx was a genuine link between dinosaurs and birds. Fossils of other feathered dinosaurs found in the Gobi Desert of Mongolia and China are very similar to the archaeopteryx fossil.

Q Were all mammoths woolly?

A The mammoth had to grow a woolly coat when the world began to get colder, about 700,000 years ago. But by the end of the Ice Age, even the woolly mammoth was extinct. The only survivor was the dwarf mammoth, which died out about 3,500 years ago. Some people believe that woolly mammoths survived the Ice Age, but died from disease or were hunted down for food.

Q Was archaeopteryx a bird or a dinosaur?

A Archaeopteryx means ancient wing. It was a prehistoric creature that had the features of both dinosaurs and birds. It had broad rounded wings and a long tail. Its feathers were just like those of modern birds. But archaeopteryx had a long jaw filled with sharp teeth. Modern birds do not have any teeth at all. Its claws were very different from the claws of any bird we know of, they resembled the claws of a dinosaur. Its tail was bony like that of a dinosaur, not feathery like that of a bird. Because archaeopteryx had half the features of a bird and half the features of a dinosaur, it is called a transitional creature.

Is that a human?

The first humans appeared about 2.4–1.5 million years ago. Called the *Homo habilis*, these people were only 1.3 metres (4 feet 3 inches) tall. But they were much more intelligent than the other animals. They made tools from stone, which they used to hunt for food. Then about 130,000 years ago, the Neanderthal man arrived in Europe. Neanderthals were about 1.7 metres (5 feet 6 inches) tall and very muscular.

Plant Life

Plants, of which there are about 350,000 species, are one of the biggest groups of living things. They include trees, shrubs, vines, ferns, grasses, mosses and lichen. Green plants can produce their own food using a combination of water and nutrients from the soil, and sunlight.

Quick Q's:

1. Do ferns have flowers?

A fern has neither flowers nor seeds. Ferns grow from spores on the leaves that are scattered by the wind. Each fern leaf can hold 750,000 spores.

2. Do some plants eat insects?

The leaves of the venus flytrap snap shut when an insect touches them. The plant then digests the trapped insect slowly, using enzymes from its leaves. It takes each leaf about ten days to digest one insect.

3. What are stilt roots?

Mangroves, tropical plants that grow near the coast, are partly covered by the sea water every time the tide flows in. To keep themselves above water, they have stilt roots which prop them up. These roots can breathe through special pores. Salt can be dangerous to the plant, but the roots filter the salt out.

▶ **Deadly trap**
Insects are attracted to the bright colours in the leaves of the venus flytrap. Once they are inside, the leaf snaps shut.

Q **What are the different groups of plants?**

A There are two major groups of plants – those that produce flowers and those that don't. Both types can be broken down into many different groups, including climbing plants and water plants.

Leaf

Stem

Root

▶ **Growing from a seed**
A seed first sends out its roots underground, and then its stem above. Leaves that grow on the stem produce food.

Q **Do all plants grow from seeds, or are there other ways too?**

A Some plants grow from a part of the parent plant, or from spores on leaves that are scattered by the wind. But most plants grow flowers, which are pollinated by insects. Then a seed forms at its base. These seeds are then scattered and grow into new plants.

Q **What kind of environment is best for plants to grow in?**

A Different plants have different needs, but all plants need food. Most plants need soil, air, water and sunlight to produce food. Plants that grow in the water need lots of water and little, or no soil. Plants that grow in the desert are used to little or no water, and would die if they were taken to a rainforest. Moss and lichen that grow in the Arctic region would not survive in warmer climates.

Q **How do plants live in a desert?**

A Plants that grow in the desert have to adapt to the scarcity of water. So, to conserve water, desert plants like cacti have few or no leaves. They store water in their fleshy stems. A layer of wax, called a cuticle, covers these stems and does not allow the water to evaporate. Some desert plants, like the ocotillo, make the most of the short rainy season to grow as much as possible, and then rest during the dry season. Some desert plants grow very long roots that reach down deep into the ground in search of water.

▶ **Slow-growing saguaro**
The saguaro cactus can take up to 75 years to develop a side shoot.

Deadly dhatura
The dhatura plant, common in Asia, contains a poison strong enough to kill humans.

Q Can plants survive in the Arctic?

A Plants that grow in the Arctic tundra (treeless plains), where the ground is permanently covered in frost, have to survive strong winds and snowstorms. The ground in the tundra contains few minerals, so there is not much food, either. The plants that grow here lie low and are much smaller than plants in other regions. While most other plants grow best when the weather is warm, plants in the tundra have had to adapt to an environment where the temperature is often below 10 °C (-50 °F). The dark colour of their leaves helps tundra plants to absorb maximum heat from the Sun. Some plants even grow hairy leaves to stay warm.

Q How do plants protect themselves from their enemies?

A Since plants cannot run away from their enemies, they devise their own protection. Plants like the cactus have spines that protect them from animals. The roots of the conifer are often attacked by beetle larvae. But the conifer has chemicals in its roots to attract worms that eat up the larvae. The wild tobacco plant uses the same tactic when it is attacked by the hawkmoth. Its leaves release chemicals, attracting killer bugs that eat up the moths. Plants like the bleeding heart and the Dhatura contain deadly poisons to kill their attackers. Some, like the rose and Himalayan blackberry, have thorns that stop any animal that wants to eat it. Other plants, like the stinging nettle, are covered with hairs and release a chemical that irritates or 'stings' the mouth of the animal that eats them.

Sharp roots
The stilt roots of the mangrove have needle-sharp points, making it difficult to walk near the plant.

Try these too...

Seasons and Climate (28–29), Food for Plants (98), Trees and Shrubs (99), Aquatic Plants (100), Climbers and Creepers (101)

What's that smell?

The voodoo lily has a flower that smells like rotten meat. This attracts flies to the plant. The flies and beetles carry pollen from one flower to another and help fertilize the flowers so that new voodoo lilies can grow. Rafflesia arnoldii has the largest flower of any plant in the world – it is over 1 metre (3 feet) across. It uses the same strategy as the voodoo lily to attract flies for pollination.

Food for Plants

Plants usually have roots, stems, leaves, flowers, fruit and seeds. The roots, stems and leaves help the plant produce food. The flowers, fruit and seeds help the plant reproduce.

◄ **Root vegetables**
Potatoes are the roots of the potato plant. The plant stores its energy in them.

Q What are the various functions of the roots?

A Plants grow from seeds or spores. With most plants, the roots grow first. They hold the plant down and keep it steady. They also absorb water and minerals from the soil and transport them up so the plant can produce food. In some plants, like the banyan, aerial roots (roots in the air) grow down from the branches to hold the plant up. They grow thickly and look like a stem or a trunk.

Q Where do the roots send the water to?

A The part of the plant that first grows above the ground is called the stem. The stem carries water and nutrients sent by the roots up to the leaves.

▼ **Food factory**
Leaves are the food factories of plants. They use chlorophyll, a green pigment, to make food.

▲ **Another carnivore**
The pitcher plant has a deep cavity filled with a liquid that attracts insects. The walls are built so that insects can climb down but cannot climb up again. Slowly, they drown in the liquid and are digested by the plant.

Q How do plants make their food?

A Leaves and green stems are the plant's 'kitchen'. They are green because they contain a substance called chlorophyll. When sunlight touches the leaves, chlorophyll converts carbon dioxide and water into a sugar called glucose. This is the basic food for a plant. As plants produce food, they give out oxygen, which all living things need to breathe. There would be no life on Earth without plants providing food and oxygen.

Q Why do plants grow flowers and fruit?

A Plants grow flowers and fruit to reproduce. The flowers contain pollen, which are carried by insects or the wind to other plants for reproduction. The fruit contains seeds of new plants, which are carried by animals, wind or water to other places where a new plant will grow.

Trees and Shrubs

A tree is a large, woody plant that has one straight central stem, called a trunk. It has branches that grow out of the trunk at different heights. There are more than 50,000 species of trees. A shrub is a woody plant that has lots of stems growing close to the ground. Rhododendron, rose and hydrangea are common types of shrubs.

Q How tall can a tree grow?

A Some trees grow extremely tall. In 1885, a eucalyptus was found in Australia that measured 143 metres (470 feet). The tallest tree alive today is a redwood called the Stratosphere Giant. It was found in the USA in 2000, and it is 112.7 metres (370 feet) tall. That's about as tall as a building 31 storeys high. The second tallest tree is in the same place and is called the Federation Giant. At 112 metres (368 feet) tall, it is not far behind the leader.

Q How long do trees and shrubs live?

A Both trees and shrubs are perennial plants, which means they live for more than two years. Shrubs live for at least three years. But trees usually live a lot longer. The oldest tree in the world is a bristlecone pine, nicknamed Methuselah, which is 4,767 years old. It is named after Methuselah in the Bible, who is said to have lived for 969 years.

▶ Autumn beauty
Many trees, called deciduous trees, have leaves that change colour in autumn and then fall off. The tree has to store food for the winter until it grows new leaves in the spring. Deciduous trees are common in temperate regions, and the beauty of the multicoloured leaves draws many visitors.

Q Why do some trees shed their leaves?

A Trees like birch, maple and oak and shrubs like hydrangea that shed their leaves every winter are called deciduous trees. Their leaves are too weak to survive extreme cold. But other trees stay green all year. Evergreen trees like pines and firs and shrubs like yew do not shed their leaves in winter. This is because the leaves of evergreen trees are coated in a wax-like substance that prevents them from freezing.

Try these too...

Seasons and Climate (28–29), Plant Life (96–97), Aquatic Plants (100), Climbers and Creepers (101), North America (110–111), South America (112–113), Europe (116–117), Africa (118–119), Asia (120–121), The Poles – The Arctic and Antarctica (122–123)

▼ Pretty shrub
The dwarf willow is a hardy shrub that lives in very cold Arctic and sub-Arctic areas. It does not grow more than 6 centimetres (2.4 inches) above the ground.

Strangling to survive

The strangler fig, or banyan tree, produces figs. Birds eat the figs and pass the seeds out with their droppings on to the branches of other trees. These seeds stick on to the branches of a tree (called the host tree) and send down roots. The roots of the strangler fig grow thicker and soon encircle the poor host tree. Then they tighten around it, cutting off its flow of nutrients. The host tree eventually dies, while the strangler fig grows.

Aquatic Plants

Plants that live in water have developed special ways to survive. They have grown so different from other plants that they cannot live on land. Plants that live in water are called hydrophytes. These plants are supported by water pressure. So they need a less rigid structure than plants on land.

Quick Q's:

1. Don't any aquatic plants have woody trunks?

Aquatic plants do not need hard, woody stems. They let the water around them support their soft stems.

2. Are aquatic plants of any use to us?

Aquatic plants are very useful. The seeds of the lotus can be eaten. The leaves can be used to wrap food in, rather than plastic or aluminium foil. A part of the water chestnut can be made into flour. Some aquatic plants, like the common mare's tail, are used to make medicine for healing wounds. Water plants absorb methane, which is a greenhouse gas. They also release oxygen into the air while making food.

3. Are water plants always good for the pond?

The water hyacinth can grow too fast, and completely fill a pond or small lake. It can double in size in 12 days. At this rate of growth, it can prevent sunlight and oxygen from reaching the water, which can cause fish and other plants and animals to die.

Q Why don't water plants sink?

A Water plants like lotus, water hyacinth and lily have large, flat leaves that help them stay afloat. All aquatic plants have fine hairs on their leaves that trap air, and air sacks that keep them buoyant. The water crowfoot has large leaves on top, plus thin thread-like leaves and feathery roots under water that spread out and help the plant to float.

Q Do water plants have the same roots as land plants?

A Since the main purpose of roots is to send water up to the leaves, aquatic plants, whose leaves are always touching the water, have smaller roots. In fact, aquatic plants have very light, feathery roots since the roots do not support the plant. These roots can take in oxygen.

▲ **Beautiful and useful**
Most parts of the lotus plant are useful. In Asia, it has been cultivated as a food plant for centuries. The flowers, seeds, young leaves and stems are all eaten.

Q Are aquatic plants special in other ways?

A Since aquatic plants are always surrounded by water and do not need to store it, their leaves only have a thin skin (waxy coating) or none at all. All plants have 'breathing' holes under their leaves that release excess water, but aquatic plants have lots of these holes, and they are always open.

◀ **Dangerous plant**
The water hyacinth grows so fast that it can choke most of the other life out of a pond. It also provides an ideal environment for mosquitoes to breed in. Originally from South America, it has now spread all over the world.

Climbers and Creepers

Climbing plants, also called vines or climbers, have developed special ways of looking after themselves. They latch onto trees or other supports and pull themselves up to reach the sunlight at the top of the forest, which they need to make food.

Q How do climbers and creepers grow?

A Climbers have different ways of getting around. Some make a few leaves grow into thread-like coils or tendrils. Other climbers, like roses, have hooks or thorns. These thorns clasp the tree they are growing on (called the host) and pull the rose plant up. Most climbers have pretty flowers, which is why they are often grown in gardens. Creepers or ramblers do not even grow tendrils. They just spread themselves over other plants or on the ground. Some plants like bittersweet and poison ivy grow as shrubs, and if they find a host, they turn into climbers.

Q Do all climbers reach out towards light?

A A few rare vines climb away from light. This is so that their tendrils can find the dark bark of trees easily, and climb up them. All climbers have softer stems than trees and do not waste their resources in growing strong, woody stems or branches. That is why they can grow much faster than trees.

▶ Green cover
People often grow climbers to cover walls with their beautiful green leaves. The ivy is the most popular plant for this purpose. Many large houses have had their outer walls covered by ivy for centuries. But we have to be careful and ensure that the climber does not push deep roots in to the wall, which can damage the structure.

Q Do climbers have any enemies?

A In a rainforest, about 40 per cent of the canopy can be covered by climbers. This robs the trees of sunlight. Some climbers are so heavy that trees can fall under their weight. Trees have their own ways of keeping climbers away. Some trees secrete unpleasant juices. Palm trees drop their heavy, prickly fronds, and the vines below are ripped off. Some, like the gumbo-limbo tree, shed their bark so that the creepers fall off with the bark.

Try these too...

Seasons and Climate (28–29), Origin of Life (88–89), Plant Life (96–97), Food for Plants (98), Trees and Shrubs (99), North America (110–111), South America (112–113), Australia and Oceania (114–115), Europe (116–117), Africa (118–119), Asia (120–121), The Poles – The Arctic and Antarctica (122–123)

◀ Itchy plant
The poison ivy is notorious for inducing an itchy rash among most people who touch it. In severe cases, poison ivy rash has to be treated by a doctor. This versatile plant can be a shrub, a creeper or a climber.

Long lianas

There are more than 2,500 species of lianas or woody climbers. Most are found in rainforests. Once a liana reaches the top of the canopy, it spreads from one tree to another. Some lianas are so thick, they almost look like trees. Others grow more than 914 metres (3,000 feet) long. Animals of the rainforest use lianas to move from tree to tree. Lianas twist upwards around their host, or grow tendrils and thorns to help them climb. Some even grow sticky hairs to hang on!

External Body Parts

The human body is operated by sensitive organs that are kept safe inside the body. The parts that can be seen outside, including hands, feet, skin, hair and nails, all have their own uses in keeping us safe and healthy.

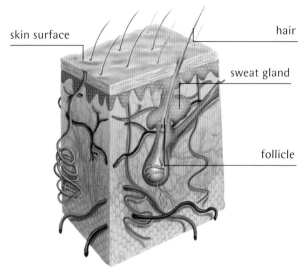

▲ Skin deep
Skin is made of layers of cells that contain nerves, blood vessels, hair follicles and glands.

skin surface · hair · sweat gland · follicle

▲ Colours of the world
A pigment called melanin decides the colour of our skin and our hair. Those who have more melanin are darker.

Quick Q's:

1. How long does it take a nail to grow?

On average, nails grow 2.5 millimetres (0.1 inches) in a month. It takes one nail cell 3–6 months to grow from the bottom to the tip of the finger.

2. What is a lunula?

The lunula is a crescent of pale skin at the base of the nails.

3. How much skin do we have?

An adult has more than 2 square metres (20 square feet) of skin. This is almost the size of a bed sheet!

4. How many hair follicles do I have?

The head has about 100,000 hair follicles and the body has about five million.

Q **Why do we need hands?**

A The human hand has five digits, four of which are called fingers, and one thumb. The thumb helps us grip things better. The hand also has a wrist, which links it to the arm. We can move and bend our fingers because each is made up of three separate bones. But the thumb is not as flexible, since it has only two bones. The fingertips have sensitive nerves that tell us what we are touching. They warn us when we are about to touch something that might harm our skin.

Q **What are feet for?**

A Feet help us to balance and move. The human foot is made up of the heel, instep, sole, ball and toes. The ankle connects the foot to the leg. The toes help us to get a balance and a good grip while we walk. They also push the foot off the ground at every step we take. The ball of the foot is the spongy part just behind the toes. The arch and the heel absorb the shock of our feet hitting the ground while we walk.

▲ All about balance
Our toes help us to keep balanced while we skip.

Q **What is skin?**

A The skin is the largest organ of the body. It holds all our other organs together. The layer of fat underneath the skin keeps our insides safe from injury. When the skin is broken, germs can attack us. Skin secretes an oil that keeps it soft and helps keep water out. Under the skin are sweat glands, which get rid of poisons that could otherwise harm us. Skin is made of layers of cells. Every minute, we lose 30,000–40,000 dead skin cells which are replaced by new ones. New skin grows from below and old, dry skin flakes off. On average, almost all of our skin is replaced every month. It is because skin replaces itself that cuts can heal so quickly.

Q **What about hair and nails?**

A Hair and nails are made of a protein called keratin. Hair grows from a tiny opening in the skin called a follicle. Nails grow from the nail root, which is hidden under the skin at the base of the nail. We have nails on our fingers and toes even before we are born. Under the nails are blood vessels that keep the nails pink. Nails are hard and they prevent the soft skin on the tips of our fingers and toes from getting hurt.

Bones and Muscles

The skeleton is like a scaffolding of bones inside us. It allows us to sit, stand, walk, run and do everything else that we do. Without it, we would be squishy, like jellyfish. The skeleton gives our body a definite shape. It protects our organs, such as the brain, heart, lungs, kidneys, spinal cord and liver. It also supports our muscles.

Q How many bones do we have?

A A human baby is born with 270 bones. Some of these join together as we grow and by the time we are adults we only have 206 bones. The central part of our skeleton has 74 bones, including 26 bones in our spine, 22 in our skull and 25 in our ribs.

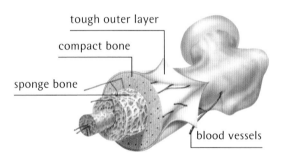

▲ Bone structure
Bones have a tough outer layer to protect them. The hard compact bone is connected to a sponge bone.

Our arms and legs have 126 bones – 62 in our legs and 64 in our arms. Our ears have six bones each. Bones are hard outside and spongy inside. This is what makes them light. Different parts of our body have different types of bones. All together we have have four kinds of bones: long, short, flat and irregular bones. In some parts of our body, there is cartilage instead of bones. The cartilge is a rubbery connective tissue. It is elastic and helps in movement.

▶ Muscle talk
Our muscles are made up of layers of fibres, one inside the other. The thicker fibres protect the thinner ones from any damage when muscles are used. It looks like thin wires inside thicker wires.

Q What are muscles?

A Muscles are tissues that can contract and return to their normal length. A muscle is made of thread-like proteins in our body. We have about 650 muscles. These muscles are connected to bones, soft tissues such as cartilage and ligaments, and to skin. The muscles in our arms and legs are long. Our chest muscles are broad and flat. Our facial muscles allow us to show our feelings through expressions. We have more facial muscles than any other animal. Muscles are voluntary or involuntary. The voluntary muscles move when we want them to. The involuntary muscles, such as the cardiac muscles in our hearts, move on their own.

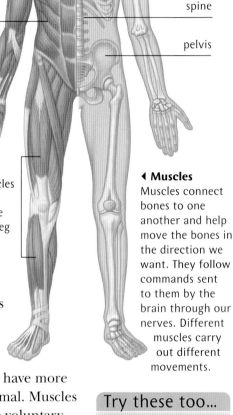

muscles that move the arm

abdominal muscles

muscles that move the leg

skull

shoulder blade

ribcage

spine

pelvis

◀ Muscles
Muscles connect bones to one another and help move the bones in the direction we want. They follow commands sent to them by the brain through our nerves. Different muscles carry out different movements.

Try these too...
Digestion and Excretion (104–105), The Brain and the Senses (107)

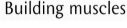
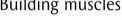

outer layer of a bundle of fibres

fibres

even smaller fibres and threads

finest muscle fibres

Building muscles

Muscles increase in size if you exercise them regularly. In fact, strong muscles show through the skin in bumps. If they are not exercised for a long time, muscles can shrink in size and grow weak.

biceps contracts, lower arm raised

triceps contracts, lower arm lowers

Digestion and Excretion

Ever wonder what happens to all that food we eat? Where does it go, and how does our body gain energy from it? Food goes through an incredible journey from the moment we take a bite. This process is called digestion and involves several organs in the body.

Quick Q's:

1. What role does the tongue play in our digestion?

The tongue has millions of tiny taste buds that help us to identify whether the food is salty, bitter, sweet or sour.

2. What is the alimentary canal?

The alimentary canal, also called the digestive tract, is a long tube that starts at the mouth and ends at the anus. It includes organs, such as the stomach, small and large intestines and rectum.

3. How does the liver work?

The liver is not a part of the digestive tract, but it plays a vital role in digestion. It releases a substance called bile that helps to break down fat. The liver also stores excess fat for later use.

4. What does the pancreas do?

The pancreas is located behind the stomach. This organ releases chemicals that help break down proteins, fats and carbohydrates. It also helps maintain sugar levels in the body and prevents diabetes.

Q Why is it important to chew food?

A An adult human has about 32 teeth. Some of these are used for biting and tearing food, while others help grind it up. The more we chew the easier it is for the body to digest the food. As we chew, the mouth releases saliva that moistens the food so that it passes through the digestive system without scraping any of the organs.

Q What happens to the food once we swallow it?

A Once swallowed, the food moves down the oesophagus, or food pipe, into the stomach. The food pipe is a long tube that connects the mouth to the rest of the digestive tract. Wave-like motions of the muscular walls of the food pipe help to push the food down the long tube.

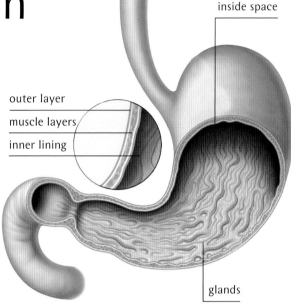

▲ **Expanding stomach**
An adult stomach is only as big as two fists, but it stretches to twice its size when filled with food.

Q Why do we sometimes choke on our food?

A The throat consists of two tubes – one for food, and one for air. A small flap called an epiglottis closes the windpipe the moment we swallow, preventing the food from entering the windpipe. However, sometimes the food accidentally enters the windpipe, causing us to choke. This usually happens when we laugh or talk while eating, or swallow food without chewing properly.

Q Is the food digested in the stomach?

A The stomach walls churn and break the food into tinier pieces. The acid in the stomach kills harmful bacteria, while other chemicals speed up digestion. Water, sugar and salt are filtered into the blood through the stomach walls. The undigested food, called chyme, passes into the small intestine for further digestion. The food is completely digested in the small intestine. Small finger-like projections, or villi, in the small intestine pass the nutrients into the bloodstream.

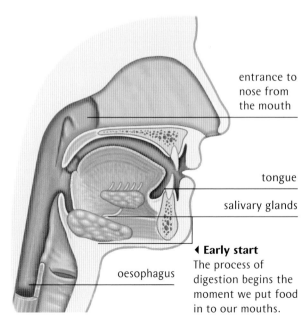

entrance to nose from the mouth

tongue

salivary glands

◀ **Early start**
The process of digestion begins the moment we put food in to our mouths.

oesophagus

Q What happens to the undigested food?

A Undigested food like fibre moves through the small intestine into the large intestine. The water in the undigested food is absorbed by the large intestine. Bacteria present in the large intestine change the waste material into faeces. The faeces are sent into the rectum where they are finally expelled through the anus.

Q What is urine?

A Urine is actually liquid waste. It contains water and a harmful chemical called urea. A pair of bean-shaped organs called kidneys filter the urine from the blood. The urine then passes into the urinary bladder through two thin tubes, known as ureters. The bladder stores the urine until it is passed out through the urethra.

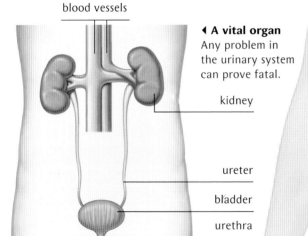

◄ **A vital organ**
Any problem in the urinary system can prove fatal.

blood vessels

kidney

ureter

bladder

urethra

Long way to go!

The alimentary canal is about 10 metres (30 feet) in length. Of this the small intestine alone makes up for almost 5 metres (16 feet). Most of the food that we eat takes about 20–30 hours to travel from one end of the canal to the other. This means that what we eat today is not digested completely until tomorrow.

▶ **Down the pipe**
Food takes about eight seconds to go down the food pipe into the stomach.

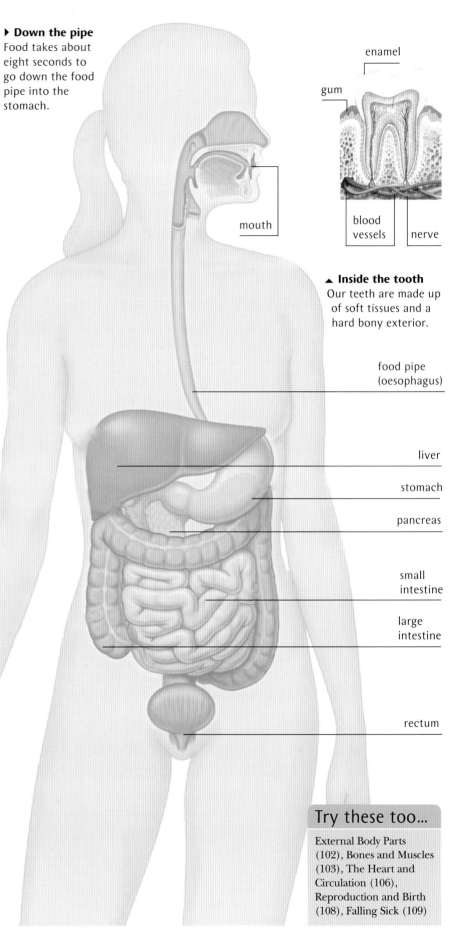

enamel

gum

mouth

blood vessels

nerve

▲ **Inside the tooth**
Our teeth are made up of soft tissues and a hard bony exterior.

food pipe (oesophagus)

liver

stomach

pancreas

small intestine

large intestine

rectum

Try these too...

External Body Parts (102), Bones and Muscles (103), The Heart and Circulation (106), Reproduction and Birth (108), Falling Sick (109)

The Heart and Circulation

The heart is a muscle about the size of a fist that pumps blood to every part of our body. It is inside our ribcage, a little to the left of the centre of our chest. Blood carries oxygen and nutrients the body needs. It also carries waste away that the body does not need. This movement of blood is called circulation.

Quick Q's:

1. How many times does the heart beat?

The heart beats about 100,000 times in one day. It begins beating from before a child is born and does not stop until the person dies.

2. Does everyone have the same kind of blood?

There are different types of human blood, so it has been divided into four groups – A, B, AB and O. Most people have a blood protein called rhesus factor. This makes their blood positive. People who do not have this protein have 'rhesus negative' blood.

3. What is bone marrow?

Bone marrow is the soft tissue inside our bones. It produces blood cells. Since red blood cells only live for about 120 days and white blood cells only for a few days, the bone marrow works constantly.

4. Are there more red blood cells than white ones ?

Red blood cells make up about 45 per cent of our blood. There is only one white blood cell for every 600 red blood cells.

Q How is the heart structured?

A The heart has four chambers, two on each side, one above the other. The two top chambers are called the left atrium and right atrium. The two lower chambers are the left and right ventricles. A wall of muscle separates the left and the right sides of the heart. The right atrium receives unclean blood full of carbon dioxide from the body. When the atrium is full, a valve opens and blood flows into the right ventricle below. From the right ventricle, the unclean blood is sent to the lungs. The lungs breathe out the carbon dioxide contained in the blood and breathe in oxygen which the body needs. The blood, now full of oxygen, enters the left atrium. When the left atrium is full, the blood flows into the left ventricle from where it is pumped to all parts of the body. This is known as the cardiac cycle.

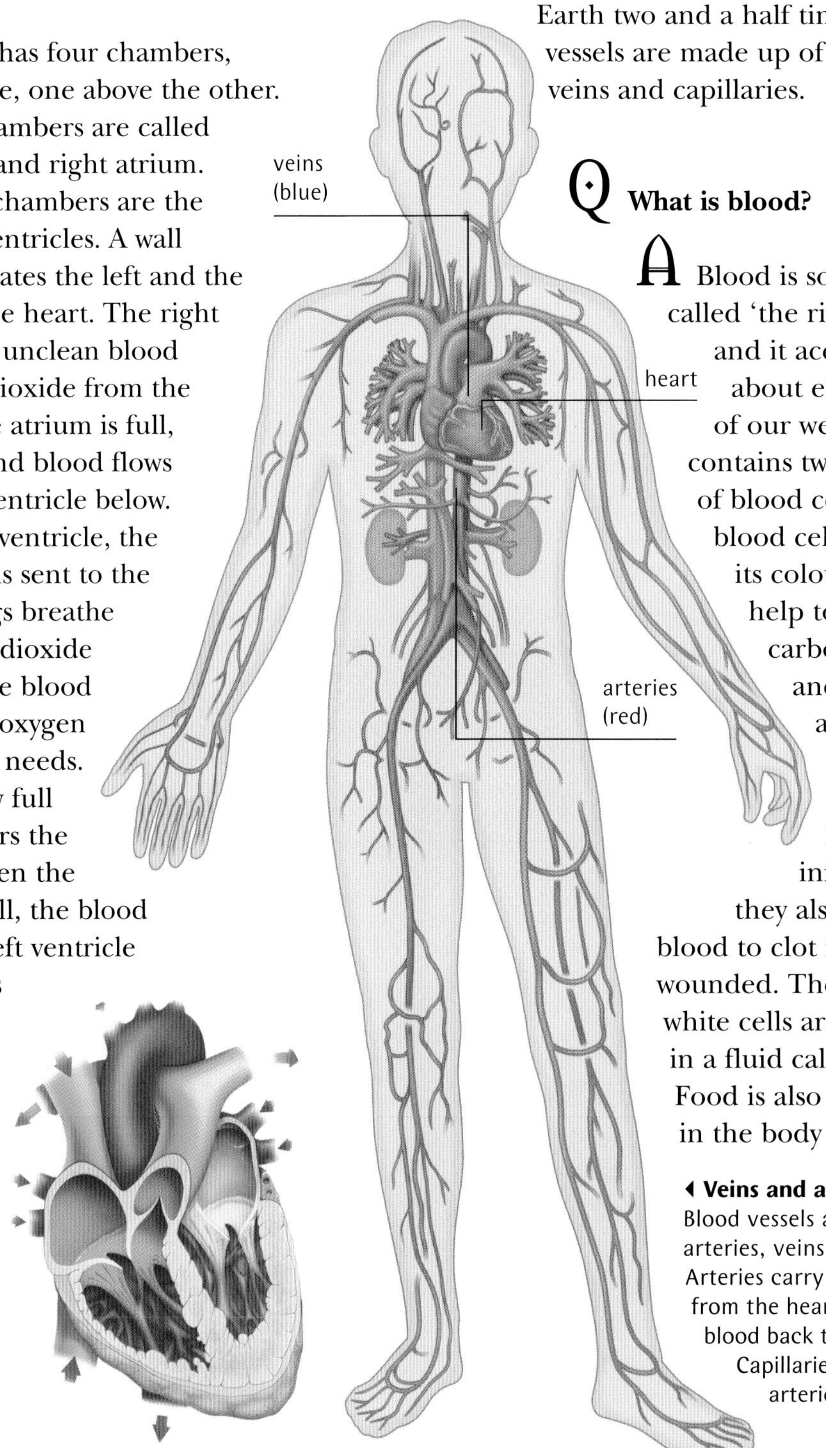

▶ Heart beat
Our heart beats because it is pumping blood. Normally it beats 72 times in a minute.

Q What is the circulatory system?

A The heart, the lungs and the blood vessels are part of the circulatory system. Humans have about 100,000 kilometres (62,000 miles) of blood vessels in their body. This is enough to circle the Earth two and a half times! Blood vessels are made up of arteries, veins and capillaries.

veins (blue)

heart

arteries (red)

Q What is blood?

A Blood is sometimes called 'the river of life' and it accounts for about eight per cent of our weight. Blood contains two types of blood cells. Red blood cells give blood its colour and also help to carry carbon dioxide and oxygen to and from the lungs. White blood cells help to fight infection and they also help the blood to clot if we are wounded. The red and white cells are suspended in a fluid called plasma. Food is also distributed in the body by blood.

◀ Veins and arteries
Blood vessels are made up of arteries, veins and capillaries. Arteries carry blood away from the heart. Veins bring blood back to the heart. Capillaries connect arteries to veins.

The Brain and the Senses

The brain, millions of nerves and the spinal cord make up the central nervous system of the human body. All the information gathered by sense organs like the eyes, ears, nose, tongue and skin is processed in the brain.

Q What is the brain?

A The brain is an organ inside the skull. It forms only about two per cent of our bodyweight, but it controls our feelings, movement, skills and every function necessary to live. The human brain is divided into three major parts; the cerebrum, the cerebellum, and the brainstem. The cerebrum gives us intelligence. It makes up 85 per cent of the brain and operates voluntary muscles that we have control over. The cerebrum is the area of the brain that allows us to dance, jump or solve puzzles. It also stores information, which we call memory. The cerebellum or 'little brain' is below the cerebrum and is just one-eighth of the size of it. The cerebellum controls balance and tells the muscles how to move. The brainstem connects the rest of the brain to the spinal cord, which runs down the neck and back. The brainstem controls involuntary muscles that work without us thinking about it, like the heart, the lungs and the stomach.

Q What are the uses of smell?

A Smell is an important sense that our nose helps to detect. Smell helps us to examine the environment around us. Our nose continuously tests the air we breathe and alerts us accordingly. It warns us in case of potential dangers like smoke or poisonous gas or tells us about the presence of other people or objects. Most importantly smell serves as a recognition function. Each of us has a unique smell and often we recognize one another by smell. This is how even a new born baby recognizes his mother!

▶ **Brainy stuff**
The brain processes the basic information that it gets from the sense organs helping us to see, hear, taste, feel, smell and react.

Q How do we actually see?

A We see through our eyes, of course, but it is due to our brain that we know we are seeing this page and not something else. When light enters our eyes, special nerves inside the eyes carry a message to the brain. Then the brain understands what we are seeing. In the same way, it is the brain that understands what we hear, smell, taste or feel.

The brain grows on

Human brains are still growing. In 1860, the average weight of a male brain was 1.36 kilograms (3 pounds). Today, a male brain weighs about 1.44 kilograms (3.17 pounds). Would you believe that the human brain is also getting smarter!

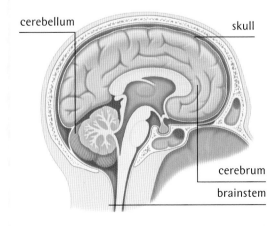

cerebellum
skull
cerebrum
brainstem

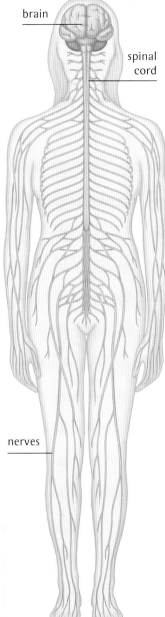

brain
spinal cord
nerves

▲ **What nerves!**
Thirty-one pairs of spinal nerves connect the spinal cord to the rest of the body. They help to deliver messages from the spine to the rest of the body.

Try these too...

External Body Parts (102), Bones and Muscles (103), Reproduction and Birth (108), Falling Sick (109), Electricity (186–187)

107

Reproduction and Birth

Like all other living creatures, human beings reproduce. Human beings are mammals, so they give birth to live children.

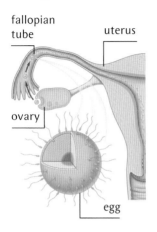

fallopian tube

uterus

ovary

egg

▲ The female egg
Once puberty begins, the ovaries produce one egg (shown enlarged here) roughly every 28 days. This egg travels into the uterus through the fallopian tubes. The uterus is connected to the vagina through the cervix.

Quick Q's:

1. How many eggs does a woman have?

The ovaries hold thousands of eggs. These are released once a month for about 30 years during menstruation. When a woman is between 45–50, menstruation stops and eggs are no longer released. This change is called the menopause.

2. For how many years can the male reproductive system produce sperm?

Unlike females, males can produce sperm thoughut their life. However, their fertility declines a lot when they are old.

Q **When can a human being reproduce?**

A It takes several years before a human being can reproduce. The body of a child goes through changes between the ages of about 8 and 15. This period is called puberty and it makes a person ready to produce children. Girls develop breasts and their hips widen. Boys grow hair on their faces and their voices grow deeper. Other changes take place in the reproductive organs.

Q **What are reproductive organs?**

A Male reproductive organs are outside the body. They include the penis, and a pair of testes inside a cover called a scrotum. The testes produce sperm and the male hormone testosterone. During sexual intercourse, sperm travels down the penis. The female reproductive system is also in the pelvic region, but it is inside the body. It is made up of two ovaries, a uterus, two fallopian tubes, the cervix and the vagina. The ovaries produce a hormone called oestrogen. They also make eggs to join with the sperm to produce a baby.

head of sperm

◀ Sperm cell
The sperm cell is either male or female. This factor determines the sex of the baby.

tail

▶ Into the world
The baby develops in the womb which backs up against the uterus wall. It comes out through the vagina at the time of birth. It is still connected to the mother through the umbilical cord, which has to be cut.

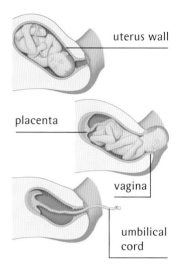

uterus wall

placenta

vagina

umbilical cord

placenta

◀ The miracle of pregnancy
The fertilized egg grows inside the mother's womb for about 40 weeks. This growth period is called pregnancy. During pregnancy, the baby gets food and blood from the mother through the umbilical cord attached to its belly button. The baby, or foetus, lies curled up inside the womb in a position known as the foetal position.

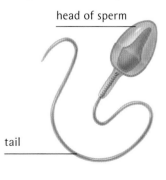

umbilicial cord

uterus

vagina (baby comes out from here)

Q **How is an egg fertilized?**

A Each of us starts from a tiny cell. Millions of sperm cells are suspended in a mixture called semen. The male body has to produce lots of sperm, since many of them die inside the uterus. One sperm cell from the father joins an egg cell from the mother. These form a new cell in the mother's fallopian tube. This is called fertilization. The fertilized egg then attaches itself to the uterus wall and prepares itself for growth. This is the beginning of a baby.

Falling Sick

When we feel good and the body and the mind are working as they should, we are in good health. When we have trouble with any part of our body, we usually feel ill.

Q Why do people fall ill?

A The human body is made up of many organs and systems. The organs include the brain and the heart, the liver, the lungs and the kidneys. If even one of these organs does not do the work it is supposed to do, we can fall ill. To work well, the body needs the right kind of food in the right quantities. It also needs exercise and a clean environment. Any imbalance in these factors can cause us to fall ill.

Exercise for health

Physical activity, which includes jumping, running, playing games, dancing and other kinds of exercise, keeps our bodies and minds healthy. It builds up muscles and strengthens bones. Physical activity makes us breathe deeply, and our lungs get more oxygen. It keeps the heart healthy and our weight in check. If you eat more food than you use up with exercise, the body stores this extra energy as fat. Too much fat can be harmful to our health.

Q What food does the body need?

A The body works best when it is fed a balanced diet with food from each of the five basic food groups – carbohydrates, vitamins, minerals, proteins and fatty acids. We get carbohydrates and starch from grains and cereals, potatoes and beans. They give us energy. We get vitamins from fruit and vegetables. Milk, cheese, yoghurt and other dairy products give us calcium, a mineral that strengthens bones and teeth. Fish, meat, poultry, eggs, nuts and pulses give us protein for building up our bodies. Butter, oil, chocolate and sugar give us fatty acids that contain the important vitamin E to protect our internal organs. Healthy oil comes from fish, nuts and vegetables.

Q What are germs?

A Germs are tiny creatures that we can only see through a microscope. These include bacteria and viruses. Harmful bacteria cause infections like sore throats and stomach upsets. Viruses are germs that can cause chickenpox, measles and influenza. We catch germs from people who are unwell, from stale and unhygienic food or water, or from our surroundings. They produce poisons that make us sick. Some of these diseases, like cholera, tuberculosis and HIV/AIDS can even kill us.

▶ **The fighter**
The image shows white blood cells (centre) surrounded by red blood cells. The white blood cells are the fighters we have within us. When germs attack, the body raises its temperature to kill them. The white blood cells attack the germs, surround and eat up the germ cells, and help us to get healthy again.

▲ **Modern diagnosis**
A modern CAT scan machine can map the electrical impulses within the brain. It is used to locate any disease in the brain or in the nervous system. Similar modern methods have made the doctor's job easier.

Try these too...

External Body Parts (102), Bones and Muscles (103), Scientific Revolution (150–151), The World after World War II (160–161), The New Millennium – 21st Century (163)

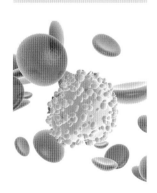

North America

North America lies north of the equator in the western hemisphere. It is connected to the the continent of South America by the narrow strip of land called the Isthmus of Panama. North America has the Arctic Ocean to the north, the Atlantic Ocean to the east and the Pacific Ocean to the south and west. It covers an area of 24,480,000 square kilometres (9,450,000 square miles), which is a little less than 5 per cent of the Earth.

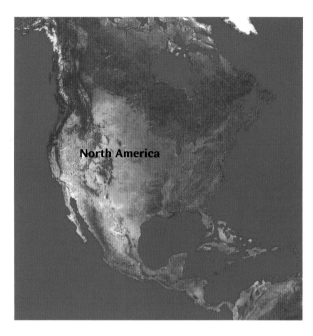

North America

▲ **North America**
The third largest continent after Asia and Africa, North America had a population of 514.6 million in 2006.

Quick Q's:

1. What languages are spoken in North America?

The United States has no official language but most people speak English and many speak Spanish. In Canada, the two official languages are English and French. But Spanish is the official language in Mexico.

2. Where is Niagara Falls?

Niagara Falls is on the river Niagara, between Canada and the United States. It is really three falls – the American Falls, the Canadian or Horseshoe Falls and the Bridal Veil Falls. In one minute, more than 168,000 cubic metres (6 million cubic feet) of water falls over its crest.

3. Where are the Great Lakes?

The Great Lakes include Superior, Huron, Erie and Ontario, on the border of Canada and the United States, and Lake Michigan in the USA. Together, these lakes make up the largest freshwater surface in the world.

Q Which countries make up North America?

A North America is made up of three countries. Canada, the largest, is in the north, followed by the United States of America in the middle and Mexico in the south.

Q What are the main geographical regions in North America?

A There are four principal geographical regions in North America. These include the Appalachian Mountains in the eastern United States and the Great Plains, which stretch from the Gulf of Mexico in the south to the northern parts of Canada. The other regions are the West, where the Rocky Mountains are found, and beyond the Rockies, the low-lying Great Basin.

Q Who discovered America?

A Native Americans have been living in the continent for thousands of years. Viking sailors may have reached there around 1000 AD, but no proof of this has yet been found. Most historians credit the discovery of America by Europeans to Christopher Columbus, who sighted land on 12 October 1492 while sailing west from Spain across the Atlantic Ocean. Columbus thought he had reached the shore of India, and that was why he named the locals Indians. The island he first sighted was San Salvador in the Bahamas.

Q What are the types of animals that live in North America?

A Animals found in the prairies include cougars, coyote, badgers, bobcat, prairie dogs, foxes and American bald eagles. The tundra (cold plains) is home to a few animals like the grey wolf and snowshoe rabbit, while birds visit the taiga (subarctic forests) to nest in the summer. The lynx, minks, red deer, elk, and moose can also be found in these regions. The desert in the south is home to a variety of insects, snakes, antelope and kangaroo rats. Grizzly bears and rattlesnakes are also found in different parts of North America.

▼ **Feared and hated**
The rattlesnake is highly poisonous but warns its enemy by rattling a special set of bones in its tail.

Q Who are the various people who live in North America?

A The first humans in North America could have been there as long as 50,000 years ago. They were probably related to the prehistoric Kennewick Man, the name given to a 9,000-year-old skeleton found in Kennewick, Washington in 1996. Different Native American tribes have claimed the remains as theirs to prove that they were the first Americans. The populations of these tribes dwindled and after the arrival of the Europeans, some were completely wiped out because of war, disease and losing their homes. When the Europeans had made North America their home, they began bringing African slaves, many of whom remained in North America after they were freed. Today North America is home to people from all over the world.

▲ **Rocky road**
The Rocky Mountains run from north to south through much of the North American continent.

▲ **Popular food**
Tortilla, or Mexican bread, is now popular all over the world.

Try these too...

Earth's Atmosphere (26–27), Seasons and Climate (28–29), Mountains, Valleys and Caves (30–31), Other Landforms (32–33)

▶ **Cat with many names**
Cougar, mountain lion, puma – these are just some of the many names for this large, solitary cat found all over North America.

A grand creation

The Grand Canyon is a steep gorge in Arizona in the United States. It has been shaped over two billion years by wind and water, where the Colorado River cuts through the Colorado Plateau. It is almost 1.6 kilometres (1 mile) deep in some places. It is about 446 kilometres (277 miles) long, and between 0.4 and 24 kilometres (0.25 and 15 miles) wide.

South America

Most of the continent of South America is in the southern hemisphere, and the equator passes through it in the north. To the west lies the Pacific Ocean, and to the north and to the east is the Atlantic Ocean. It is 17,840,000 square kilometres (6,890,000 square miles) – almost 3.5 per cent of the Earth. This makes it the fourth largest continent. It is about two and a half times the size of Australia.

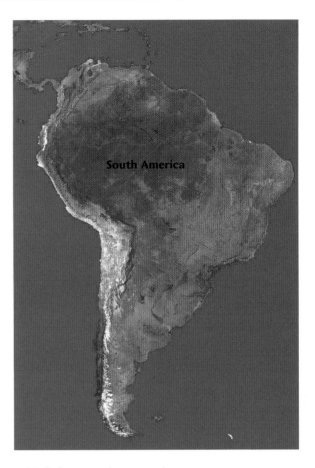
South America

Quick Q's:

1. Which is the highest peak in South America?

The Aconcagua peak rises 6,960 metres (22,834 feet) in the Andes range in western Argentina. It is the highest peak in the western and southern hemispheres, the highest in the world outside Asia.

2. Which is the highest waterfall in South America?

Angel Falls on Auyan Tepui river in Venezuela falls 979 metres (3,212 feet). It is the highest waterfall in the world. It is named after James Crawford Angel, who first saw it from his aeroplane in 1933. The local name is Churún Merú, which means Devil's Mouth.

3. Which is the longest mountain range in South America?

Stretching for 7,000 kilometres (4,400 miles), the Andes is the longest mountain range in the world. It starts near the equator and goes on almost to Antarctica. In some places, it is 500 kilometres (300 miles) wide.

Q How many countries make up South America?

A The 12 countries in South America are Argentina, Brazil, Bolivia, Chile, Colombia, Ecuador, Guyana, Paraguay, Peru, Suriname, Uruguay and Venezuela. French Guiana is controlled by France. The Galapagos islands in the Pacific Ocean are a part of Ecuador.

Q What are the main geographical regions in South America?

A In the north and west are the Andes, the second highest mountain range in the world. On the eastern coast are the lower mountains of the Guiana plateau, the Brazilian massifs and the Patagonian plateau. The most important lowland is the Amazon Basin, with the world's largest rainforest.

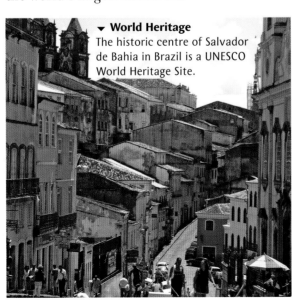

World Heritage
The historic centre of Salvador de Bahia in Brazil is a UNESCO World Heritage Site.

▲ Varied geography
South America contains tropical rainforests, high mountains, temperate grasslands and sub-polar regions. Chile is home to the world's driest desert – the Atacama. The Andes mountains are home to the highest lakes in the world.

Q What types of climate are found in South America?

A With the equator passing through the continent, much of South America has a warm and tropical climate, with wet summers and dry winters. The northern coasts of Venezuela and Colombia are dry and prone to droughts. The Pacific coasts of Colombia and Ecuador have a tropical climate, but the coastal regions in Peru and northern Chile are very dry. The cold currents off these shores do not carry moisture. In the high Andes mountains there is an alpine climate, and the areas around them are cool. South of the tropic of Capricorn, the climate is temperate – summers are cool and winters are cold. Patagonia in southern Argentina has an almost polar climate.

Q What vegetation grows in South America?

A South America has the largest rainforest in the world, which lies along the equatorial region. Palms, tall trees, ferns, bamboos, and lianas (vines) grow there. There are also large areas of savannah, where tall grass grows. This gives way to the brushlands along the Venezuelan coast. Brazil has both deciduous and evergreen forests as well as prairie (grassy plains). The Pampas of Argentina are the largest grasslands in South America.

Q What are the main animals found in South America?

A South America has animals that are special to the continent. These include bloodsucking bats, the spectacled bear and the tapir. South America is famous for its alpacas and llamas. It also has jaguars, anteaters and coati. The rainforests are home to hundreds of species of birds, including macaws and 500 types of hummingbirds. The more unusual birds include the rhea and the flamingo. Rainforests are also home to snakes like the anaconda and other types of boas, as well as iguanas and crocodiles. The green anaconda, the largest boa, can grow up to 10 metres (33 feet) long. The Galápagos Islands, near the coast of Ecuador in the Pacific Ocean, are known for their unique animals like the Galápagos tortoise.

▼ World's largest tortoise
An adult Galápagos tortoise can weigh 300 kilograms (661 pounds) or more.

When it's that huge, it's Amazonian!

In terms of the amount of water it carries, the Amazon is the largest river in the world. It starts in Peru in the Andes and flows into the Atlantic Ocean after crossing into Brazil. Tributaries from Bolivia, Colombia and Ecuador join it. Along its banks are 6,000,000 square kilometres (2,300,000 square miles) of rainforests. These forests contain about 2,000 species of birds and mammals, several thousand varieties of plants and almost 2.5 million types of insects. It was given its name after a battle that Spanish explorer Francisco de Orellana fought with a tribe of Tapuyas women. They reminded Orellana of the ancient female warriors or Amazons of Greek mythology.

▼ Tango in harmony
Various styles of the tango dance developed in different parts of Argentina and Uruguay. It is now popular all over the world.

▲ Delicious food
Shrimp stew in a mud pot – a typical dish of Brazil. People from all over the world brought their cuisine to South America.

Try these too...

Earth's Atmosphere (26–27), Mountains, Valleys and Caves (30–31), Other Landforms (32–33), Oceans (34–35), Volcanoes (36–37)

Australia and Oceania

Oceania is a group of about 10,000 islands that lie in the Pacific Ocean between Asia and America. It includes the continent of Australia. Unlike the other continents, Oceania is a region linked by water rather than land. It was given its name in 1831 by French explorer Dumont d'Urville.

Australasia

Quick Q's:

1. How crowded is Australia?

Australia is the sixth largest country in the world, but it has the lowest population density, with only two people living in every square kilometre.

2. What is special about Australian sheep?

Australia has more than 101 million sheep. Most of them are merinos which produce an excellent light wool. They give us more than 70 per cent of the world's wool.

3. What is a dingo?

The dingo is a wild dog of Australia. The dingo fence, which keeps sheep safe from dingoes, is the longest continuous fence in the world. It is 1.8 metres (5.9 feet) high and runs through Queensland for 5,531 kilometres (3,437 miles).

4. What is special about Hawaii?

Except for Easter Island in the South Pacific, Hawaii is furthest from any other body of land. These volcanic islands are still expanding as more lava pours into the seabed.

Q **Other than Australia, what are the islands included in Oceania?**

A Oceania has four regions: Micronesia, Melanesia, Polynesia and Australasia. These regions are divided into thousands of islands. Fiji, Indonesia and Papua New Guinea are in Melanesia. Micronesia is a chain of tiny islands that forms the Federated States of Micronesia. The Cook Islands, Samoa and Tonga are in Polynesia. Australia, New Zealand and Christmas island are part of Australasia. Hawaii, in the middle of the Pacific ocean, is also part of Oceania.

Q **Why is Christmas Island so-called?**

A Christmas Island was given its name by the British captain William Mynors of the ship the Royal Mary, because he arrived there on Christmas Day in 1643. This small island in the Indian Ocean is so far from any other landmass that its plants and animals are quite unique. People did not live there earlier, so there has been no human interference. As a result, it is of immense interest to scientists.

▲ **An unknown continent**
The early inhabitants of Australia are believed to have come from Southeast Asia about 48,000 years ago.

Q **What is the Australian climate like?**

A Australia is the driest and flattest continent inhabited by people. Most of it is desert, arid land or hummock grasslands. The north has a warm, tropical climate with rainforests, mangrove swamps and grasslands. The south-east and south-west have a cool and temperate climate. Australia is an island with an area of 7,686,850 square kilometres (2,967,909 square miles), surrounded by the Indian and Pacific Oceans. It has a coastline of 25,760 kilometres (16,007 miles) where nearly 90 per cent of its population lives.

▼ **Natural beauty**
New Zealand (left) is known for the beauty of its mountains and lakes. The beaches of Australia (right) are very popular with surfers.

Q How long have people lived in Australia?

A Humans began to live in Australia about 48,000 years ago. They were hunter-gatherers. Their descendants are Aborigines and Torres Straight Islanders. There were about 350,000 Aborigines when the Europeans first landed in 1606. Today, most Aborigines live in the desert-like central part of Australia called the 'outback', having been pushed out of the more fertile areas by the European settlers.

Q Who discovered Australia?

A The first European to find Australia was the Dutch navigator Willem Jansz, who sighted Cape York Peninsula in 1606. On 26 January 1788, the British established a penal colony in New South Wales to house convicts whom they could no longer lock up in the overcrowded British jails. After 1864, they stopped shipping convicts to Australia. The Aborigines were forced off their land by the Europeans and several died in their new homes. Today, they make up 2.2 per cent of the total population. Many of the 20.6 million Australians are immigrants from Great Britain and Ireland.

Q Why do koalas live only in Australia?

A Australia and the islands of Oceania are ancient lands that have been isolated from other continents for millions of years. That is why 84 per cent of Australia's mammals and plants and almost half of its birds cannot be found anywhere else in the world. These include the koala, kangaroo, platypus, echidna, brush-tailed possum and wombat, and birds like the emu and the kookaburra. Other native animals include reptiles like crocodiles, snakes and lizards. The saltwater crocodile of northern Australia is the largest reptile in the world. The tuatara, the most ancient reptile, is found in New Zealand. It can live for up to 100 years.

▲ **Corroboree**
An Aboriginal word, Corroboree means dance, music and theatre.

▲ **Sports crazy**
Australians are reputed to be a nation of sports lovers. Whether it is cricket, Australian-style football, tennis, swimming, surfing or athletics, stadiums are almost always full.

Try these too...

Earth's Atmosphere (26–27), Seasons and Climate (28–29), Mountains, Valleys and Caves (30–31)

That's some barrier

The Great Barrier Reef, the longest coral reef in the world, stretches for over 2,000 kilometres (1,250 miles) in the Coral Sea off north-eastern Australia. It is made up of 3,000 reefs and 900 islands. The Great Barrier reef is a precious environmental site because it is home to many thousands of species of fish and marine animals. In 1981, it was made a World Heritage Site. However, life on the reef is still under threat from over-fishing and pollution.

Europe

Europe is the sixth of the seven continents in terms of size. It covers 10,390,000 square kilometres (4,010,000 square miles), which is 2 per cent of the surface of the Earth. To the north of Europe lies the Arctic Ocean, and to the west, the Atlantic Ocean. To the south, Europe is separated from Africa by the Mediterranean Sea. To the east, the boundary is not clear, but it is around the Ural Mountains and the Caspian Sea.

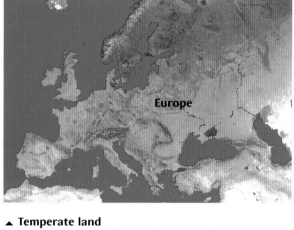

Europe

▲ **Temperate land**
The Gulf Stream that flows in from the Atlantic Ocean keeps north-western Europe warmer than other places at the same latitude.

Northern Ireland
Scotland
England
Wales

▲ **British Isles**
The United Kingdom is made up four countries: England, Scotland, Wales and Northern Ireland.

Quick Q's:

1. Is the Vatican City a country?

Vatican City, which is an enclave in Rome, is the world's smallest independent country. It is the seat of the Roman Catholic Church. It is ruled by the Pope.

2. Why is Norway called the land of the midnight Sun?

One-third of Norway lies north of the Arctic Circle. From May to the end of July, this region has continuous daylight.

3. Where is Istanbul?

Istanbul is in north-west Turkey. It is the only city in the world to be in two continents – Europe and Asia. It is divided in to two by the Bosporus Strait.

Q **What is the landscape of Europe like?**

A Europe is more mountainous towards the south, which also has some of the best beaches, on the Mediterranean coast. The Alps cover parts of Austria, Slovenia, Italy, Switzerland, Liechtenstein, France and Germany. Although the Alps have high peaks like Mont Blanc and Piz Bernina, the highest peak in Europe is Mount Elbrus in Russia, 5,642 metres (18,510 feet), in the Caucasus range. Moving beyond the Alps, the Pyrenees and the Carpathians, the land rolls into the Great European Plain. The British Isles are separated from the rest of the continent by the English Channel and the North Sea.

Q **When did people start living in Europe?**

A Neanderthal man reached Spain by sailing, floating or swimming across the Strait of Gibraltar from Africa. They disappeared mysteriously about 30,000 years ago when homo sapiens (modern man) began to arrive. The first humans probably came to Europe about 10,000 years ago. Although Europe is relatively small, more than 710,000,000 people – about 11 per cent of the world's population – live here. Only Asia and Africa have more people.

◄ **Flamenco dancer**
The flamenco of Spain is one of the many traditional dance forms popular in Europe.

▼ **City of canals**
Venice, a city off the coast of north-eastern Italy, has canals instead of roads.

Q What languages are spoken in Europe?

A As many as 41 languages are spoken in different parts of Europe. Some of the languages, such as English, French, Spanish, German and Russian, are spoken by millions of people in many countries all over the world.

Q Does Europe have forests?

A Centuries ago, about 90 per cent of Europe was covered in forest. Now, more than half of this has been felled. However, in countries like Finland, 72 per cent of the land is still covered by forests. Evergreen and deciduous forests cover most ground. Conifer forests are found in Scandinavia and parts of Russia and Ukraine. Further north is the taiga region with forests of spruce, birch and pine. The Mediterranean region has cork oak forests, cypress trees and olives.

▲ **Wild cat**
The lynx is the largest wild cat found in Europe. Apart from the bear, it is the prime predator in the forests of the continent.

One Europe

Europe has about 47 countries, some of which, like Liechtenstein, are among the smallest in the world. Of these 47 countries, 27 are part of the European Union (EU). The EU is the largest political and economic group in the world. It has its own currency called the euro.

Q Are the forests full of animals?

A Europe's forests are home to brown bears and wolves, which are now protected by law. Smaller animals include lynx, badgers, hedgehogs, wildcats, jackals and foxes. Snakes like the viper and birds like the vulture, eagle and owl are also found here. The northern parts of Scandinavia have herds of reindeer, some of whom have been domesticated for centuries. The forests of Scotland are famous for the red deer. Europe is home to many bird species that spend their winters in warmer Africa, and return to their European homes every spring.

▲ **Traditional food**
Steak (left) and Yorkshire pudding (above) are among the traditional foods of Europe. Switzerland is famous for its dairy products, especially cheese. The cuisines of all countries on the Mediterranean coast are famous around the world.

Try these too…

Earth's Atmosphere (26–27), Seasons and Climate (28–29), Mountains, Valleys and Caves (30–31), Oceans (34–35), Volcanoes (36–37), Ancient Greece (128–129), Ancient Rome (130–131), Medieval Europe (136–137), The Renaissance (142–143)

◀ **Prickly spines**
The little hedgehog with its prickly spines is common but shy, nocturnal and tough to spot.

Africa

Africa is the second largest continent in the world. The Romans named it 'Africa terra', which means land of the Afri, after a tribe who lived in North Africa. Africa has around 840,000,000 people. It covers about 30,300,000 square kilometres (11,700,000 square miles) including the islands. This is roughly 6 per cent of the total surface of the Earth.

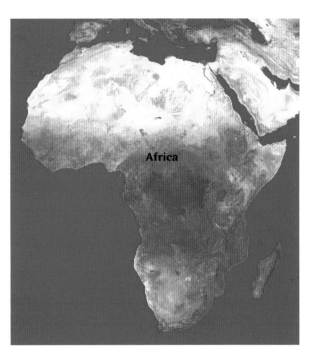

Africa

▲ **Many climates**
Africa has several different climate zones. The Sahara keeps the north hot and dry. The centre has the rainforests, the south-east the savannah.

Quick Q's:

1. Which is the highest point in Africa?

Kibo on Mount Kilimanjaro is the highest peak. It is 5,895 metres (19,341 feet) tall. Although close to the equator, the peak is so high it is covered with snow.

2. Does Africa have any big lakes?

Lakes Victoria, Tanganyika, Albert, Edward and Kivu are the Great Lakes of Africa, in the Great Rift Valley. Lake Victoria covers 69,500 square kilometres (26,836 square miles) and is the world's second largest freshwater lake.

3. Does Africa have major rivers?

The Nile River, at 6,825 kilometres (4,241 miles) long, is the longest river in the world. Other rivers in Africa include the Congo, the Zambezi and the Niger.

4. Is the Sahara the only desert in Africa?

Three major deserts cover one quarter of Africa. The Sahara covers 11 countries. The Kalahari desert and the Namib desert are in the south.

Q **Where can I find Africa on the globe?**

A Africa is the only continent straddling the tropic of Cancer, the equator and the tropic of Capricorn. It lies to the south of Europe and the Mediterranean Sea and to the west of Asia, beyond the Red Sea. To its west is the Atlantic Ocean and to its east is the Indian Ocean. It is a long continent, stretching 8,000 kilometres (5,000 miles) from the tip of Tunisia in the north to its most southern point in South Africa, the Cape of Good Hope. It is widest at the centre, with 7,400 kilometres (4,600 miles) between its most eastern point in Somalia and its western coast. Africa's coastline is 26,000 kilometres (16,100 miles) long.

Q **How many countries are there in Africa?**

A Africa is home to 54 countries. The largest is Sudan and the smallest is the Seychelles, a cluster of islands to its east. Of all the islands, Madagascar is the largest, covering 587,000 square kilometres (226,658 square miles).

▼ **Tribal dance**
Different tribes in Africa have different traditional dance forms. This is a dance in Nigeria, western Africa.

Q **How long have humans lived in Africa?**

A The first human life on Earth started in Africa more than 7 million years ago. Our ape-like ancestors lived there. The 'cradle of humankind', a series of limestone caves near Johannesburg in South Africa, is the oldest sign of human civilization that we know of. People who live north of the Sahara desert are called North Africans and people who live south of the Sahara are called sub-Saharan Africans. One of the earliest tribes, the Berbers, were pushed into the Sahara and the Sahel (the area bordering the Sahara) in the seventh century by the Arabs, who settled on the northern coast. Other tribes still found in sub-Saharan Africa include the Bushmen of the Kalahari Desert, the Masai of Kenya, the Twa pygmies and the Tutsi of west and central Africa. Europeans, people from the Middle East and Asians have also settled in Africa, where they colonized several countries. In the last century, most European countries handed these colonies back to the local people. There are now people from all over the world who live in Africa.

Q Is there poverty in Africa?

A Africa is the world's poorest continent. Of the 175 countries ranked in the 2003 United Nations Human Development Report, 25 African countries ranked lowest. Sixty per cent of the people depend on agriculture, and they have been getting less and less money by exporting their crops. The situation has been worsened by poor rainfall since the 1980s in many countries south of the Sahara.

Q What plants and animals might I see on an African safari?

A Cypress, pine, oak, orange and olive trees grow along the Mediterranean coast of North Africa. The date palm is the common plant in the Sahara oases. Rainforests in north-west and central Africa have hundreds of species of plants and animals, including elephants, gorillas, snakes, okapi and crocodiles. The baobab and the acacia are common trees in the mixture of grassland, desert and mountains that cover much of eastern and southern Africa. This is home to the lion, elephant, cheetah, rhino, zebra and many kinds of monkeys, apes, deer and antelope.

▼ **Haven for animals**
The African savannah – now a series of national parks – is home to a huge variety of wild animals.

What-a-fall!

Victoria Falls, locally called Mosi-oa-Tunya (meaning 'smoke that thunders'), is on the Zambezi River between Zambia and Zimbabwe. The falls are about 1.7 kilometres (1 mile) wide and 128 metres (420 feet) high – the largest single sheet of water in the world. In 1855, David Livingstone named the falls after Queen Victoria. They are a World Heritage Site.

Try these too...

Earth's Atmosphere (26–27), Seasons and Climate (28–29), Mountains, Valleys and Caves (30–31), Other Landforms (32–33), Oceans (34–35), Volcanoes (36–37)

▶ **Traditional decoration**
A woman of the Himba tribe in Namibia, south-western Africa, wears a traditional headdress and jewellery. The decorations have cultural significance.

Asia

Asia is the largest continent in the world. It spreads over an area of 44,390,000 square kilometres (17,139,000 square miles). This is 8.7 per cent of the total area on Earth, or 29.8 per cent of the total landmass. Over 3.5 billion – six out of every ten – people live in Asia, in some of the most populated countries in the world like China and India. Except for a few of its islands, Asia is in the northern hemisphere – north of the equator.

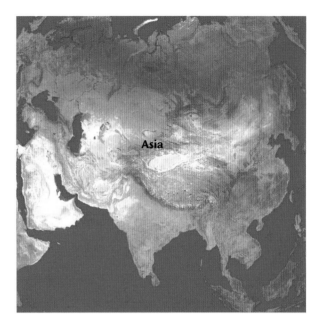

▲ Large and populous
The continent of Asia accommodates about 60 per cent of the world's total population.

Quick Q's:

1. Which are Asia's largest cities?

Seoul, Mumbai, Jakarta, Tokyo and Shanghai are some of the largest cities, not only in Asia, but in the world!

2. What languages are spoken in Asia?

There are more languages spoken in Asia than on any other continent – over 100 in the Philippines and more than 500 in Indonesia alone. Chinese, Hindi, Arabic and Bengali are among the languages spoken by over 100 million people. Chinese will soon be spoken by more people than any other language. People in most Asian countries speak more than one language.

3. What are the most famous architectural structures in Asia?

There are old cities, forts and monuments all over Asia. The Great Wall of China is the only man-made structure that can be seen from the moon! The Taj Mahal in India and the Angkor Wat in Cambodia are among the world's famous monuments.

Q **Who are Asia's neighbours?**

A To its west, Asia borders Europe. If you drew an imaginary line along the Ural mountains to the Caspian Sea, the Black Sea and the Aegean Sea, it would be the western border of Asia. Asia has the Arctic Ocean in the north, the Indian Ocean in the south, and the Pacific Ocean in the east.

Q **What is the landscape of Asia like?**

A Asia is home to Mount Everest, the highest point on Earth and to the Dead Sea, the lowest surface on Earth. Along the coast and in river valleys are fertile plains.

They include the valleys of the Yangtze and Hwang Ho rivers in China; the Ganges, Brahmaputra and the Indus rivers in south Asia; and the Tigris and Euphrates rivers in west Asia. The Yangtze is the longest river in Asia, covering 6,380 kilometres (3,964 miles). The highest mountain ranges in the world are in Asia – the Himalayas, Hindu Kush, Kunlun and Tien Shan mountains.

▼ Modern cities
Many Asian cities such as Dubai (seen here), Tokyo, Shanghai, Hong Kong and Singapore are full of high rise buildings.

Q What kind of plants grow in Asia?

A Asia is so large, it contains various biomes (climate areas with similar plants and wildlife). In the northern sub-polar regions, grasses and moss grow. Away from the coast, the coniferous forests form the taiga. Central Asia has vast grasslands known as the steppe. South-west Asia is arid and desert-like. Further south and east, in countries such as India, Sri Lanka, Malaysia and Indonesia, tropical rainforests abound.

Q Do people live all over Asia?

A Most people live along the river valleys and grow crops like rice and wheat. Many others work in mines, since Asia is rich in petroleum, iron and bauxite. Asia is the world's largest producer of bananas, cotton and tea. With such a long coastline, fishing is also an important source of income. In China and India, where industry is booming, many people are moving away from rural areas to live in densely populated cities.

Q Does Asia have a lot of wildlife?

A There are some animals in Asia that are not found anywhere else in the world. The giant panda of China, the orangutan of Borneo and Sumatra and the komodo dragon of Indonesia are all unique to the continent. The tiger, the Asiatic lion and the rhino are all under threat of extinction.

Sitting on a seabed

During the Paleozoic and Mesozoic eras, 570 million to 65 million years ago, the Tethys Sea covered most of what is Asia and parts of Europe. The Indian subcontinent broke off from Africa and drifted towards the north-east. As the land pushed north, it crumpled and folded to form the Himalaya mountains. Gradually, the islands of eastern Asia, such as Japan and Taiwan, began to grow. The plates that make up Asia are still moving and settling, which makes this region prone to volcanic activity, earthquakes and natural disasters such as the 2004 tsunami that devastated many countries around the Indian Ocean.

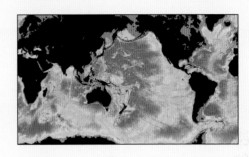

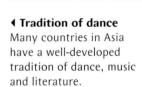

Try these too…

Earth's Atmosphere (26–27), Seasons and Climate (28–29), Mountains, Valleys and Caves (30–31), Other Landforms (32–33)

◀ **International tastes**
The cuisines of China, India and Japan are famous all over the world.

◀ **Tradition of dance**
Many countries in Asia have a well-developed tradition of dance, music and literature.

▼ **Tea ceremony**
Asian countries like Japan have very formal traditions like that of the tea ceremony.

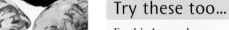

The Poles – The Arctic and Antarctica

The North and South Poles are at the two ends of the Earth's axis. The North Pole is the northernmost part of the Earth, and the most southern tip of the Earth is the South Pole, in Antarctica. The Arctic and the Antarctic are the most arid (dry) places on Earth.

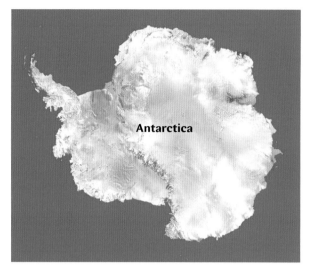

Antarctica

▲ **Discovering the south pole**
For centuries, people kept searching for the 'Southern Continent'. Antarctica was finally discovered in 1819.

Quick Q's:

1. Why is 21 June an important day around the Arctic Circle?

On 21 June or the summer solstice, the Sun does not set north of the Arctic Circle. That is why this area is called the land of the midnight sun. For the local residents, this is a time to celebrate. On the other hand, on 21 December – the winter solstice – the Sun does not rise at all.

2. What lies below the ice and snow?

Many minerals have been found in the Arctic, although mining is difficult. Russia and the US have found deposits of coal, copper, nickel, gold, uranium, tungsten, diamonds, natural gas and oil. Antarctica may also be rich in minerals.

3. Do people live in the Arctic?

Hunters from Siberia were the first people to live in the Arctic, arriving about 5,000 years ago. The Inuit of North America, the Greenlanders, the Lapps of western Europe, and some groups of people in Russia and Siberia live in the Arctic. They hunt, fish and keep herds of reindeer.

Q What is the Arctic?

A From the air, the Arctic would look like a blob of ice surrounded by ocean and rock, with a scattering of islands. The Arctic Circle is an imaginary line around the Earth which represents the southern limit of the Arctic region. The average summer temperature north of the Arctic Circle does not rise above 10 °C (50 °F).

Q Which countries are in the Arctic?

A Parts of Canada, Alaska (the largest state in the USA), Russia, Norway, Sweden, Finland, Iceland and Greenland lie within the Arctic circle. The Arctic landmass is made up of mountains, plateaus and tundra plains. The tundra is flat and marshy and covered by permafrost (permanent ground frost). The sea in the Arctic, known as the Arctic Ocean, is frozen over for much of the year.

Q Does it rain in the Arctic?

A The climate in the Arctic is polar. It has a short, cool summer and long, freezing winter. In the outer edges of the Arctic – the tundra – the average summer temperature is between 0 and 10 °C (32–50 °F). Among the ice caps, it is below 0 °C (32 °F) throughout the year, and there is a permanent cover of snow. Most of the precipitation (rainfall) is frozen and falls as snow, but it does occasionally rain.

▼ **Continent of ice**
Huge cliffs of ice are found at the edge of the Antarctic continent.

Q Who lives in Antarctica?

A Antarctica has no local population. It is the least populated continent. In 1819 William Smith discovered a landmass which he called the South Shetland Islands. He believed it to be a group of islands, but in 1840 it was declared a continent.

Q Are the polar ice caps melting?

A Polar ice caps have been melting at an increasing rate since the 1990s due to the increasing level of greenhouse gases like carbon dioxide in the Earth's atmosphere. In 2005, 221 cubic kilometres (53 cubic miles) of the Greenland ice cap melted and fell into the sea, compared to 92 cubic kilometres (22 cubic miles) in 1996. One cubic kilometre is three times the amount of water used in a large city in a year. This water is raising sea levels, threatening coasts all over the world.

▼ Icebreaker
Many ships have been surrounded and immobilized by ice in Arctic and Antarctic seas in the past. Modern ships that sail in these waters are specially built to ram their way through thick sheets of ice.

▶ Maximum distance
Every year, the Arctic tern migrates from the Arctic to Antarctica and back! This is the longest regular migration by any animal that we know about. For its effort, the Arctic tern does get to enjoy two summers every year.

▼ Hole in the ice
The Arctic ringed seal is the only seal that can make a breathing hole in ice and live under it throughout the year.

Try these too...

Earth's Atmosphere (26–27), Seasons and Climate (28–29), Mountains, Valleys and Caves (30–31), Other Landforms (32–33)

Night light

The aurora is a coloured glow seen in polar regions at night. In the Arctic, it is called the aurora borealis or northern lights, and in the Antarctic, the aurora australis, or southern lights. These colourful lights are caused by magnetic fields, when high-energy particles from the Sun react with atmospheric gases.

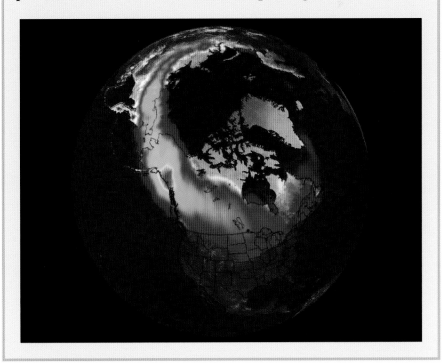

Ancient Mesopotamia

A large part of ancient Mesopotamia is now covered by the country of Iraq. The fertile land near the Euphrates and Tigris rivers is known as the 'Cradle of Civilization', and it was here that the first ever Mesopotamian civilizations were born. Mesopotamia was home to the ancient cultures of the Sumerians, Akkadians, Babylonians and Assyrians.

◀ Location of the ancient civilizations in Egypt and Mesopotamia.

▼ **Watering the land**
Mesopotamians were very clever. They built elaborate canals and dams to irrigate their dry farm lands.

▲ **Symbols of the past**
The cuneiform is the oldest script in the world.

Quick Q's:

1. Which was the oldest Mesopotamian civilization?

The Sumerians settled in Mesopotamia about 4000 BC, making them the first civilization in the world.

2. Who ruled Mesopotamia?

Every Mesopotamian city was ruled by a king, who was thought to have been chosen by the god of the city.

3. Were there wars in ancient Mesopotamia?

Mesopotamians fought with each other over land, water and power. The first ever war probably took place between the cities of Lagash and Umma.

Q What did the Mesopotamians do for a living?

A A large part of the Mesopotamian society consisted of farmers. The Sumerians were the world's first farmers. They cultivated a variety of crops including wheat, barley and flax. The climate in Mesopotamia was dry, so the people living there had to depend on the rivers for irrigation. They built canals to carry water from the rivers into large reservoirs, where it was stored. The farmers also built dykes to protect their houses from floods.

Q Why did the Mesopotamians build boats?

A Apart from farming, Mesopotamians also traded in goods like stone and metal. They realized that these materials could be transported easily along the rivers and across the sea using boats. So the Mesopotamians built different types of boats. They had wooden boats with triangular sails, a wooden raft called a *kalakku,* and a tub-like boat made of reeds and covered with animal skin known as a *guffa.*

Q What is a *ziggurat*?

A The Mesopotamians believed that their cities and towns were protected by gods. They built temples to these gods on top of large, pyramid-like structures called *ziggurats.* These were made of mud bricks and had between three and seven storeys. The ziggurat was often built at the centre of the city.

▲ **Down the river**
Boats were used for transport and trading goods in ancient Mesopotamia.

Q Were the Mesopotamians really the first people to develop writing?

A The Sumerians were the first to develop a written language. Their script is known as cuneiform and was composed of a series of symbols. These were carved on to clay tablets using a reed called a stylus. They used the tablets to keep records of trade and land ownership. There were some religious texts too. The Sumerian script was adapted by the later civilizations including the Akkadians.

Ancient Egypt

The civilization of ancient Egypt on the banks of the Nile lasted for more than 3,000 years and was the longest continuous civilization in the world. During this period there were many political and economic changes, but the basic culture, religion and lifestyle remained the same throughout.

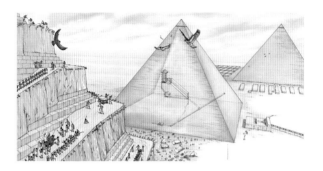

Q Why is the Nile River known as the lifeline of Egypt?

A It was the fertile banks of the Nile that attracted early settlers to Egypt. These settlers formed two different kingdoms – Upper Egypt in the south, and Lower Egypt in the north, with the Nile Delta. People fished in the Nile and farmed on its banks.

Q Why did ancient Egyptians build pyramids?

A Ancient Egyptians built pyramids as a final resting place for their kings, called pharaohs. They believed that their pharaohs continued to look after the affairs of the kingdom even after death. It was therefore necessary to make their souls comfortable. The Great Pyramid of Khufu, made out of stone, is the grandest of all pyramids. This amazing monument is over 146 metres (480 feet) tall and has survived for more than 4,000 years!

Q What is a mummy?

A The ancient Egyptians believed in life after death. They thought that each person had three souls – *ka, ba* and *akh.* It was said that the body had to remain intact even after death for *akh* to exist happily. So, the ancient Egyptians preserved dead bodies by a process called embalming. The process was known only to some priests. The embalmed body is called a mummy, and some have survived until today!

Deciphering sacred carvings

The ancient Egyptians used a form of writing that was made up of pictures. This was known as hieroglyphics. The word hieroglyphic means sacred carving in Greek. For years, no one could read these strange-looking symbols. Then in 1799, the famous Rosetta Stone was discovered at Rashid (Rosetta), in Egypt. This stone contains an order issued by the priests of Ptolemy V in 196 BC. The order is written in a mixture of Egyptian hieroglyphics, Greek and other ancient scripts. With the help of the Greek texts, experts were soon able to decipher the hieroglyphic script.

▲ **Massive effort**
Many people were needed to build a pyramid.

▲ **Comfortable afterlife**
Ancient Egyptians buried food, furniture, jewellery and everything else that was thought necessary for the afterlife along with the mummies. It was believed that the dead had to be well-provided for if they were to perform their duties effectively after death.

Try these too…

Africa (118-119), Discovery of New Lands (144-145), Architecture (164-165), Art and Artists (166-167), World Religions (176-177)

Ancient India and China

Most ancient civilizations developed in river valleys. The Indus Valley civilization, from 3000 to 1500 BC, covered Afghanistan, Pakistan and western India. The Chinese civilization developed along the banks of the Hwang-ho River in about 2100 BC and was governed by various dynasties, or ruling families.

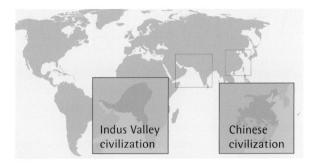

Indus Valley civilization

Chinese civilization

▲ **Unknown script**
A seal of the Indus Valley civilization, with its unknown script.

Quick Q's:

1. What is Mohenjo-Daro?

Mohenjo-Daro was the largest city in the Indus Valley and means mound of the dead. It had been abandoned for many centuries. Then in 1924, while a railway line was under construction, workers started digging near the mound. When archaeologists saw the ancient bricks the workers were digging up, they realized they had hit upon an important ancient site.

2. Who was Empress Xi Ling-Shi?

Empress Xi Ling-Shi is said to have discovered silk when a cocoon fell into her cup of tea and the silk unravelled. By 3000 BC, silk was worn by Chinese royalty.

Q What was special about the ancient Indus Valley civilization?

A The Indus Valley civilization grew up around 3000 BC along the banks of the Indus and Ghaggar-Hakra rivers. Before this, people generally lived in the forest or in small villages. When the civilization developed, great cities were built, with populations of up to 35,000 people. These cities were very advanced and carefully planned with straight roads. The people knew how to make baked bricks out of mud and they built homes two storeys high. Each home had a well and a bathroom from which waste drained in to sewers through clay pipes, some of which were covered and were high enough for a man to walk through. The sewers drained in to a river or the sea.

◄ **Ancient priest**
Scholars think this is the statue of a priest from the time of the Indus Valley civilization.

Q What did the people of the Indus Valley do for a living and for recreation?

A Farmers grew barley, peas, melons, wheat, cotton and dates and herdsmen kept sheep, pigs, cows and water buffalo. Fishermen caught fish using hooks like modern fishermen do today. Grain was stored in a large town granary. Specialized writers kept records of trade and land ownership on the terracota seals. The people were expert artists and potters, and could weave. They could work metal to make jewellery, statuettes and weapons. There were market days every week, to which people came from far away. Colourful clothes and jewellery were sold in the markets. The women wore lipstick made out of vegetable dyes. The men went hunting, sometimes with falcons. Children played with different toys like small carts, whistles shaped like birds, and monkeys that slid down a string.

▼ **Swimming pool or religious bath?**
The great bath of Mohenjo-Daro may have been used for ritual bathing before prayers. But some scholars think it was also used for recreation.

Q What are the early Chinese dynasties known for?

A The Xia dynasty is the earliest known Chinese dynasty (2100–1600 BC). It lasted for about fourteen generations. During the Shang dynasty (1600–1027 BC), a written language began to take shape and history started to be recorded. At this time, people also learnt to make things out of bronze.

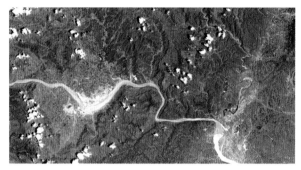

The Shang dynasty in China was followed by the Zhou dynasty (1027–221 BC), when the Chinese learnt to use iron. The rulers during this period encouraged their people to grow crops, spin silk, make pottery, build boats and carts, and hunt with bows and arrows. In 221 BC, Emperor Qin Shi Huang became the first king to rule over the whole of China. He made sure that all Chinese people spoke the Qin language. A written language with over 3,000 characters was developed.

Q Who was Confucius?

A Confucius was born in 551 BC during the rule of the Eastern Zhou dynasty. He was a teacher and a philosopher. He travelled widely, giving advice to different rulers and trying to convince them to be more caring towards their people. He believed in the family and in peace, truth and cooperation. He also believed that the king should be just and fair. The years of Confucius are known as the Golden Age of Chinese philosophy. His teachings were followed by generations of rulers and officials who governed China.

Teatime

The ancient Chinese knew all about tea. Tea, which they called *tu*, was grown in China from at least 1000 BC. It was often used in religious ceremonies. For a long time, the leaves were eaten like vegetables. Gradually, from the time of the Western Han dynasty around 207 BC, people began to use tea as a medicine and as a royal drink. But it wasn't until the Tang dynasty that began in 618 AD that drinking tea became an important part of Chinese life.

◀ **River valley**
An aerial view of part of the Yangtze river and its valley, where the ancient Chinese civilization was developed over many centuries.

▼ **Destroying knowledge**
Emperor Qin Shi Huang ordered the burning of most books in the country in 213 BC, destroying very valuable information about ancient China. He believed that those who wrote books were spreading dissent against him.

Try these too...

Asia (120–121), Discovery of New Lands (144–145), Architecture (164–165), Art and Artists (166–167), World Religions (176–177)

Ancient Greece

The ancient Greek civilization is the oldest in the western world. This civilization thrived about 3,000 years ago. One of the earliest cultures to flourish in the Greek islands was the Minoan civilization on the island of Crete, which began around 2700 BC. The ancient Greek civilization we know today emerged around 800 BC.

◀ Location of the ancient Greek civilization.

Quick Q's:

1. Did ancient Greeks know about democracy?

Democracy – a form of government elected by the citizens of a country – was first introduced in Athens.

2. Who was Homer?

Homer is one of the best-known Greek writers. He wrote the two famous epic poems – *The Iliad* and *The Odyssey*.

3. What is the Parthenon?

The Parthenon is the most famous building of ancient Greece. It was a temple to Athena, the Greek goddess of war and wisdom. The Parthenon has been renovated many times. The latest round started in 1975, and has been going on since then.

4. Did ancient Greeks make pottery?

Ancient Greeks made pottery for their daily use. Some of the most commonly used vessels included amphora (wine jars), hydria (water jars) and krater (mixing bowls). These vessels were often painted with beautiful scenes from famous Greek legends.

Q What are city-states?

A Ancient Greece was divided into many small, self-governing communities. This was largely because of the geography of Greece, where every island and many cities are cut off from their neighbours by mountain ranges or sea. These smaller independent communities formed what were known as city-states. Each city-state had its own customs and laws. The most important city-states were Athens, Sparta, Corinth and Thebes.

Q What caused the Peloponnesian war?

A Around the fifth century BC, the Athenians became very powerful. They began to dominate all the other city-states, especially in war.

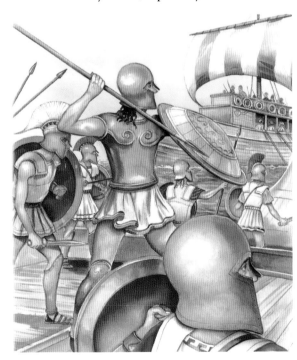

▲ **Pottery class**
Ancient Greeks had a system of training in all the arts.

The city of Sparta became jealous and, supported by Corinth, went to war against Athens in 431 BC. The Peloponnesian War lasted for 27 years. Athens was defeated. It was stripped of its navy and lost its colonies.

Q Were ancient Greeks good at art?

A The Statue of Zeus at Olympia by Phidias was one of the seven wonders of the ancient world. The statues made in ancient Greece showed detailed knowledge of the human anatomy. Ancient Greek architecture consisted mainly of temples. They had simple square or rectangular shapes, surrounded by tall columns. Greek art has had enormous influence on the cultures of many countries.

◀ **War**
The ancient Greeks were well-known for the many wars they fought on land and sea. City-states fought one another, then united to fight Persian invaders.

Q What did the ancient Greeks do for fun?

A Ancient Greeks enjoyed watching plays. Almost every city had open-air theatres where drama festivals took place. Awards were given to the best playwright. Greek tragedy and comedy have had a lasting impact on western drama and culture.

Q When were the first Olympic Games held?

A The ancient Greeks were keen sportsmen. The Olympic Games were an athletic and religious celebration held in the town of Olympia. The first Olympic Games were held in 776 BC, in an attempt to bring all the city-states together in friendly competition.

Q Did girls in ancient Greece go to school?

A Only boys went to school in ancient Greece. Girls were not sent to school. They were taught housework and married by the age of 13. Women were not allowed to go out to work, or even to vote. Only men took part in the affairs of the state.

▼ **Ancient Olympics**
A discus thrower takes part in a competition in ancient Greece.

Try these too…

Europe (116–117), The Renaissance (142–143), Architecture (164–165), Art and Artists (166–167), Theatre (170–171), World of Sports (172–173)

▼ **Birth of democracy**
In the city-states of ancient Greece, men openly debated and voted on many issues.

Living in slavery

Slaves in ancient Greece had no rights at all – they didn't even have their own names! They used the names their masters gave them. People became slaves in many ways; some were children of slaves, some were abandoned as infants; some were children sold by their families for money. Prisoners of war also became slaves.

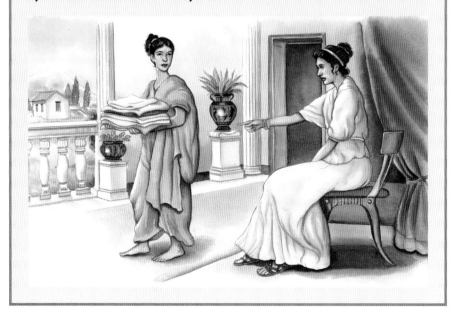

Ancient Rome

The ancient Roman civilization was the most powerful of all ancient civilizations. In the beginning Rome was a small city-state that was under the control of the Etruscans. It soon grew to become the largest empire in the ancient world. Ancient Rome was greatly influenced by the ancient Greek culture.

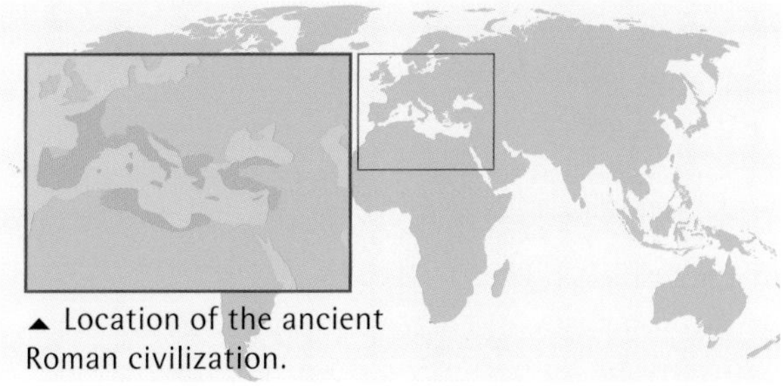

▲ Location of the ancient Roman civilization.

Quick Q's:

1. What was special about the Colosseum?

The Colosseum is a huge open-air theatre in Rome. It was built by Emperor Vespasian and his sons. It held 50,000 people. Gladiatorial games and mock naval battles were the main events held in it.

2. Did all ancient Romans wear togas?

A toga was a long piece of cloth worn by men in ancient Rome. It was usually draped over the tunic. The toga was a symbol of the person's position in society. Therefore, slaves and most poor men did not wear togas.

3. What are *insulae*?

The poor people in ancient Rome lived in small, crowded apartments known as *insulae*. These apartments had only 2–3 rooms, and large families lived in them.

4. Who were the *bestiarii*?

Sometimes, criminals who had been sentenced to death and prisoners of war were forced to fight wild animals with their bare hands in the Roman arena. They were called *bestiarii*.

Q When was Rome founded?

A According to legend, Rome was founded on 21 April 753 BC by Romulus and Remus, who were twins born to Mars, the Roman god of war. A fight broke out between the two brothers regarding the exact location of the city of Rome, and Romulus ended up killing Remus. Romulus then completed building the city that was later named Rome after him.

Q Was ancient Rome ruled by kings?

A Romulus was the first of the Seven Kings of Rome to rule the city. Around 509 BC, Tarquin, the last of the Seven Kings, was made to step down from the throne and the Roman Republic was established. Under this system, Rome was ruled by magistrates and other representatives who were elected by the people. The Republic of Rome dominated all of western Europe. However, by 30 BC, Rome once again came under the rule of kings and became known as the Roman Empire. The Roman Empire was later divided into two parts – eastern and western.

▲ **Roman soldiers**
Roman soldiers were the best trained, the most disciplined and the most feared in the ancient world.

Q Who were the Five Good Emperors?

A The Five Good Emperors ruled ancient Rome between AD 96 and 180. They were Nerva, Trajan, Hadrian, Antoninus Pius and Marcus Aurelius. The Five Good Emperors were so-called because ancient Rome prospered the most under them. They were known for their fair policies and good rule.

◄ **Army officer**
An army officer was an important citizen in Rome, especially during the time the Roman Empire was expanding. They held titles that showed the number of soldiers they commanded. For example, a centurion commanded a hundred soldiers.

Q Were the ancient Romans good at engineering?

A Ancient Romans were brilliant architects and engineers who constructed magnificent buildings throughout the Empire. However, they are best known for their amazing public baths, roads, aqueducts and drainage systems. Baths were a very important part of life in ancient Rome. Both men and women visited the baths at least once a day. The water in the baths was channelled through aqueducts.

▲ **Roman bath**
The Roman bath had many rooms, with water at various temperatures and facilities for exercise.

Q Why did ancient Romans build aqueducts?

A The Romans built aqueducts to carry water to the cities. Sometimes, the water would be carried from rivers or streams as far as 95 kilometres (59 miles) away! They used natural gravity to carry the water over such long distances. Wherever there was a depression, walls or arches were built over it to keep the water flowing. The water was stored in a large tank, or *castellum*, in the city, from where it was distributed to public fountains and baths.

Q What did ancient Romans do for recreation?

A Ancient Romans loved dance and music. The rich held elaborate feasts in which they served exotic food like oysters, pork and snails and entertained their guests. All the people were very fond of gladiatorial games.

▲ **Roman banquet**
Roman banquets went on for hours.

Try these too...

Europe (116–117), Architecture (164–165), World of Sports (172–173)

▼ **The scribe**
The scribe was an important part of ancient Rome. He wrote down all the laws and the debates in the senate.

Paving the way

Apart from baths and aqueducts, ancient Romans also built roads, some of which still exist today. Roads in ancient Rome had multiple layers. The bottom layer, called *pavimentum*, was made of mortar. This was covered with a layer of stones and cement. A layer of concrete and slabs of stone was added to this. Finally, the upper layer of concrete and smooth pebbles was laid. This method of building roads is known as paving.

Ancient Americas

Middle America, also called Mesoamerica, is the region that stretches from central Mexico to northern Honduras. In ancient times, it was home to some highly developed civilizations like the Maya and the Olmec. These civilizations prospered until the arrival of the European settlers in the sixteenth century.

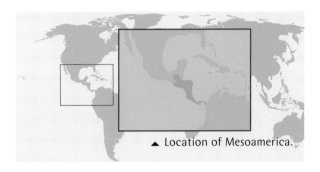

▲ Location of Mesoamerica.

Quick Q's:

1. What type of gods did Mesoamericans believe in?

Ancient Mesoamerican gods were part human and part animal. They represented natural elements like the Sun and the Moon, rain, lightning and the various planets.

2. Who discovered the cocoa that we all love?

The Maya loved to drink hot cocoa. They believed cocoa was a gift from their snake god Quetzalcoatl and that it could cure them of illness. Chocolate is made from cocoa.

3. Why did the Mesoamericans bury jewellery with their dead?

The Mesoamericans believed in life after death. They buried their dead with jewellery, vases and toys they thought were needed in the afterlife. The Mayans believed that ordinary people went to the underworld when dead, but when kings died, they went to heaven and were reborn as kings in another world. When rich people died, they were buried under their own homes, while kings had elaborate tombs.

Q How did the various civilizations in Mesoamerica develop?

A Farming in Mesoamerica goes back to 5000 BC. Various tribes knew each other and traded in food, animal skins and jewellery. Sometimes their armies raided each other's villages. Gradually, large cities with big palaces, temples and flat-roofed pyramids were built for the rich. The rulers were also the priests. The workers grew crops, built houses for the rich and fought as soldiers.

Q Besides farming, what were the other kinds of work in Mesoamerica?

A People wove cloth and made rope, baskets and fishing nets. Traders took their wares to other villages. Huge temples, pyramids and tombs were built. Artisans carved and painted designs on their walls.

▼ **Stepped pyramid**
The huge stepped pyramid built by the Maya at Chichen Itza (Mexico).

Q Who were the Olmec?

A The Olmec were the first group of people to arrive and settle in Central America. They made the area their home by 1200 BC. They had a calendar and calculated time by studying the stars and a written language which they engraved on stone. Later civilizations learnt many things from them, such as how to build houses. This is why they are the mother culture of Mesoamerica.

▲ **Big heads**
Enormous statues of helmeted heads are the best-known examples of Olmec art. Some were 3 metres (10 feet) tall.

Q Why are the Maya special?

A The Maya took the study of astronomy and mathematics much further than the Olmecs had done. They built huge observatories to study stars. They were excellent artists and built grand structures like palaces and ceremonial platforms. They made tools and weapons from volcanic glass.

Native Americans

People have lived in North America for more than 12,500 years, since before the end of the last Ice Age. Scholars believe that these people moved from Asia to America through the Bering Land Bridge during the last Ice Age.

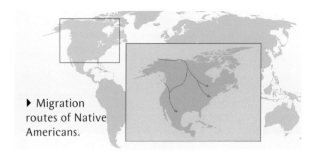

▶ Migration routes of Native Americans.

Q Where did these people come from?

A Most people believe that the early Americans crossed the Bering Land Bridge from central Asia. This bridge now lies underwater. Gradually people spread out across North America. The people of different regions developed different ways of life.

Q Who were the Mississippians?

A The Mississippians were hunter-gatherers who lived in the south-eastern part of what is now the United States. They began to grow crops about 5,000 years ago. About 2,400 years ago, they learnt how to grow maize crops. They also grew beans, squash and sunflowers. They buried their dead under huge mounds. They knew how to bake pottery and they built four-walled homes of clay and thatch. Some of them lived in a city called Cahokia.

Q Did people live in other parts of North America?

A The Delaware, Mohegans, Mohawks and Abenaki lived in the north-east of America. They were good hunters and used spears, bows and arrows and clubs. They fished with spears, hooks and nets and lit flares to attract fish to the surface. They knew how to make two types of homes – the longhouse covered with bark, and the wigwam covered with reeds and animal skins.

Try these too...

North America (110–111), Incas and Aztecs (141), Discovery of New Lands (144–145)

◀ **Classic teepee**
Native Americans in the Great Plains designed a wigwam that could be put up and dismantled very quickly.

▼ **Warrior**
Native American warriors often dressed to look like the animals with which they felt a spiritual bond.

The story of Hiawatha

The Iroquois people were constantly fighting among themselves. After the death of his family a heartbroken chief, Hiawatha, was wandering in the forest when he met the Peacemaker, who helped him to overcome his grief. The Peacemaker took Hiawatha and visited all the Iroquois tribes and convinced them to live in peace. The tribes got together to form the Iroquois Confederacy. This Confederacy continues and is one of the oldest political groups in North America, far older than the government of the United States.

▲ God of fertility
Kokopelli is a fertility god who was worshipped by Native Americans in the south-western part of the United States.

Quick Q's:

1. Why are Native Americans also called American Indians?

Columbus believed he had landed in India when he reached America. He called the locals Indians.

2. Why did their population fall?

Europeans carried diseases which the native Americans had not known. They were unable to fight smallpox, measles, bubonic plague, cholera, typhoid fever, scarlet fever, pleurisy, mumps, diphtheria, pneumonia, whooping cough, malaria and yellow fever. Some groups were wiped out.

3. Were they prepared for Europeans?

Battles with the better-armed Europeans killed many Native Americans. As the Europeans wanted more land, the tribes were pushed back. Many could not adjust to their new homes and died.

Q Who were the Apache Indians?

A The deserts of what is now the south-western United States were occupied by nomadic hunter-gatherers and farmers. The people who lived here included the Apache and Navajo. The farmers grew maize, squash and beans. They often lived in pueblos or terraced stone and adobe brick homes built around a square. They were good farmers who could grow enough crops in a dry place to support entire villages. Each clan had a headman. Most Apache lived in a *wickiup*, a hut shaped like a dome or a cone of grass and reed mats over a frame. Each wickiup had a fire pit and a smoke hole. Navajo lived in cone or dome-shaped *hogans* which had six or eight sides. The doors of hogans always faced east. A hogan was almost a sacred place since the Navajo believed the roof symbolized Father Sky and the floor was Mother Earth.

Q Why did the Navajo paint sand?

A The Navajo made beautiful sand paintings depicting their gods as part of a healing ceremony. The paintings were done with coloured powder made from grinding stones and other objects they found around them. They used five shades: white, black, red, yellow and blue. The colours were dribbled on to sand. The sand painters were guided by the Navajo priests, called shamans. The paintings were done at dawn and wiped out at the end of the day.

▶ The shaman
Native American priests, called shamans, were often the local doctors as well.

▲ Cave dwellings
The cave dwellings of Mesa Verde (Colorado) in which the Pueblo lived in the twelfth and thirteenth centuries.

Q Were the Native Americans religious?

A Religion was an important part of daily life for Native Americans. Priests called shamans practised medicine and performed rituals. There were rituals for planting and harvesting. The Green Corn Ceremony was a Cherokee thanksgiving festival. Nothing was taken for granted. Most Native Americans were forgiving people and pardoned all crime except murder. The Navajo believed in ghosts, who they thought were the spirits of their ancestors.

Q Who are the Inuit?

A Inuit means 'the people'. The Inuit people settled in the Arctic zone in the extreme north of America. These people, who probably migrated to America from central Asia, adjusted well to the extreme cold conditions. Since they could grow little food, they became expert hunters. They also became experts at building igloos, houses made with blocks of ice.

Q How did the Inuit hunt?

A For fishing, the Inuit learnt how to use a harpoon, or a spear with a strong line attached to it, that could be hauled back from the water. They also fished with hooks, lines, or spears with three prongs. In summer, they dug out roots and berries, the only plant food in their diet. For meat, they ate whales, walruses, polar bears and musk oxen. They often ate meat raw, since there was little fuel to cook with. The Inuit trained packs of dogs to work for them, pulling their sledges and helping them to hunt. They used the skins of the animals they hunted to make kayak boats, sleds, tools, clothes and even homes. The Central Inuit group or the Caribou Inuit, only hunted land animals and caught freshwater fish.

Q Who is the Kennewick man?

A In 1996, the skeleton of a man was found on the shores of the Columbia River near Kennewick, in the state of Washington, USA. Radiocarbon dating showed that the Kennewick man was at least 8,500 years old. His is one of the earliest human skeletons to have been found in North America. Five Native American tribes, led by the Umatilla of the Columbia River Basin, have argued that scientists have no right to disturb the dead. They want the Kennewick man to be buried once again.

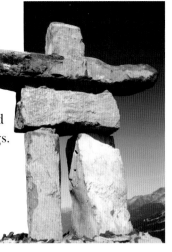

▲ **An Inuksuk**
An Inuksuk is a direction marker used by the Inuit.

▲ **Newspaper Rock**
On Newspaper Rock in Utah (USA), people have been recording their activities on stone for 2,000 years.

Frozen home

For centuries, the Central Inuit people have lived in a igloos or snow homes. The igloo was made of blocks of ice laid in a circle like a dome. The ice bricks were covered with soft snow to keep out the freezing wind. Stale air went out through a hole at the top. The people inside could look out through a window made of clear ice. The bed was a platform of ice on which the residents piled fur sheets. People could enter and leave through a covered passage. Most igloos had a smaller room for storage. What most of us do not know is that the igloo was just the winter home of the Inuit. In summer, they lived in tents made of caribou hide and in huts made of earth and grass.

▼ **A new monument**
The Crazy Horse Memorial, a mountain monument being built in South Dakota to honour Native Americans.

▲ **Dreamcatcher**
The dreamcatcher is a cultural object among many Native Americans. It has a willow hoop and a net, decorated in different ways. There was a belief that it would protect children from nightmares.

Try these too...

North America (110–111), Incas and Aztecs (141), Discovery of New Lands (144–145), The American Revolution and Civil War (152–153)

Medieval Europe

The Middle Ages fell between the time of the ancient Romans and the Renaissance, lasting from about AD 500 to 1450. By AD 500, the western parts of the Roman Empire had begun to break away. It was a time of endless battles, bloodshed and struggles for power. During this period, Christianity began spreading throughout Europe.

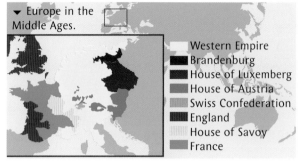

▼ Europe in the Middle Ages.

- ☐ Western Empire
- ■ Brandenburg
- ■ House of Luxemberg
- House of Austria
- Swiss Confederation
- ■ England
- House of Savoy
- France

▲ **Joust**
Duels between armed knights, known as jousts, were common during the Middle Ages.

Quick Q's:

1. What was a castle?

A castle was the home and fortress of a lord or king. They had ramparts from which soldiers could attack the enemy if the castle was besieged. Many people besides the lord lived in it, including servants, soldiers, cooks, blacksmiths and falconers. Cows, horses, pigs and chickens were also kept there for food.

2. What did people wear?

Knights wore sleeveless coats decorated with their coat of arms. Rich men wore cloaks. Rich women wore tunics that reached to their ankles. Married women tied their hair in a bun and wore tight caps and nets over it. Unmarried women could leave their hair loose or braided.

Q How did the spread of Christianity affect medieval Europe?

A Although other religions existed in Europe, the Catholic Church ruled the lives of most people. It laid down its own laws, owned land and levied taxes. The Church was based in Rome and headed by the Pope, but it also ruled from monasteries located in different parts of Europe. The Church was all-powerful, and people who openly spoke out against it risked being branded heretics and burned alive at the stake.

▼ **The power of religion**
The Catholic Church ruled every aspect of life in medieval Europe. It decided who lived where and how. It also controlled marriages and burials.

▶ **The keep**
Most forts had a high and strong keep to which defenders could retreat if necessary. Many of the keeps had secret tunnels for escape.

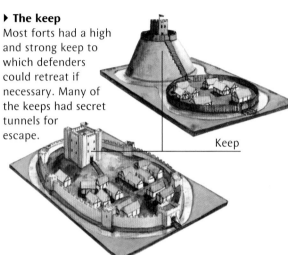

Keep

Q How were the various kingdoms governed?

A Much of western Europe was ruled by the feudal system. The king distributed land among noblemen in return for services and loyalty. Poor peasants rented this land from the nobles, and often paid them with livestock, eggs, firewood or wine. The nobles lived in a castle or a manor house.

Q How did the Crusades begin?

A The Crusades were a series of battles fought between Christians and Muslims. In AD 1095 Pope Urban encouraged Christians to free Jerusalem from Muslim rule. Several unorganized groups set off before they could be formed in to an army. Most of them died along the way. The main Crusaders left for Jerusalem in late 1096. They captured Jerusalem and other cities. This started a series of wars that went on for over 300 years, known as the Crusades.

Heroic thief

Robin Hood is a legendary hero whose story began in medieval England. He and his band of 140 men lived in Sherwood Forest in Nottinghamshire. They fought against the poverty and injustice of the feudal system by robbing the rich and giving what they stole to the poor.

Q What was the Black Death?

A In the mid-fourteenth century, the bubonic plague broke out in Europe. It began as a disease of flea-infested rats, but quickly moved to people and spread like wildfire. It is likely that it was carried from the East along trade routes and by Crusaders returning to western Europe. It killed around 25 million people within five years. It was called the Black Death because of the black-coloured boils that appeared on the victims' skin.

Q Did King Arthur exist?

A Historians are not sure whether King Arthur was a legend or based on a real king. Some think he may have been a Celtic warrior who fought the invading Anglo-Saxons in the late fifth century. Stories about him have been popular since the twelfth century.

Q Who were the Vikings of Scandinavia?

A The Viking Age occurred between the eighth and eleventh centuries. The Vikings came from Denmark, Norway and Sweden. Most Vikings were farmers who were also great travellers and explorers. They travelled in winter when they could not farm. They were fierce warriors who attacked the coasts of Europe in their longboats, capturing new lands to farm. Many of these attacks were very violent and earned the Vikings a reputation for being barbaric. The Vikings settled in colonies in Scotland, Iceland, Greenland, Newfoundland in Canada, and many other places along the shores of the Atlantic Ocean.

Try these too...

Europe (116–117), Ancient Greece (128–129), Ancient Rome (130–131), The Renaissance (142–143), Architecture (164–165)

▲ **Couple from the Middle Ages**
Rich people wore long and heavy cloaks.

▼ **Garbage disposal**
The habit of throwing garbage on to the street led to many diseases.

Medieval China and Japan

By about AD 500, the world was becoming more connected. Technology had improved, allowing people to travel more and learn from each other. With more trade and travel, religions started to spread. This was the period during which Buddhism spread in China and Japan.

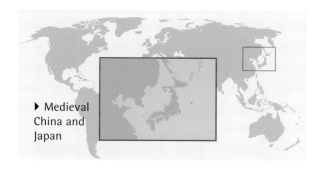

▶ Medieval China and Japan

Quick Q's:

1. What was the Silk Route?

The Silk Route was an important trade route that began in China and ran across Central Asia, all the way to Europe. Silk was the cloth worn by royalty in China. This land route was important until the early sixteenth century.

2. What is origami?

The Japanese perfected the art of folding paper into three-dimensional figures and shapes. Origami may have come to Japan with Buddhist monks from China. Others believe Origami is an art form that was developed in Japan. Only a few folds are used in Origami, but the folds can be combined in a variety of ways to make complicated designs. Most Origami designs begin with a square sheet. The two sides may be in two different colours. Usually, the paper is not cut.

Q **Which was the first major dynasty to rule China during this era?**

A The Han dynasty had a long rule from 206 BC to AD 220. This was enough time for a strong dynasty to bring most of modern China together. Under a long line of strong rulers, stability and peace spread. The Han dynasty saw the development of Chinese philosophy. This was also the time when a new religion came to China. Missionaries from India brought Buddhism, a religion that preached peace. Many Chinese people converted to Buddhism.

Q **Why is the Tang dynasty famous?**

A During the Sui dynasty (AD 589–618), cultural changes began in China. Then came the Tang period, between AD 618 and 907. This is known as the Golden Age of China. Learning and the fine arts developed like never before. When the young king Tang T'ai-tsung took over in 618, he made the government stable and strong. This encouraged agriculture and trade, and China grew prosperous. The arts flourished. Talented people did a lot to improve landscape painting, music, poetry, ceramics and metalwork. Sculpture became popular. Buddhist art was developed. Tang stone pagodas and paintings from the Dunhuang caves are fine examples of art from this age.

◀ **Folded paper**
Origami, the Japanese art of folding paper, uses a small number of different folds. They can be combined in a variety of intricate designs.

Q **What were the major developments of this period?**

A As early as AD 105, the Chinese knew how to make paper and how to print. They perfected printing and used wooden blocks to print books. Science was also prospering. China gave the world the compass. While Europe struggled to fight the plague, China, Korea and Japan were developing rapidly. However, some strange ideas also crept in.

◀ **Mongol emperor**
Genghis Khan (1162–1227) was the first of the great Mongols. He brought China, Tibet, Burma, Iran, Eastern Europe, and parts of Russia under Mongol control. In 1234, the Mongols had northern China in their grip. It took them some time to bring the rest of this vast country into their fold.

During the Sui dynasty, around AD 500, the emperor ordered that only the rich would wear colours and the common people would wear blue or black. During the Sung dynasty, around AD 1100, a painful sign of nobility was used. The feet of little girls were bound so tight that they never grew more than 7.6 centimetres (3 inches) long. The bandages broke the toes of girls as young as five years old. The toes bent under the feet. As women, they could barely walk. These lily feet were in fashion for over 1,000 years until they were banned in 1912.

Try these too...

Asia (120-121), Ancient India and China (126–127), Discovery of New Lands (144–145), Architecture (164–165), Theatre (170–171)

◀ Delicate work

The artefacts made in medieval China were of porcelain stone. China clay was added in the eighteenth century. It increased the strength of the artefacts.

Q Why is the Ming dynasty so famous?

A The Mongols, who ruled China for 89 years, were overthrown by Hung-Wu in AD 1368. That marked the start of the Ming dynasty, which lasted until 1644. The Ming dynasty is remembered for making the administration strong, widespread and fair. Judges had to take a test to get a job. Chinese literature, art and philosophy reached new heights during Ming rule. Some of the best Chinese porcelain was manufactured at Jingdezhen. The yellow imperial bowls, red vases and highly decorated painted ceramics became popular. For the first time, both cotton and silk production did very well.

Q Who were the shoguns?

A Across the sea, Japan saw a long period of peace under the Seii Tai shogun or shoguns, military dictators who ruled from 1192 to 1867. The term means 'barbarian-subduing generals'. Minamoto Yoshinaka was the first modern shogun, who came to power after defeating the Taira dynasty. The shogun rulers had loyal warrior servants known as samurai. Samurai is from the Japanese word *saburau*, which means 'to serve'. Japan developed far slower than China because it was a group of islands, cut off from the mainland of Asia. It was only in AD 405 that the Japanese adopted a written language and even then they developed a writing system based on the pictorial alphabet of the Chinese.

Q What did the Chinese take to Japan?

A Around the fourth century, Chinese settlers taught the Japanese how to grow and weave silk. The Japanese wore hemp clothes before that. In the sixth century, Buddhism spread among the Japanese from China. Japanese art of this period includes wooden and bronze statues of Buddhist figures, landscape paintings and scroll paintings. The Japanese built magnificent pagodas. Literature developed. The Chinese also taught them a form of theatre. The Japanese combined it with their own comic plays and created a new form, the *noh*. The Japanese learnt about tea from the Chinese in the ninth century. They later developed a ceremony around it. The *Tale of Genji*, one of the earliest Japanese classics, dates to the eleventh century.

▲ World heritage

Built in stages between 1346 and 1601, Himeji Castle is one of the best examples of medieval Japanese architecture.

National dress

Kimono, in Japanese, means clothing. In recent years, it has come to mean a traditional Japanese robe. Kimonos came into fashion during the Heian period (794–1192). Before that, the Japanese wore separate upper and lower garments, or one-piece robes. In the Heian period, a new stitching technique led to the kimono. Cut in straight lines, these kimonos were suitable for all weather. As techniques improved, so did the kimono. They even became family heirlooms. The kimono was the most popular garment in Japan until about 50 years ago. Today, the kimono is only worn on special occasions like the tea ceremony.

Mughal India

In 1526, Babur, a Turk from central Asia, occupied Agra in northern India. He expanded his influence throughout the region and founded the Mughal Empire. The Mughal Empire continued until 1857.

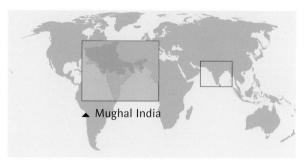

▲ Mughal India

▶ Inlay work
Inlay work on stone reached its height in Mughal India. It was used to decorate mosques, mausoleums and palaces.

Quick Q's:

1. What does Mughal mean?

Mughal comes from the Persian word for Mongol. The first Mughal Emperor Babur was from a Mongol family.

2. What is the Taj Mahal?

The Mughals loved architecture. They built complicated and intricately decorated mosques, tombs and strong forts at Agra and Delhi. They also studied the science of landscaping and created beautiful gardens. Shah Jehan built the Taj Mahal as a tomb for his beloved wife, Mumtaz Mahal.

3. Who were the *navratna*?

Navratna means nine jewels in the Hindi language. These were nine talented men in the court of Akbar. They were given special powers. They included Tansen the singer, Todar Mal the administrator, Abul Fazl, the emperor's chief advisor, and Maharaja Man Singh, Akbar's trusted general.

Q Who was Akbar?

A Babur's grandson Akbar was the greatest of the Mughal emperors. He expanded the empire to cover most of northern India. His reign brought peace and prosperity. Although Akbar could not read or write, he encouraged philosophers, poets, artists, architects and musicians. He died in 1605. His son Jehangir and Jehangir's son Shah Jehan enjoyed long and prosperous reigns. For the first time, the Mughals gained control of western India. Under Shah Jehan's son Aurangzeb the Empire covered almost all of south Asia.

Q How did the Mughals keep the Empire together?

A The Mughals had a central government. The Emperor was supreme. The highest nobles were mostly central Asians, Persians, Afghans, Indian Muslims and Rajputs. The Mughals won over the powerful Hindu Rajputs partly through conquest, and partly by respecting their customs. Akbar married Joda Bai, a Rajput woman. He even tried to start a new religion that included elements of all existing faiths in India. No single group was allowed to become powerful enough to threaten the Emperor. Tax was paid in cash, which was spent on creating new towns and markets. European traders visited Mughal India frequently and trade prospered.

▼ Poetry in stone
The Taj Mahal in Agra, India.

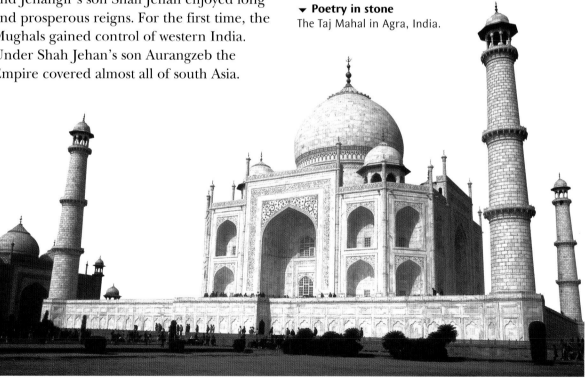

Incas and Aztecs

The Incas and the Aztecs ruled the last ancient empires of Latin America. The Incas expanded their kingdom in the twelfth century, and by the early sixteenth century, they had more land than any other people in South America. The Aztecs had their empire in Central America, in today's Mexico.

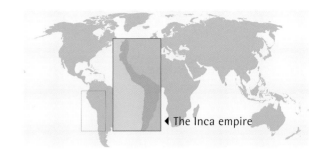
◀ The Inca empire

Q What did the Incas do for a living?

A The Incas were good farmers, even though farming was difficult in the Andes mountains, where they lived. They carved terraced fields, where they grew corn, chilli peppers, beans, squash, peanuts, cassava, quinoa and potatoes. They knew how to irrigate their fields. They used tools like spades, clubs, hoes, sticks and foot ploughs. The Incas domesticated animals like the llama and alpaca for wool and to use as transport. They were good at construction and fitted gigantic stone pieces together without using mortar. They built bridges and tunnels through the mountains. They studied medicine and performed operations. They worshiped many gods and believed in heaven and hell. Of all the gods, the Sun God was the most important, and they built many temples in his honour. When an Inca king died, his body was mummified. People would offer the mummy food and consult it to solve problems. Ordinary people were also mummified, but they were buried.

Q What happened to the Incas?

A In 1531, a Spanish General named Francisco Pizarro invaded the Inca with only two hundred soldiers. He tricked the Inca ruler, Atahualpa, into meeting him in Cajamarca. Pizarro then kidnapped him and killed hundreds of his family and followers. Atahualpa was killed in 1533. Different Inca tribes did put up resistance for 30 years, but the Spanish defeated them. This ended the largest and richest South American empire.

Q Who were the Aztecs?

A The Aztec were the last tribe to arrive in Central America. In 1325, they founded the city of Mexico-Tenochtitlan. They built one of the strongest armies in the region. Between 1428 and 1521, they had the largest empire in Central America. The Aztec Empire fell in 1521, when they were defeated by the Spanish General Hernan Cortes.

◀ **Spanish invader**
Spanish General Francisco Pizarro defeats the Incas in battle. The Incas had a large and disciplined army, but they could not hold out against the Spaniards.

Try these too...

North America (110–111), South America (112–113), Ancient Americas (132)

▲ **Terraced farming**
Terraces on mountain slopes held soil and water and allowed the Incas to farm the slopes. The Incas developed new techniques to build the terraces.

A bridge made of grass

The Incas were good with their hands. They knew how to plait grass into strong rope. They built suspension bridges with this rope which they wove together (as shown here). Some bridges were 61 to 91 metres (200 to 300 feet) long. Although made of grass, they lasted several hundred years.

The Renaissance

The European Renaissance lasted from about 1450 to 1650. The French word Renaissance means rebirth. This period brought an end to the Middle Ages and marked the start of the modern world. Every part of life, including art, politics, trade and learning took a new turn. The Renaissance began in Italy, and spread throughout western Europe.

Quick Q's:

1. Did the Renaissance change music?

During the Renaissance, musicians learnt many things about the science of sound waves, which helped them to create the kind of music they wanted. Composers studied Greek drama and were inspired to create the opera.

2. Who was Mona Lisa?

The Mona Lisa is probably the most famous painting ever created. It was painted by Leonardo da Vinci. The model is said to be Lisa Gherardini, who was the wife of a nobleman. The painting is in the Louvre, Paris.

3. What was in fashion in Renaissance Florence?

Women shaved or plucked off their eyebrows. Even the Mona Lisa has none.

Q **What led to the Renaissance?**

A Italy, surrounded by sea on three sides, was a centre of trade. More money and exposure to other cultures led people to expand their ideas. They were also inspired by the ancient cultures of Greece and Rome. People were eager to learn, and they studied literature, art, history and science. For the first time, art and literature were not restricted to religious subjects.

Q **What was Renaissance literature about?**

A Renaissance literature was based on Greek and Roman classics. The poetry of Francesco Petrarch and the stories of Giovanni Boccaccio in Italy, as well as the witty writing of Desiderius Erasmus in Holland and François Rabelais in France were among the new forms of literature that recalled the Greek and Roman classics. People realized that there were many forms of literature apart from religious books. Major authors like Shakespeare changed the way people looked at themselves and at the world around them. Many forms of literature today, like the novel, owe their birth to Renaissance ideas.

◀ **Hans Holbein the Younger (1497–1543)**
A German painter famous for his portraits, Hans Holbein the Younger painted the king and many of the nobles in the court of England.

▶ **The Last Judgment**
This is a detail from the famous fresco painted by Michelangelo on the ceiling of the Sistine Chapel in the Vatican.

▲ **Statue of Dante in Verona, Italy**
Dante (1265–1321) was an Italian poet, famous for his work *The Divine Comedy*. He had a major influence on later Renaissance poets and writers.

Q **What was special about Renaissance art?**

A Artists became interested in drawing the human figure as it really is. They learned to use light and shadow. Wall paintings on wet plaster (called fresco paintings) became common, as did tempera paints that were mixed with egg yolk. Oil painting became popular towards the end of the Renaissance.

Q Who were the most famous artists?

A Leonardo da Vinci, Michelangelo and Raphael in Italy, and Durer in Germany, were the most famous artists of the Renaissance. Leonardo da Vinci created paintings like the *Last Supper* and the *Mona Lisa*. Michelangelo created sculptures such as the *Pieta* and painted the roof of the Sistine Chapel in the Vatican. Raphael painted the Pope's apartments, also in the Vatican. Durer created engravings like *Knight, Death and the Devil*. All these are still admired by millions of people today.

Q Who was Gutenberg?

A Gutenberg invented Europe's first printing press with moveable type in 1445. The first book he printed was the Bible. The printing press meant books were much cheaper and easier to produce than before. It allowed people to read the work of ancient scholars, whose work had been forgotten during the Middle Ages. It also meant that books were available to many more people. People who had never seen books before could now learn to read and expand their horizons and their ambitions.

Q Did science play a part in the Renaissance?

A During the Renaissance, Italians were able to travel further because of tools they had invented, like the astrolabe and the magnetic compass that helped sailors figure out where they were going. More travel meant more trade, which made the Italians richer. These rich Italians commissioned artists to paint their portraits. During the Renaissance, science played a part in other ways too. The famous painter Leonardo da Vinci started dissection of dead bodies, and that increased the knowledge of the human anatomy many times over.

◀ **Master painter**
The Marriage of the Virgin – a painting by Raphael (1483–1520), one of the best artists in Italy during the Renaissance. This famous painting is now in Milan.

▼ **Martin Luther**
Martin Luther (1483–1546) reformed the Church, founding what became known as the Protestant Church.

Try these too…

Europe (116–117), Ancient Greece (128–129), Ancient Rome (130–131)

Shakespeare was a Renaissance man

The Renaissance in England is also known as the Shakespearean age. It was England's golden age of literature, architecture, science and exploration. Literature prospered more than any other form of art. William Shakespeare was one of the most important English playwrights during this period. He wrote about 38 plays and hundreds of poems. His plays are still loved and performed today, almost four hundred years after his death.

Discovery of New Lands

Between the fifteenth and the seventeenth centuries, Portugal and Spain stepped up their exploration of sea routes. France, Germany, England and the Netherlands also sent out explorers to find new lands. This period became known as the Age of Exploration. Apart from the spirit of adventure, the explorers were driven by the desire to spread Christianity and the hope of getting rich.

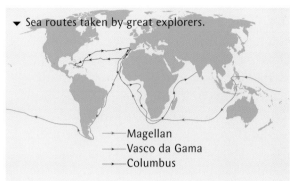

▼ Sea routes taken by great explorers.

→ Magellan
→ Vasco da Gama
→ Columbus

Quick Q's:

1. How did technology help improve sailing?

New gadgets made sailing more accurate and safe. The chronometer was a special clock that kept time even on rough seas. The compass helped the sailor find his way. The astrolabe helped predict the position of the Sun, Moon and stars as well as tell time.

2. How did the Pacific Ocean get its name?

Ferdinand Magellan gave the Pacific Ocean its name, which means peaceful or calm. After battling past the fierce Cape Horn at the tip of South America, he found the Pacific Ocean unusually still.

3. What did the sailors bring home with them?

The sailors brought riches and spices from the new lands. Foods like potato, tomato and chilli were introduced. Animals like jaguar and tapir, and birds like macaw and toucan were brought for the zoos of Europe. Many shipowners became very rich carrying gold and other treasures for the government.

Q How did these navigations begin?

A The Vikings of Scandinavia were the earliest seafaring people to cross the Atlantic Ocean. They discovered Iceland, Greenland and Newfoundland, and sailed along the coast of Canada long before other European countries set out in search of new lands. During the period from 870–930 AD, the Vikings began to settle in Iceland. In 930 the ruling chiefs established a parliament there. In 982, a Viking called Eric the Red sailed from Iceland and discovered Greenland. Nearly 20 years later, his son Leif Eriksson discovered Newfoundland.

◀ **Essential device**
The invention of the astrolabe allowed European sailors to travel around the world. This model has been kept in a park as an exhibit.

Q Who were the most adventurous sailors from western Europe?

A The Portuguese were the first to begin exploring sea routes in the fifteeenth century. Portugal's Prince Henry the Navigator was a great patron of seamen. He was a devout Christian and dreamt of spreading the religion to new lands. In 1434, his ships landed on the west coast of Africa. Various Portuguese ship captains kept going further and further south along that coast. About fifty years after the first landfall in western Africa, another Portuguese explorer, Bartholomew Diaz, was the first to go around the southern tip of Africa – the Cape of Good Hope. In 1497, Vasco da Gama followed this route to reach India. He first went around the Cape of Good Hope and then reached the island of Madagascar off the eastern coast of Africa. Then, with the help of an Arab pilot, he followed the trade winds and crossed the Indian Ocean. Vasco da Gama became the first European of his age to reach southern India. Ferdinand Magellan set out in 1519 to find a western route to the Spice Islands. He reached the Philippines in 1521 where he was killed in a battle. However, three of the ships he led returned to Europe. This was the first expedition to sail around the world and return home in triumph.

◀ **Vasco da Gama reaches India**
A contemporary sketch showing the meeting between the Portuguese explorer Vasco da Gama and the ruler of Calicut in southern India.

Q Who was Christopher Columbus?

A Born in Genoa, Italy, in 1451, Christopher Columbus began sailing when he was just 14 years old. He had read that the world was round. While most explorers were going east on the longer and more dangerous route discovered by Diaz, he decided to go west and come all the way round to the Far East so that he could find new trade routes to Asia. After petitioning for funds for ten years, Columbus was given a grant by King Ferdinand and Queen Isabella of Spain. The grateful Columbus promised to bring back gold, spices and silk from the Far East and to spread Christianity. In return, he asked to be made a governor of all the lands that he discovered. On his first voyage he discovered an island in the Bahamas and Cuba. Between 1493 and 1502, Columbus made three more voyages, hoping to see more of what he thought was Asia. During these trips he came upon more Caribbean islands including Jamaica, Trinidad and Tobago and Grenada. He also discovered Honduras, Nicaragua and Costa Rica in Central America and Venezuela in South America. Until he died, Columbus thought he had reached India, when in fact he had discovered America!

Q How was America named?

A America was named after the Italian traveller Amerigo Vespucci. Vespucci had studied books and maps under Michelangelo. Vespucci was a banker. He went to Spain in 1492 where he became interested in sailing. His first expedition was in 1499 as a navigator. He and his crew reached the mouth of the Amazon River and explored the coast of South America. He calculated how far west he had travelled. In 1501, he sailed around most of South America. He was the first to realize that the 'New World' of North and South America was not in Asia. He made three trips to the New World and made a number of calculations before he died of malaria.

Q Where did the British expeditions go?

A John Cabot led the first British expedition to the West. Like Columbus, he wanted to find a shorter and safer route to the spice-producing countries of the East. In 1497 Cabot landed in Newfoundland, Canada. Between 1576 and 1578, Martin Frobisher made three voyages to Canada and claimed a large part for England. In 1580, Sir Francis Drake was the first Englishman to sail around the world. His fleet of five ships sailed nearly 57,936 kilometres (36,000 miles) in 34 months. James Cook made three voyages between 1768 and 1779. On the first he charted New Zealand and the east coast of Australia. On the second he found several South Pacific islands and crossed the Antarctic Circle. On his last voyage he discovered Hawaii and then sailed up north to Alaska.

Try these too...

Oceans (34–35), North America (110–111), Mughal India (140), The Renaissance (142–143), The British Empire (146–147), The Industrial Revolution (148–149), Scientific Revolution (150–151)

▲ **Spicy trail**
Europeans sailed all over the world in search of the spices of the East.

All for a name

The German cartographer Martin Waldseemüller liked to make up names. He even created his own surname. In honour of Amerigo Vespucci's discovery, Waldseemüller printed a map called *Carta Mariana*. He named the southern part of the New World America. The northern part was called Indies at this time. A thousand copies of this map sold out. Waldseemüller changed his mind about the name America a few years later, but by then, it had already become popular.

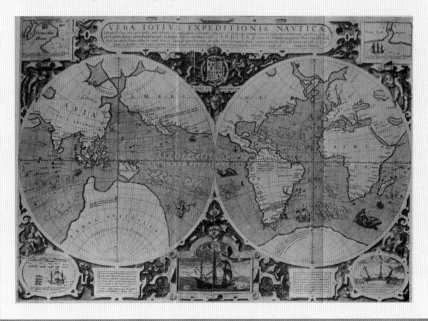

The British Empire

In the fifteenth century AD, the Age of Exploration led to the Age of Imperialism. Europe became rich and powerful because of its conquests of various countries in other continents. Spain and Britain were great rivals for overseas territories. In 1588, the British defeated the Spanish Armada and became a major world power due to the strength of its navy. English merchants were also tempted by the spices, silk and gold of the Far East.

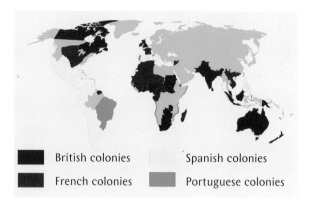

■ British colonies		Spanish colonies	
■ French colonies		Portuguese colonies	

Quick Q's:

1. Which was the first British colony to gain independence?

In 1776, thirteen British colonies in North America signed the Declaration of Independence. They formed the United States of America.

2. What was special about the colony in Australia?

Between 1788 and 1853, thousands of English criminals were shipped off to Australia because the English jails were too full to house them. These were the first British settlers in Australia.

▲ **Company flag**
The British East India Company was given the Royal Charter by Queen Elizabeth I in 1601 to trade in India. In 1617, the company was given trade rights by the Mughal Emperor who then ruled much of India. It established its military power in parts of India after winning the Battle of Plassey in 1757.

Q Did the English monarchy encourage sailors to find new territories?

A In the 1490s, when Spain and Portugal were charting new sea routes, British sailors were also busy. Encouraged by Henry VII, John Cabot was looking for a trade route to China across the Atlantic. He reached North America in 1498, while searching for an alternative route to India. In the sixteenth century, Sir Francis Drake set out to look for the East Indies. He was a favourite of Queen Elizabeth I, who not only encouraged explorers to find new lands, but also to establish British settlements in these regions.

Q Who were the first people to settle in the United States?

A The colonization of North America really started with the Plymouth Company of religious pilgrims. It was the first permanent English settlement overseas. The pilgrims left England in their ship, the Mayflower, in September 1620 and headed for New England in the United States. They set up their first village and named it Plymouth.

▶ **Defeating the Armada**
The defeat of the Spanish Armada at the hands of the British paved the way for the British Empire.

Q When did the British go to India?

A At the end of the sixteenth century, the East India Company was formed. The first Indian warehouse to store spices, textiles and a textile dye called indigo was built and the first ship left with this cargo for England in 1615. During this period, the British fought the Dutch and the Portuguese repeatedly in the Indian Ocean.

Q How far did the British Empire reach?

A By 1687, the British in India moved on to Bombay, which Charles II was given as a wedding gift by his Portuguese bride, Catherine of Braganza. With colonies from North America to Africa, India, Sri Lanka, some Southeast Asian countries, several South Pacific Islands, and all of Australia and New Zealand, Britain became the largest imperial power between the sixteenth and the nineteenth centuries. It held nearly one-third of all the land in the world.

Q Did other countries have colonies?

A The Portuguese had the large colony of Brazil in South America, as well as Angola and Madagascar in Africa. They also held small enclaves in many other parts of the world. The French colonized much of northern, western and central Africa; Lebanon and Syria in the Middle East; Vietnam, Cambodia and Laos in Southeast Asia. They also had small colonies in the Caribbean islands, South America and some of the islands in the Pacific Ocean. The Dutch had a large colony in what is now Indonesia, a group of islands in Asia.

Q How did Britain govern such a large territory around the world?

A Britain was able to hold on to so much land so far from home since her officials dealt with each of the colonies as the situation demanded. In Asia and Africa, Britain first set up trading companies, which started by dealing with local rulers and setting up trading posts. With time, these companies grew and supported organized armies. At that stage, local rulers were won over or defeated, while the British gained territory. Britain also sent thousands of its citizens to colonize North America, Australia and New Zealand.

Q How did the Empire collapse?

A The British needed educated people to work for their trading companies in the colonies. So, they taught the native people English and provided all branches of western education in the colonies. This education, especially in the social sciences, exposed the residents of these countries to ideas of democracy and self-rule. As a result, political parties were formed in the colonies, and these parties began to demand independence from British rule. On top of this, the two World Wars left Britain economically weaker than it had been for centuries, Britain found it difficult to raise the money required to administer the colonies. In 1947 India became independent. Most other Asian and African countries became independent by the 1960s.

Try these too...

Discovery of New Lands (144–145), The Industrial Revolution (148–149)

▲ **Sceptical statesman**
Benjamin Disraeli was a nineteenth-century politician sceptical about the benefits of the Empire.

A common history

Fifty-three countries, which have all been colonies of Britain, form the Commonwealth of Nations. These are independent states that have their own governments. These countries help each other in trade and other areas. The Queen of England is still the queen of 16 former colonies, which are called the Commonwealth Realms. These countries compete in the Commonwealth Games every four years – the world's second-largest sporting event after the Olympics.

The Industrial Revolution

Towards the end of the eighteenth century, western society experienced major changes because of new and improved machines that helped make more goods faster. This period of change lasted for about a century and is known as the Industrial Revolution. In other parts of the world, replacing manual work with machines began later. In some places, it is still going on.

▶ The iron horse
The steam engine was improved by James Watt (1736–1819) so that it could be used to pull trains and in factories. Trains opened up vast new areas to development.

Q. Where did the Industrial Revolution start?

A The home of the Industrial Revolution was in Britain. By the eighteenth century, Britain was one of the richest nations in the world. It had supplies of coal and iron, two of the most important raw materials of industry. Inventions like the steam engine had improved transportation. More roads were built. Canals were dug for barges and these were used to move raw materials to factories and take finished goods to cities and ports.

Q. How did manufacturing change?

A Machines took over most types of manufacturing. Before the Industrial Revolution, about 70 per cent of the work was done by muscle power and with simple tools. During the Industrial Revolution, people began to burn coal instead of wood. This provided more energy to produce more goods.

Iron – the most important metal in industry – could now be made into different shapes. Iron was used to make more machinery and other industrial equipment.

Q. How did the Industrial Revolution change society?

A The effects of machinery were first seen in agriculture. In 1708 Jethro Tull's seed sower helped plant seeds in neat rows very quickly. The machines did the work faster and better than people. Many farmers had to move to cities and work in factories. Things that used to be made at home or in small workshops were now mass-produced. Handicraft that had developed over hundreds of years died out. Cities grew larger. Soon, the Industrial Revolution spread to other parts of Europe and America. Since countries were rivals for buying and selling goods, they needed larger armies to help them.

◀ Bicycle factory
One of the early factories of the Industrial Age, this bicycle factory used methods of mass production originally developed in the United States by Henry Ford for the Model-T Ford car. Mass production allowed factories to make many products exactly like one another, far more quickly and cheaply than before. A greater range of products was manufactured, and more people could afford them.

Q What were the major areas of manufacturing that changed?

A Once people learnt to use iron in different shapes and forms, rail tracks and engines improved. They made transportation of men, machinery and raw materials easier and faster. The first steam pump was developed in 1689. James Watt improved on it and used it for trains. It was also used for steamboats. Textile manufacturing really improved in the early part of the Industrial Revolution. In 1733, John Kay came up with the flying shuttle that speeded up weaving. In 1770, James Hargreaves invented the Spinning Jenny, which could spin a number of threads at once. By 1779 Samuel Crompton had made The Mule to spin finer thread. With so many improvements, Britain could supply cloth throughout the world.

Q Did other countries benefit from the Industrial Revolution?

A Britain's financial success encouraged other countries to turn to industry. France, Germany, Holland, Belgium and the United States joined the Industrial Revolution. The United States soon overtook Britain as a global industrial power, to become the world leader. This period of growth is called the Second Industrial Revolution. In the United States, land and other natural resources were available in plenty. By 1851, the United States had the most advanced mechanical inventions to show at the industrial fair at Crystal Palace in London. Germany had huge deposits of iron and coal needed by industry.

So iron and steel and other heavy industries grew quickly there. The Industrial Revolution spread across Europe, often helped by inventors in other European countries and in the United States.

Try these too...

Discovery of New Lands (144–145), Scientific Revolution (150–151)

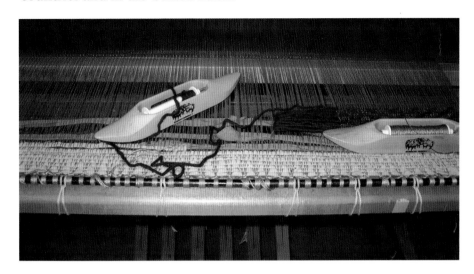

▲ **Flying shuttle**
The shift from handloom to power loom for weaving made the manufacture of cloth much faster.

▲ **Communication revolution**
The first telegraph machine developed by Samuel Morse. This made it possible to send messages over long distances almost instantly.

In good company

Technical companies started springing up in the eighteenth century. In 1775, James Watt joined Matthew Boulton to start an engine-building and engineering company that would solve technical problems in factories. There were many such companies that helped to improve industry. Businesses had to develop new ways of working and become organized into corporations. People were employed to manage these businesses. Management became a profession and a course of study at many universities, especially in the USA.

Scientific Revolution

The Scientific Revolution between 1550 and 1727 marked a change in the way that people thought about science. It was sparked by Copernicus and then spread across western Europe. Sir Francis Bacon spurred on this change when he said that science should be based on observation and experiments. To this day, these are the foundations of science and a scientific temperament.

▲ **Bloodletting**
During the Middle Ages, it was believed that removing blood would cure diseases.

Quick Q's:

1. How important was the Scientific Revolution?

Before the Scientific Revolution, people did not question the way things worked and many people were superstitious. The Scientific Revolution challenged such ideas.

2. What was the most important scientific study of the time?

In 1687, in his *Mathematical Principles of Natural Philosophy*, Isaac Newton explained ideas such as gravity, force, mass and acceleration. People now understood how substances attract each other and how the Earth exerts gravity.

Q **Who was Copernicus?**

A Nicholas Copernicus (1473–1543) is regarded as the father of the Scientific Revolution. He claimed that the Sun is at the centre of the universe and that the Earth rotates on its axis once a day and revolves around the Sun each year. At the time, this claim shocked and upset people because they had always believed that the Earth was at the centre of the universe and that the Sun went around the Earth.

Q **Who coined the term Scientific Revolution?**

A The term Scientific Revolution was given to this period of change in 1939 by Alexandre Koyre. The Scientific Revolution began with astronomy and then shifted to physics and anatomy. The most astounding progress in chemistry and biology only came in the early eighteenth century. Changes happened in theory and experiments as well as in the way scientists worked and thought.

Q **Were there any new discoveries in the life sciences at this time?**

A In 1543, Andreas Vesalius found that blood circulated in the body because the heart acted like a pump to push it around. He worked with dead bodies and put together the first complete human skeleton. William Harvey also dissected human bodies to show how blood circulates through the body.

▲ **Revolutionary man**
Nicholas Copernicus, seen here with his model of the solar system, changed the way we see the world.

Antony van Leeuwenhoek made a single lens microscope which made studying the tiniest details of the world around us possible.

Q **Who were the first scientists to study electricity?**

A William Gilbert studied magnetism and its relationship to electricity in 1600. He discovered the Earth's magnetic field, which makes the Earth act like a huge magnet. The needle of a compass always points north because of this magnetic field. Gilbert was the first person to use the term electricity.

◀ **Knowing the direction**
Once it was discovered that the compass points to the magnetic north, navigation improved.

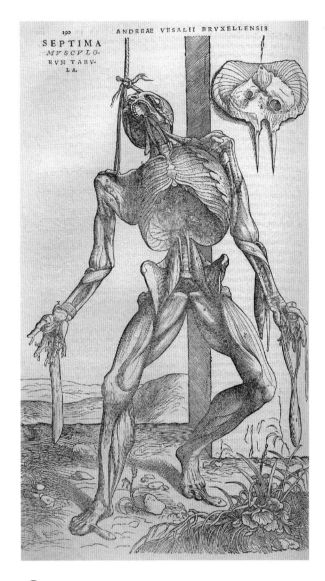

◀ **Medical textbook**
An early drawing of human anatomy by Andreas Vesalius (1514–1564) in his book *De Corporis Fabrica* (What The Body Is Made Of). The book changed the way medicine was studied.

Q **When did the Scientific Revolution end?**

A The Scientific Revolution is said to have come to an end with the death of Isaac Newton in 1727. He took the work of Johannes Kepler and Galileo further. He developed calculus and showed how mathematics could be used in science. He also established the laws of gravity.

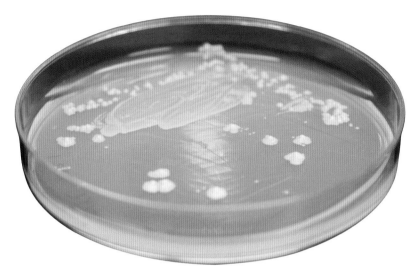

▲ **Bacteria culture**
The legacy of the Scientific Revolution, modern medicine depends on observation and experiments for diagnosis.

Try these too...

Discovery of New Lands (144–145), The Industrial Revolution (148–149), The World after World War II (160–161), Computer Revolution (162), The New Millennium – 21st Century (163)

Q **Who was Galileo?**

A Galileo Galilei was an Italian astronomer and physicist who supported the theories of Copernicus. He improved the telescope and made so many new observations about the planets that he has been declared the father of science. He discovered the four biggest moons of Jupiter. However, during his lifetime, Galileo struggled against the Roman Catholic Church. The Church banned his work on the planets because it was so different from what the scriptures said. He was put under house arrest for insisting that the Sun is at the centre of the solar system and remains in one place. The Church forced him to change his views in public, but he held on to them in private.

The science of preserved food

Sir Francis Bacon was a lawyer and philosopher. Once, he was also put in debtors' prison for owing people money. He is best known for an experiment he carried out to see if snow could preserve meat. In March 1626, while he was stuffing a chicken with snow, he caught pneumonia. He died on 9 April 1626, a martyr to science.

The American Revolution and Civil War

The American Revolution and the Civil War were two of the most important events in the history of the United States. The Revolution established the United States as an independent and democratic country. The Civil War was fought to gain equality for all by abolishing slavery. The United States of America became an example of enterprise and justice.

▶ **Founding father**
Benjamin Franklin (1706–1790) played a key role in the American Revolution. He was in the team that drafted the Declaration of Independence. He was the ambassador to France and made sure that this transatlantic ally supported the American Revolution.

▲ **Battle of Bunker Hill**
This battle on 17 June 1775 may have seen the maximum casualties during the American Revolution.

Quick Q's:

1. Which thirteen colonies formed the original United States of America?

New Hampshire, Massachusetts, Rhode Island, Connecticut, New York, New Jersey, Pennsylvania, Delaware, Maryland, Virginia, North Carolina, South Carolina, and Georgia were the original thirteen colonies of the United States.

2. When did the USA get its Constitution?

The Constitution of the USA was adopted in March 1789.

3. How bloody was the Civil War?

More than 600,000 lives were lost and property worth $5 billion was damaged during the Civil War.

Q **Why did Britain and France clash in North America?**

A By the eighteenth century, word of North America's wealth had spread throughout Europe. France called its colony in the north New France. The British settlers came by the shiploads. They colonized the south. Their colonies grew fast. In Europe, Britain and France were fighting the Seven Years' War and so tensions were high between the two countries. Eventually, the British defeated the French. A treaty was signed in 1763, which gave the British control over all of North America except Québec.

Q **Why did the colonists in the United States want to be independent of Britain?**

A After the end of the Seven Years' War, the British government demanded heavy taxes on imports and trade items – which included sugar, indigo dye, wine, coffee, textiles, paper, glass and tea. The colonists protested. Even pamphlets, newspapers and playing cards were to be taxed. Britain also refused the United States permission to print their own currency notes. The colonists wanted more political freedom. This led to riots. On the night of 16 December 1773, about fifty colonists disguised themselves as Mohawks and raided three British ships anchored in Boston harbour. They dumped 342 containers of tea, which was taxed heavily, into the sea. This act of defiance was known as the Boston Tea Party and started the Revolution.

Q **What was the Declaration of Independence?**

A On 4 July 1776, representatives of the thirteen colonies met in Philadelphia and declared independence. Britain was not happy and refused to give up such profitable colonies. The War of Independence began. Fierce battles were fought right up until 1783. George Washington led the Continental Army, which finally defeated the British.

▲ **The life of a slave**
Slaves were worked hard, fed little and treated cruelly. Many who tried to escape were caught and punished.

Q What was the Civil War?

A The American Civil War was fought between the US government and eleven states in the southern United States who refused to give up slavery. These eleven states called themselves the Confederate States. The war started in 1861 when the president of the USA Abraham Lincoln declared that slavery would be ended and the Confederates decided to break away from the USA in protest.

Q Which were the states that formed the Confederates?

A South Carolina was joined by Florida, Mississippi, Georgia, Texas, Alabama, Louisiana, Tennessee, North Carolina, Virginia and Arkansas. Most of the states were controlled by slave-owners. They formed the Confederate States of America.

Q How did the Civil War end?

A The Federal army, made up of the northern states, won after four years of fierce fighting. The Confederates surrendered on 9 April 1865. Lincoln was assassinated by a Confederate supporter just five days later.

The Loyalists

The Loyalists were faithful to Britain during the American War of Independence. They believed they owed loyalty to Britain and fought the rebels. Historians estimate that about 20 per cent of the white population in the thirteeen states were Loyalists, though exact numbers are difficult to come by. After the Declaration of Independence in 1776 the Loyalists were regarded as traitors. As a result, many of them changed their allegiance. But many of those who remained Loyalists were exiled and lost their land and possessions. Between 1775 and 1783, over 70,000 Loyalists were forced out of the United States. Of them, 50,000 went north to what is now Canada. These Loyalists called themselves the United Empire Loyalists. A few other Loyalists returned to Britain and many settled in other British colonies like the Bahamas.

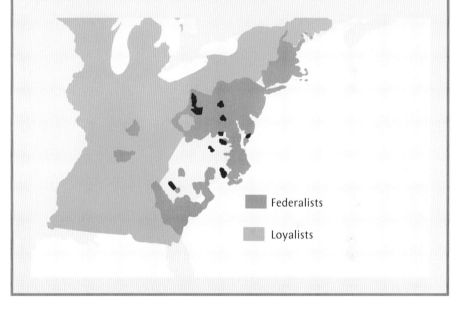

Federalists

Loyalists

◀ **Marching to war**
Union soldiers marching to join the Civil War and ensure that the United States of America remained one country. The Civil War witnessed very heavy casualties on both sides. The Confederates registered some victories in the beginning. But the better-equipped Federal forces prevailed at the end.

Try these too...

North America (110–111), The British Empire (146–147)

The French Revolution

The French Revolution, which lasted for ten years from 1789 to 1799, changed the entire political system and society of France. Before the Revolution, the king held all the power. The Revolution transferred this power to the citizens, who ruled through a governing body. The effects of the French Revolution were felt across most of the world.

Quick Q's:

1. Who was Robespierre?

Maximilien Robespierre was an important leader during the French Revolution. He was part of the Commune of Paris that overthrew Louis XVI. Under his orders, protesters were paraded and guillotined in public. On 28 July 1794, Robespierre himself was guillotined without a trial.

2. Did Marie Antoinette really ask the people to eat cake?

When there was a shortage of bread in Paris, the queen Marie Antoinette is believed to have said, 'If they have no bread, then let them eat cake!' There is no evidence of this.

3. Why was the storming of the Bastille important?

It was the first open rebellion against the king. While most people know that prisoners were set free, few know that there were only seven prisoners in the Bastille at that time. The event of 14 July is still celebrated in France as a national holiday.

Q What led to the French Revolution?

A The French Revolution had been building up for years. The king of France at the time was Louis XVI. He was young and inefficient as a king. A long, hard winter had killed most of the crops and lots of people were unemployed. The king was spending huge amounts of money on wars so taxes had to be raised. The majority of people were getting poorer and poorer while the rich were living it up. At around this time, the Age of Enlightenment was in full swing. Philosophers were becoming interested in equality, human rights and liberty for everyone. These philosophers encouraged scientific thought and looked down upon the old traditions held in place by the king. The people became passionate about these ideas and rose in protest.

Q Was it only the poor who revolted against the king?

A Almost all the classes were against the King. France was teeming with 25 million people, the largest population in Europe. Most were starving peasants. Paris was crowded with merchants, traders and factory workers, all seeking more power and privileges from the king. The clergy (priests) held 10 per cent of the land, but many parish priests were very poor, so they supported the Revolution too. The middle classes supported it because they wanted more say in elections.

Q How did the Revolution break out?

A On 14 July 1789, an angry mob stormed the Bastille prison in Paris, set the prisoners free and started the Revolution. The National Assembly was taken over. On 26 August 1789, the Assembly published the *Declaration of the Rights of Man and of the Citizen*, which gave equal rights and freedom to all Frenchmen. It abolished the old system of land ownership and changed the justice system.

◀ **Storming of the Bastille**
A crowd of people stormed the Bastille prison near Paris and effectively started the French Revolution. The event was of enormous symbolic significance, because it was first open act of rebellion against the king. After storming the prison and freeing the seven prisoners, the attackers concentrated on looting the large quantities of arms and ammunition stored there, including over 13,600 kilograms (30,000 pounds) of gunpowder.

Q What happened to King Louis XVI?

A At the start of the Revolution, the Emperor Louis XVI was forced to move from his palace in Versailles to Paris. The rulers of Austria and Prussia sent soldiers to support Louis and help him to escape. But he was captured and returned to Paris. In August 1792, Louis XVI was forced to step down from the throne, his family was imprisoned, and France was declared a republic. In January 1793, Louis XVI and his wife, Marie Antoinette, were beheaded. Many other noblemen who had sided with the royal family also lost their lives in the French Revolution. Some fled to other countries and worked against the new government.

Q What was the effect on the people?

A The Revolution did not improve the life of the poor. Food was still scarce and there was rioting. The days of the week were renamed and a new calendar was adopted, which caused chaos. Churches were closed. With no king and a sudden change in government, there was confusion about who was in charge. Several ambitious people fought for power. Those who lost were beheaded. And so began the Reign of Terror.

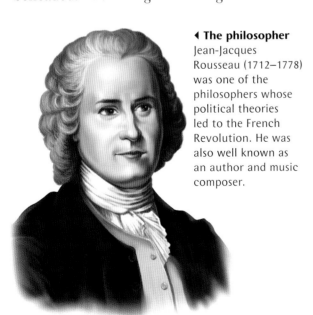

◀ **The philosopher**
Jean-Jacques Rousseau (1712–1778) was one of the philosophers whose political theories led to the French Revolution. He was also well known as an author and music composer.

Q What was the Reign of Terror?

A The Reign of Terror lasted from 5 September 1793 to 28 July 1794 when over 20,000 people opposed to the Revolution were killed. The Reign of Terror effectively ended a day after two of its most important leaders, Robespierre and Marat, were killed themselves.

Try these too...

Napoleonic Wars (156–157), The World Wars (158–159)

▼ **The guillotine**
The guillotine (seen here) was the killing machine of the Reign of Terror.

The killing machine

The guillotine was a machine used for executing prisoners by chopping off their heads. The first known guillotine-like instrument was used in 1307. However, it wasn't until the French Revolution that it became a common way to kill people. It was named after a French doctor, Joseph-Ignace Guillotin (pictured), who recommended it as a more humane way to execute prisoners than the other methods of the time. At least 20,000 people were executed by the guillotine during the French Revolution.

Napoleonic Wars

Napoleon Bonaparte or Emperor Napoleon I of France conquered almost all of Europe before being defeated by the British. Napoleon received the biggest compliment any army officer could hope for, when his arch enemy, the Duke of Wellington, called him the greatest general ever. It changed for ever the way wars were fought.

▲ **Royal resting place**
Napoleon's tomb in Les Invalides in Paris.

Quick Q's:

1. Did Napoleon inspire other leaders?

Napoleon has inspired many leaders. He didn't hesitate to take a tough decision, even if it meant destruction. He never accepted a treaty that gave him less than what he thought war could get him.

2. Where is Napoleon's throne?

Napoleon's red and gold throne is kept in the Louvre museum in Paris.

3. How did Napoleon die?

The causes of Napoleon's death are a mystery. Some people believe he died of arsenic poisoning, and others say he suffered from cancer of the stomach, like his father before him.

Q Who was Napoleon?

A Born on 15 August 1769 in Corsica, Napoleon rose to power as a general during the French Revolution. He became the First Consul – the virtual ruler of France, on 11 November 1799. In May 1804, he took the title of Emperor Napoleon I.

Q Why is his Italian campaign so famous?

A In 1796, Napoleon led the French troops in an invasion of Italy. A true General, he mingled with his soldiers and won their trust. He defeated the Pope's army and took over some of the papal land. The following year, he took Pope Pius VI prisoner, and the Pope died in captivity. The Treaty of Campo Formio with the Italians was made in 1797.

It gave Napoleon power over most of northern Italy. The Italian campaign was one of his greatest, during which he captured 160,000 prisoners and 2,000 cannons. His military success made him a popular political figure in France.

Q Where did he go after that?

A Napoleon spent 179–99 trying to conquer Egypt, which was then a part of the Ottoman Empire. Napoleon wanted to protect French trade interests in Egypt and to provide an obstacle to Britain's access to India. He reached Alexandria on 1 July. Napoleon gained the upper hand on land, and the many scientists who had gone with the military expedition made a number of discoveries. This included the finding of the Rosetta Stone, which enabled scholars to read the ancient Egyptian script. But the British Navy, under Admiral Horatio Nelson, captured all but two of his ships in the Mediterranean. Napoleon returned to Paris in 1799, leaving his troops in Egypt. The British now defeated the French troops, who were sent back to France in British ships.

◀ **Napoleon's Waterloo**
The battle of Waterloo took place on 18 June 1815 at a site in today's Belgium. This was Napoleon's last battle, where he was finally defeated by the allies. The Duke of Wellington led the British forces in battle, while the Prussians were led by Gebhard Leberecht von Blücher. The battle raged for most of the day without any side being able to get the upper hand, until the British forces withstood a final French attack in the evening and the Prussians broke through Napoleon's right flank.

Q What did Napoleon do after Egypt?

A Following the Egyptian campaign, Napoleon set his sights on political power at home. He seized control of the ruling council in France in November 1799. In 1804 he drafted the Code Napoleon, covering virtually every subject from the church to the military, education and government. Some of the suggestions from the Code are still followed in many countries. In 1804, Napoleon also became Emperor of France. There were several battles over the next eight years. Napoleon continued to be the most powerful general in Europe, forcing treaties on Austria, Britain, Russia and Prussia. His greatest victory was at Austerlitz in 1805, when he defeated the joint forces of the Russian and Austrian empires. The battle is often considered a masterpiece of war strategy and tactics on the part of Napoleon.

Q Did Napoleon conquer Russia?

A In 1812 Napoleon turned on Russia with a huge army of over 400,000 soldiers. To keep such a large force on its feet, he needed another 400,000 people who provided food, clothing, tents and so on. Rather than face Napoleon's troops, the Russians chose to retreat. As they moved back, they destroyed crops and resources so that the French army would not find any supplies to plunder. The French reached Moscow on 8 September after the Battle of Borodino. It was one of the bloodiest battles of that age, killing 80,000 soldiers on both sides. But the Russians refused to be defeated. They would rather destroy their own land. So, they set fire to Moscow. Napoleon could do little but retreat. Crippled by the lack of food, the French army lost thousands of men to disease. As winter set in, Napoleon's Grande Armée was also up against the extreme cold of Russia. By the end of 1812, only 10,000 of the original 400,000 soldiers survived. It was a major blow to Napoleon.

Q How did Napoleon's reign end?

A While Napoleon was away on the Russian campaign, his enemies in Europe became strong once again, and grouped together to remove him. By 1813, Napoleon knew he was in a tight spot. Even the British had reached France. Now, the people of France lost confidence in him. On 30 March 1814, Paris surrendered to the allied forces of Britain, Russia, Prussia and Austria. Napoleon stepped down from the throne of France. He was exiled to the Mediterranean island of Elba. But Napoleon still had many supporters in France, who continued to work for his return. In 1815, just 11 months after being imprisoned in Elba, Napoleon escaped to France and regained his throne. But his enemies in Britain, Russia, Prusssia and Austria would not accept Napoleon as emperor. After several more battles, he was defeated at Waterloo on 25 June 1815. This time, Napoleon was exiled to the island of St Helena in the Atlantic Ocean. On 5 May 1821, at the age of 51, Napoleon died while in captivity. But well after his death, the legacy of Napoleon continued, especially in the area of military strategy.

Try these too...

Europe (116–117), The French Revolution (154–155), The World Wars (158–159)

▲ **Admiral Nelson**
The British Admiral defeated the French Navy in the Mediterranean and did not allow any supplies to reach the French troops in Egypt.

A matter of inches

Napoleon is said to have been one of the shortest generals in history. For years people believed that his height was just 1.58 metres (5 feet 2 inches). However, what most historians forgot was that Napoleon's height had been measured in French units. When converted to Imperial units, this is 1.69 metres (5 feet 6.5 inches). His personal guards were part of an elite force of very tall soldiers. This also made him look smaller than he was.

The World Wars

The two World Wars took millions of lives. In the 31 years from the beginning of World War I to the end of World War II, the world changed in a more fundamental way than it had in the hundreds of years before that. New nations were created and old nations were divided by the political interests of powers thousands of kilometres away.

Quick Q's:

1. What was the blitzkrieg?

The Germans introduced a new and effective military operation during World War II. The blitzkrieg was a quick and strong surprise assault on the enemy, using a combination of tanks, aircraft and motorized infantry vehicles.

2. Did Germany surrender after World War II?

Germany surrendered just eight days after Hitler shot himself on 30 April 1945.

3. What was the Bismarck?

On 24 May 1941, the British battle cruiser Hood was sunk by the German battleship Bismarck near Greenland. The British chased the Bismarck across the Atlantic and sank it on 27 May.

4. What was the SS?

The SS or *Schutzstaffel* (Defence Staff) was Hitler's personal army. The Gestapo or Secret Police was a part of it. The SS were also in charge of the Nazi concentration camps.

Q What led to World War I?

A World War I was fought between 1914 and 1918. It was the longest, costliest and most violent war the world had seen. It involved most European countries and the United States. In the nineteenth century, growing overseas colonies and trade rivalries led to intense nationalistic feelings throughout Europe. The Industrial Revolution led to a need for more and more raw materials. Once the goods were made, their makers needed new markets to sell these goods to, and countries rivalled each other for markets. Each country built up a large army to safeguard its interests and to strike fear into its opponents.

Q Did anyone think of peace talks?

A There were attempts to defuse the situation at the Hague Conferences of 1899 and 1907. But they had little effect. Fearing war, Germany, the Austro-Hungarian Empire and Italy formed the Triple Alliance.

▲ D-Day
In World War II, the Allied forces carried out a major invasion of German-held France from the area of Normandy in 1944.

On the other side, Great Britain, France and Russia formed the Triple Entente. Germany supported Morocco's independence from France in 1905–6. There was more tension when Austria-Hungary took over Bosnia and Herzegovina in the Balkans in 1908. On 28 June 1914, Archduke Francis Ferdinand, heir to the Austrian and Hungarian thrones, was assassinated in Sarajevo, Bosnia by a Serb called Gavrilo Princip. It was this act that sparked the war.

Q What were the trenches?

A Very early during the course of World War I, the armies found out that with new weaponry, they could dig even a shallow hole in the ground and stop the advance of the enemy. That was why both Germany and the Allied powers (mainly Britain and France) started digging trenches in the ground, where their soldiers could stay and defend their territory. As the war went on, the trenches became deeper and more complex.

◄ Trench warfare
World War I saw the large-scale use of trenches for the first time. The area between the trenches of the opposing armies was often filled with barbed wire to make an enemy advance even more difficult.

Q How long did the peace last after World War I?

A In 1918, World War I finally came to an end. In 1919, the Allies – the United States, Britain, France and Italy – worked out the Treaty of Versailles. But the peace did not last long. In 1933, the Nazi leader Adolf Hitler came to power in Germany. He promised to make up for the defeat of Germany in World War I. In 1935, Hitler defied the Treaty of Versailles and began building up an army. Germany began a military campaign, taking over Austria and a part of Czechoslovakia. On 1 September 1939, Germany attacked Poland. On 3 September, Britain and France declared war on Germany and World War II began. It was even fiercer than World War I. The Allied Powers included Britain and its colonies, and the Soviet Union and the USA. Germany, Italy and Japan formed the Axis powers. Battles took place across the world.

Q What were the consequences of World War II?

A Over 62 million people, or 2.5 per cent of the world's population, died in World War II. Eight out of every ten deaths were on the Allied side. The Soviet Union lost at least 23 million people. People around the world died of disease and starvation caused by the war. Adolf Hitler unleashed racial hatred against people who were from other races or religions. Two-thirds of his victims were Jews. Hitler's Nazis began by shooting thousands of Jews. Later, they built death camps where people were shot or gassed or simply allowed to waste away. Chemical weapons were used in this war as never before. Under orders from Emperor Hirohito, Japan used toxic gas 375 times. Thousands of British, Australian and other Allied troops died in the harsh conditions of the Japanese prisoner camps. The political map of the world was completely changed by the war – it led to the end of colonialism.

Q How did the Second World War end?

A The war in Europe ended in 1944, but it continued in Asia. President Harry Truman of the USA ordered the world's first atomic attack. On 6 and 9 August 1945, two atomic bombs were dropped on the Japanese cities of Hiroshima and Nagasaki, killing thousands and injuring thousands more. Japan surrendered on 14 August 1945.

Try these too...

North America
(110–111), Europe
(116–117), Asia
(120–121), The
World after World
War II (160–161)

▼ **Enola Gay**
The B-29 Superfortress
that dropped an atomic
bomb on Hiroshima.

Pearl Harbour

Pearl Harbour is in Hawaii. It was one of the important military bases of the United States of America. On 7 December 1941, Japanese submarines and aircraft attacked the US Pacific fleet at Pearl Harbour. Eight American battleships and thirteen other naval vessels were sunk or badly damaged. Nearly 200 American aircraft were destroyed. About 3,000 military personnel were injured or killed. It was this attack that brought the USA in to World War II on the side of the Allies.

The World after World War II

When World War II ended, almost everyone, everywhere, had been affected by it. Maps were redrawn, and people living in the new territories were suddenly thrown into new societies. Old countries ceased to exist.

Quick Q's:

1. Why was the United Nations Organization formed?

The Allied nations got together after World War II to form the United Nations in 1945. An organization of all countries, it is meant to prevent wars and to help in overall development around the world.

2. Why do people fight over oil?

With more automated transport like cars, buses, trains and aircraft being used, more and more oil is required. Vast oil fields were found in the Middle East which the Western world needs to use to maintain their current lifestyle. Oil has become the cause of world-wide conflict.

3. Why do we need to look for new fuel?

The supply of oil and coal is limited. We need to look for new fuel sources that are renewable, so that there can be no risk of running out of fuel. Scientists are studying various renewable sources of energy such as solar power, wind power and biogas to reduce the cost of producing usable energy from these sources.

Q What was the most important task after World War II ended?

A Millions of people had lost their lives. Millions more had fled their home countries as refugees. Countries had lost most of their money buying arms and keeping huge armies fed and clothed. Industries had been bombed out and had to be rebuilt. Most countries spent the second half of the twentieth century trying to rebuild what was lost.

Q How has modern science affected everyday life?

A The World Wars inspired scientists to think of bigger and better machinery. All wars fought after World War II have used more machinery and fewer humans. Since so many people had died in the World Wars, scientists wanted to develop machines that would take over much of the work. Also, after World War II, factories began producing cheaper goods in larger numbers. This changed transportation. From animal-drawn carriages, which had been the only land vehicles for thousands of years, trains, cars and aircraft became common. Space studies also improved, originally for military reasons. Within 25 years of World War II ending, man had landed on the moon. Wired communication and signalling like Morse code and semaphore were not used any more. Satellites speeded up communication and personal computers connected millions of homes to the Internet. Machines such as washing machines, dishwashers, vacuum cleaners and microwave ovens speeded up household work.

▲ **A modern assembly line**
Assembly lines in modern factories have improved efficiency. In a modern car factory, most of the work consists of assembling parts made by others.

Q How did the spread of liberal ideas change the world?

A Ideas of liberal democracy spread around the world after World War II, partly as a result of the Allied victory in the war. The first result was that colonies of European powers started to demand their freedom, and most of them had gained independence by the 1960s. Also during the 1960s, there were protest movements by some American and European university students against the involvement of the USA and European countries like France in the Vietnam War. The liberal ideas of these youth leaders gave rise to large-scale anti-war movements around the world. New forms of music pioneered by bands like the Beatles helped these ideas to spread, leading to a sense of rebellion against the establishment and traditional society. This had a far reaching impact in many countries – attendance in churches declined and age-old social institutions such as marriage lost a lot of their significance.

◀ **Bringing social change**
Musicians like Bob Dylan (left) have influenced modern society greatly.

Q What was the Cold War?

A At the end of World War II, the victorious Allied countries found themselves divided into two distinct camps – one led by the USA and the other by the former Union of Soviet Socialist Republics (USSR). As the USA and the USSR had both started to make many nuclear weapons, the tension between the two camps became a matter of concern all around the world. The USA and the USSR fought through other countries – in Korea, Vietnam and Afghanistan. Both superpowers tried their best to include more countries in their camps. But they did not go to war against each other directly, which was why the state of affairs was described as a Cold War. The Cold War lasted till 1990, when the USSR collapsed into a number of independent countries and most of the countries in this camp chose to move towards a system of liberal democracy.

Q What was apartheid?

A Apartheid was established in 1948 by the South African government, run by descendants of European settlers. This was a regime in which black South Africans did not have the same rights as the whites and were treated very unfairly. In 1994, the fight against apartheid succeeded and Nelson Mandela became the first non-white President of South Africa.

Q Did human health improve in the twentieth century?

A New medical research during the twentieth century has helped people in many ways. Surgery has improved and organs including the heart, liver and kidneys can now be transplanted, so that the failure of a vital organ need not necessarily lead to death. Doctors have become better able to diagnose problems with improved technologies such as X-rays and sonograph and various kinds of imaging of the body and the brain. Doctors can also examine the health of foetuses through techniques such as ultrasound sonography. Antibiotics that followed the discovery of penicillin now help fight diseases that earlier killed thousands. Life expectancy improved in the twentieth century. However, new viruses like HIV/AIDS are spreading throughout the world. In the West, where food is plentiful, obesity (excess fat) has created new health risks.

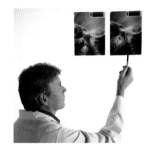

▲ **The X-ray**
Methods of medical diagnosis have vastly improved in the years since World War II. Today, doctors have many tools like X-rays, sonography, magnetic imaging and so on to look inside the bodies of their patients, find out exactly what has gone wrong, and treat the patients accordingly.

Try these too...

The World Wars (158–159), The New Millennium – 21st Century (163)

◀ **Modern messiah**
Nelson Mandela, a leader of the African National Congress, spent 27 years of his life in the infamous Robben Island prison on an island off the Cape of Good Hope for his opposition to apartheid. But on becoming the President of South Africa, he implemented a policy of reconciliation with supporters of the earlier apartheid regime.

A telly in every home

The period after World War II saw major developments in broadcasting through television, though it had started before and during the war years. The first colour broadcast on network television took place in the USA on 25 June 1951. Since then, the availability of satellite communication has made it possible to watch 'live' television programmes from around the world. The number of television channels has increased many times. Television receiver sets have also improved and new technologies like liquid crystal display and plasma display have been developed. An old (left) and a new (right) TV receiver set are shown here. Towards the end of the twentieth century, television programmes started to be distributed over the Internet.

Computer Revolution

The Industrial Revolution made work so much faster that people needed machines to help them keep track. Adding machines and cash registers helped them. Modern wars also required arms, ammunition and plans that were more precise than ever. Governments needed efficient and safe machines to store and process information. The computer was the answer.

▲ **Data carriers**
Compact disks can carry data between computers.

Quick Q's:

1. Who was Grace Hopper?

Grace Murray Hopper, nicknamed Amazing Grace, worked on the Harvard Mark I computer. She coined the term 'bug' for a computer fault, because a moth had led to a fault in the Mark I. She was also the first person to debug a computer.

2. What was the first computer game?

The first computer game, called Spacewar, was invented in 1962. It was a two-player game. Each player controlled a spaceship and fired at each other.

3. Who invented the floppy disk?

A team of IBM engineers led by Alan Shugart invented the floppy disk in 1971.

Q **What were the very first computers like?**

A The first mechanical computer was invented by Wilhelm Schickard in 1623. It was a calculating machine that could add and subtract six digit numbers. Charles Babbage is known as the father of computing. He designed the Difference Engine, which could calculate tables. In 1833, he invented the Analytical Machine, which could add in three seconds and multiply and divide in two to three minutes. Konrad Zuse, a German engineer, is called the inventor of the modern computer. He built automatic calculators that had memories and could show him the results of previous calculations. In 1936, he made Z1, a machine with a control, a memory, and a calculator. It was the first binary computer, which means it used the numbers 0 and 1 to carry out its calculations. Today's computers are all binary – everything is finally translated to 0 and 1 for them. In 1941 Zuse also made Z3, the world's first electronic, fully programmable digital computer.

Q **What was the 4004?**

A In 1971, scientists in Intel made the first single chip microprocessor. It was called Intel 4004. This put the central processing unit, memory, input and output controls on to one small chip. The development of personal computers became easier due to the chip. The first personal computer was sold in March 1974. The number of PCs multiplied many times in the 1990s with the development of the Internet.

▼ **The familiar mouse**
The mouse makes it easy to select the item that we want to use on screen. It was named the mouse because the thin wire that connects it to the computer looks like the tail of a mouse.

Q **What is the Internet?**

A The Internet is a worldwide network that is accessible to all computers with an Internet connection. This network allows computers from all over the world to communicate with one another, so that users have access to a bank of information. Now people can communicate with each other through e-mail on the Internet. They can also chat, share music, play with others, show photographs and write diaries for anyone in the world with Internet access to read. The Internet has created a 'global community' that was unimaginable just a few years ago.

The New Millennium – 21st Century

Despite advances in science, medicine and technology, the new millennium is not without its troubles. Terrorism, when people wreak havoc by killing and injuring innocent people, is an increasing threat. On top of the fear of terrorism, pollution and global warming are serious threats in the new century. But many countries also expect to join the developed world in this century.

▶ In memory
Memorial lights of the World Trade Center, whose twin towers were destroyed by terrorists. Thousands of people were killed by the terrorist act.

Q Did the new millennium bring countries together?

A In 2002, the euro became the common currency of some of the member countries in the European Union. In 2007, the number of members rose to 27 countries. Meanwhile, other countries gained their independence. East Timor in Southeast Asia became the youngest nation in the world when it gained independence from Indonesia on 20 May 2004.

Q Has the world become warmer in the twenty-first century?

A Increasing use of fuel for industry and transport is warming up the Earth. As a result, natural disasters have become more frequent and more deadly. On 26 December 2004, an earthquake and tsunami in the Indian Ocean killed over 310,000 people in many countries. On top of such disasters, the amount of ice at the North and South poles is decreasing due to global warming. So sea levels will rise and swamp coastal areas all around the world, according to scientists.

Q Why is the twenty-first century called the Age of Terrorism?

A On 11 September 2001, nineteen terrorists hijacked four passenger airplanes in the United States. They flew American Airlines Flight 11 and United Airlines Flight 175 into the twin towers of the World Trade Center in New York. Another aircraft hit the Pentagon building in Washington. The passengers and crew of United Airlines Flight 93 attacked the hijackers and saved many lives when the plane crashed into a field instead of a public building. Almost 3,000 people were killed in the attacks. George Bush, the President of the United States, declared a war on terror that took American troops to Afghanistan and Iraq. Since 2001, terrorist attacks have occurred in other cities around the world. Bombs are detonated in busy market places and city centres, killing innocent people. Terrorism is particularly bad in the Middle East, where Israel has been fighting most of its neighbours for many years, and in Iraq. With an increasing clash between Western and Islamic lifestyles, many people talk of an Age of Terrorism.

Try these too...

The World Wars (158–159), The World after World War II (160-161), Communication and Satellites (192–193), Air Transport (198–199)

◀ Wind power
Using traditional power sources such as coal and oil is adding to pollution. Cleaner ways to produce energy like windmills are now becoming more and more popular around the world.

Poor Pluto

Pluto was called the ninth planet of our solar system since its discovery by Clyde Tombaugh in 1930. But on 25 August 2006, the International Astronomical Union said it was not a planet, but a dwarf planet. Changes like this show how astronomy is becoming more accurate.

Architecture

Architecture is what goes in to designing a building. It can influence anything from a tool shed to a monument like the Taj Mahal. Architects also design buildings such as the Taipei 101 Tower in Taiwan, which stands 509 metres (1,670 feet) tall and was the tallest completed structure in the world in 2006.

Quick Q's:

1. Why is the Parthenon famous?

The Parthenon was a temple to the Greek goddess Athena. It was built between 447 and 433 BC and still stands at the Acropolis in Athens. Its decorative sculptures made of white marble make it an example of the best Grecian architecture.

2. What is Stonehenge?

Stonehenge, built between 3000 and 1500 BC, is the best known prehistoric stone structure in England. It is formed of tall standing stones, or megaliths, set in a circle within even older earthworks. It has been declared a World Heritage Site.

▲ **Stones in a circle**
Modern scholars believe Stonehenge was an ancient observatory, used for predicting phases of the Moon.

Q Have the earliest buildings lasted?

A The earliest buildings were of bark, leaves, mud and straw. They did not last long. But later, people began to build temples and palaces of stone. The earliest structures that we know of were built in about 9000 BC in the Neolithic or New Stone Age. These include the world's oldest stone temple, the Gobekli Tepe, in Turkey. Around 7000 BC the Sumerians, Assyrians and the Egyptians made huge improvements in building. Some of the most remarkable early buildings, including Sumerian *ziggurats* (temples) and the Egyptian pyramids, were made around 3000 BC. As people grew more confident in architecture, the buildings got bigger and more decorative.

▼ **Building a cathedral**
Stones unloaded by boats for the making of a cathedral were raised through a system of pulleys. They were dressed by expert stonemasons before being put in place.

Q What were medieval buildings like?

A With the spread of Christianity, some of the best medieval architecture was seen in churches. Churches were built in two styles: Romanesque and Gothic. The Romanesque style typically used brick vaults and rounded arches. Gothic churches like the Salisbury Cathedral in England and Notre Dame de Paris in France are tall churches with pointed-arch windows and doorways. They are supported by buttresses and they have beautiful stained-glass windows to let light in. During the Renaissance, architecture was inspired by the classical age of Greece and Rome.

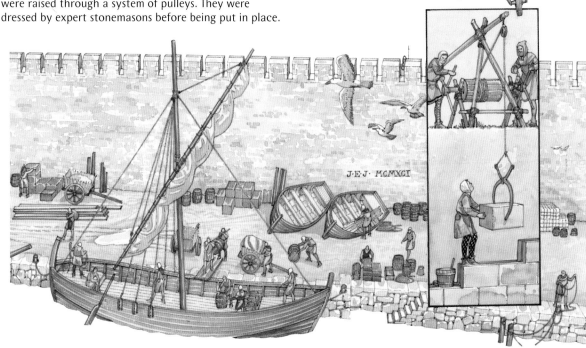

J·E·J· MCMXCI

Q How did modern architecture come about?

A The Industrial Revolution gave architects many new materials to build with, like iron and steel, concrete and strong glass. In 1779 English ironmonger Abraham Darby built the first iron bridge over the river Severn. It proved that cast iron could be used as a strong building material. The Crystal Palace that Joseph Paxton put up at the Great Exhibition in London in 1851 was entirely made of glass and iron. Modern architecture became widespread in the twentieth century. It was much simpler than the ornamental style of the past. Buildings were more practical and designed to make the most of space.

Q Where was the first skyscraper?

A In the United States, tall buildings were called skyscrapers as early as the 1880s. They were built on a steel structure and had central heating, electrical pumps and lifts. In 1890, Major William Le Baron Jenney and Louis Sullivan built the first skyscraper in Chicago. This was the Home Insurance Building. It had ten floors, including the basement. Two floors were added in 1891. Skyscrapers could house so many people that they changed the way people lived and worked.

Q What is different about architecture now?

A In contemporary architecture, the materials often decide the design. There is little decoration. It is simple and uncluttered and often, the supporting pillars and beams are shown. Reinforced concrete and steel allow architects to use fewer columns, beams and thick walls. This means that buildings can now be lighter and taller. Modern buildings often use glass walls, which allow more heat and light inside. The latest trend among architects is to design buildings where the need for heating and lighting is minimized. These are called energy-efficient buildings.

▲ **Modern city skyline**
Modern cities around the world are dominated by skyscrapers. Cities like New York, Hong Kong and Singapore are full of them. But there has been a reaction and in the last few years low buildings are being designed again.

Try these too...

Ancient Mesopotamia (124), Ancient Egypt (125), Ancient Greece (128–129), Ancient Rome (130–131), Medieval Europe (136–137)

▲ **The first modern building**
The Crystal Palace was built in London's Hyde Park for the Great Exhibition in 1851. It was the world's first large iron and glass building. After the exhibition, it was kept in Upper Norwood, where it was destroyed by a fire in 1936.

Touching the sky

The Eiffel Tower was designed by Maurice Koechlin and made by Gustav Eiffel. It is 300 metres (1,000 feet) high. It took 300 workers two years to put together 18,038 pieces of iron with 3.5 million rivets. It is the tallest structure in Paris. It was built as an entrance arch to a world fair held in 1889 to celebrate the 100th anniversary of the French Revolution.

Art and Artists

Art is the way people represent themselves and the world visually. They do this by drawing, painting, sculpture and other means. The earliest art that we know of are rock and cave paintings which date back about 40,000 years. The artists used natural dyes extracted from plants and stones.

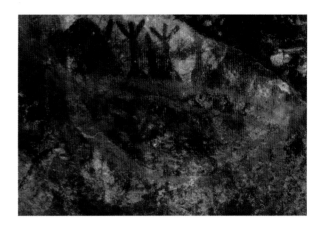

▲ **The ancestor of all artists**
A cave painting in Brazil shows life as it used to be. The painter used colours made from vegetable dyes.

Quick Q's:

1. What is Minimalism?

In the 1950s, Frank Stella of the United States painted white pinstripes on a black canvas and called it *The Marriage of Reason and Squalor*. When asked what it meant, he said 'What you see is what you see'. This style, where painted objects are not a symbol for anything else, is Minimalism.

2. What is pop art?

In the 1960s, American painters like Andy Warhol and Roy Lichtenstein created art from everyday objects. They used soup cans, comic books and advertisements to comment on modern life.

3. What is earth art?

In the 1960s and 1970s, artists like Robert Smithson used bulldozers instead of brushes to create art from natural things outdoors. These works were called earth art. The earth art movement was influenced by concerns about the deterioration of the environment through pollution and deforestation. The ideas of the earth art movement have been used in movies.

Q What were the earliest paintings about?

A The earliest paintings were about things people did every day like hunting, and about the wild animals they saw. Horses, bison, deer and even human hands were drawn. These paintings were often made with pieces of coloured stone. The painters were probably holy men or shamans. Some of these paintings were of such a high standard that they were believed to be fakes. When the Altamira caves in Spain were found and studied in the nineteenth century, many people believed the historians themselves had painted them. The first sculptures also date back to the prehistoric age. One of the most famous statues is the stone image of a woman, named Venus of Willendorf (Austria). It was carved 22,000 to 24,000 years ago.

Q Did different ancient civilizations have their own art?

A Each ancient civilization, including Egypt, Mesopotamia, China, Greece, Rome and India, had its unique art style. Art was used for worship, but it also came to be seen as a form of beauty. Paintings of Egyptian gods and goddesses covered the insides of pyramids. The Mesopotamians covered the walls of their temples with paintings. The Greeks studied the human body closely, and their paintings and sculptures include details of muscles and proportion. The Chinese were among the first to paint on paper and used painting to develop the script for the Chinese language. Indian artists were highly skilled at carving and painting on walls.

Q How was art important during the Middle Ages?

A Art and sculpture of the Middle Ages can be divided into the Romanesque period and the later Gothic period. The spread of Christianity meant that more churches were built. These churches were decorated with images from the Bible. To show their respect for God, painters used a lot of gold colour, made out of real gold. While statues from the Romanesque period are still around, little of the fresco art survived. Gothic art gained ground gradually. Art was also used to decorate hand-written books.

Q Did the Renaissance affect art?

A The Renaissance, lasting from the fourteenth to the sixteenth century, was a great period for artists and sculptors. Much of the inspiration came from the temples and statues of ancient Greece and Rome. Renaissance artists believed in the importance of the human being. They explored the human form and captured scenes from things around them. They learnt about perspective, or the importance of size and distance in a painting. They painted landscapes and developed new styles as well as new material to paint with. The invention of oil painting meant that pictures lasted far longer without fading.

Q How did art change in the nineteenth century?

A During the Romantic period in the nineteenth century, artists began to use their work as a form of expression. Like poets, Romantic artists used art to share their pain, fear and sorrow through nature and landscapes. Unlike Renaissance artists, they did not portray human beings as the ultimate in perfection. Instead, humans were seen as imperfect creatures. English painter JMW Turner and French painter Eugène Delacroix were two of the most famous Romanticists. French painters like Claude Monet captured the wonder of natural light with soft, swift strokes. He and his fellow artists like Camille Pissarro, Paul Cézanne, Edgar Degas, Edouard Manet and Pierre-Auguste Renoir were deeply moved by how the same landscape reminded them of different feelings at different times of the day. This school of art was called Impressionism. The Impressionist movement had a major influence on later artists, and even on music and literature.

Q What is modern art?

A Art from the late nineteenth and twentieth centuries is called modern art. It is made up of a number of art movements. The twentieth century began with artistic movements like Cubism, Futurism and Expressionism. Never before had art of every form been given such freedom. Artists could express any feeling through any form of art, not just painting. The Industrial Revolution, which reduced man to another machine in a factory and the violence of the two World Wars deeply influenced twentieth century art. The Dada movement of World War I was a protest against set ideas in society. In the 1930s, the Surrealist movement explored human psychology. Many Surrealist artists wanted to show the pain and despair of those who suffered in the war.

Moving masterpieces

Michelangelo (1475–1564) was an Italian painter, sculptor and architect during the Renaissance. He was a master of technique. The *Pieta*, a sculpture of Mary with the dead Christ in her arms, took him three years to finish. It was completed in 1500 and stands in Saint Peter's Basilica in Vatican City. Michelangelo was just 25 when he finished this masterpiece. His next major sculpture was the statue *David* (see right). Perhaps the greatest honour for him was to build the tomb for Pope Julius II, for which he made a statue of Moses. Beginning in 1508, he painted the ceiling of the Sistine Chapel over a period of four years. In 1534, he painted the *Last Judgement* on the wall above the altar of the Sistine Chapel.

Q Has technology influenced art?

A Artists in Europe and the United States were influenced by art from other societies. Paul Gauguin and Henri Matisse were inspired by Japanese silk-screen prints. Pablo Picasso tried to show the many views or angles in any subject. This style became known as Cubism. Many recent art shows include photography, film, objects or installations, music and even voices, along with the paintings.

Try these too...

Ancient Egypt (125), Ancient Greece (128–129), Medieval Europe (136–137), Mughal India (140), The Renaissance (142–143)

▼ **Earth art**
The *Spiral Jetty*, an artwork created by Robert Smithson in Great Salt Lake, Utah, in 1970.

Music

Music is a combination of sounds that is usually pleasing to the ear. It can be produced by a singer, a musical instrument, a bird or even a wind chime. It is an art form that has been used in worship, as entertainment or as an accompaniment to dance. It can express different emotions, from joy to sorrow. Human beings made music before they could write.

Quick Q's:

1. What were the first musical instruments?

The earliest musical instruments were probably percussion instruments that kept a beat. These were made of material ancient man found easily, such as stones, branches and animal bones.

2. Are some musical instruments really made of vegetables?

Traditional flutes are made of reeds and bamboo. Gourds and coconuts are dried to make various string instruments, as well as drums and castanets. Jug bands and skiffle music use washboards, metal buckets and glass jugs. The musician blows across the opening of the jug to make a vibrating noise.

Q What is classical music?

A Music composed between the mid-1700s and the early 1800s in Europe is called classical music. This music includes great detail, showing how every note should be played. Classical musicians require years of guided training. Classical music began with church music and later included music for the royal court. In other parts of the world, different countries have their own classical music. Classical Qin music of China is over 1,000 years old and is played with a seven-stringed zither. In India, classical music is not written, but is set to basic 'ragas' or a pattern of notes in a scale.

Q Who invented opera?

A Opera is a form of theatre in which the drama is conveyed through music and singing. Opera singers develop special vocal techniques. They are accompanied by an orchestra. The musicians are in a pit in front of the stage. Opera emerged in Italy around 1600 AD. *Daphne* by Jacopo Peri, written in 1597, was the first opera production. The work is now lost. The first opera that we have today is a 1600 production, also by Peri. It was called *Euridice*. The first opera that is still performed regularly is *Orfeo* by Claudio Monteverdi, composed in 1607.

◀ **Playing the trumpet**
Louis Armstrong was one of the top jazz musicians of the twentieth century.

▲ **Superstar**
Modern musicians like Bon Jovi (above) have millions of fans around the world. They also have a major influence on fashion trends.

Q What is Blues music?

A Blues music grew out of the songs and chants of the African-American slaves in the southern United States. This vocal and instrumental musical style has inspired several other popular genres like pop, rock and roll, ragtime, rhythm and blues and jazz. The Blues get their name from 'feeling blue' or sad.

Q How did jazz develop?

A Jazz was also developed by African-Americans around the first decade of the twentieth century. Jazz, blues and pop music developed at virtually the same time and are similar genres of music in many ways. Blues singers like Bessie Smith, Ma Rainey, Louis Armstrong and Benny Carter were also jazz musicians. Jazz is mostly instrumental and encourages improvisation. The saxophone, trumpet and trombone are popular jazz instruments.

Warbling on

Millions of children have played the recorder, which is a type of folk flute. Recorders have six finger holes and a hole for the left thumb. Recorders have been played in Europe since the fourteenth century. King Henry IV of England had a recorder and King Henry VIII of England had 76. Today, recorders are often the first instrument for children to learn music. They were an important part in the music of composers like Bach and Vivaldi.

▲ **Portable music**
With the development of digital technology, personal music players have become small and portable. They can record music from the Internet.

Q What is pop music?

A Pop is short for 'popular'. Popular music includes music from films and musical comedies, and even country music and rock music. The lyrics are often about everyday life. Country music is inspired by the outdoors: it is simple and tells a bit of a story. Rock 'n' roll began in the 1950s, inspired by Rhythm and Blues (R&B). Elvis Presley and Buddy Holly mixed in blues and country with their own music to produce yet another genre – rockabilly. Famous modern music stars include Bob Dylan, Joan Baez, Eric Clapton, Sting, Elton John, groups like the Beatles, Queen and U2, the hard-rock group Deep Purple and the heavy-metal band Mötley Crüe. Rock music led to Heavy Metal, a loud style of music in which the guitar is important. Recent music stars include Eminem, Beyonce Knowles, Shakira and the group 'NSync.

Q Did science help music?

A Developments in science led to the creation of new musical instruments like synthesizers and drum machines. Electronic music, which has been growing since the 1960s, is played on these instruments. Electronic music has given rise to different styles like techno and house music. Rap developed in 1979 from R&B with rhythmic vocals. It is recited to electronic drum beats and digital recordings of other music. Famous rappers include Eminem and Jay-Z. Hip-hop includes rap and break-dance. Like rap, it is often played by the disc jockey (DJ), who mixes sounds, adds his own electronic effects and creates new music. Advances in technology also made music popular and accessible to wider audiences. The microphone magnified sound and the gramophone, which came in about 1910, allowed music to be recorded and played over and over again. The earliest records were made of rubber or shellac. Nowadays, music is recorded on cassettes, CDs and DVDs and using digital technology.

▲ **Music sheet**
A part of a music sheet written by the famous composer Wolfgang Mozart. Musicians have to learn how to read the notations and follow the score while playing.

Try these too...

The Renaissance (142–143), Computer Revolution (162), Sound (182–183), Communication and Satellites (192–193)

Theatre

The word drama comes from the Greek *dran* which means to perform. Drama usually involves actors on stage, performing a story through dialogue or song. Drama and theatre include acting, pantomime, mime, opera, musicals and ballet.

Quick Q's:

1. Why are some plays staged again and again?

Some plays are so popular that many people want to see them. *Life with Father* by Clarence Day Jr was staged in the USA about 3,200 times and *Oklahoma* by Richard Rodgers and Oscar Hammerstein had 2,000 performances.

2. Did European theatre allow women performers?

Acting was considered disgraceful for women, so even Shakespeare's plays had young boys playing the part of women. Women started acting in the seventeenth century.

3. Which is the longest-running musical?

The Broadway musical *A Chorus Line* was performed for the last and 6,137th time on 28 April 1990 at the Shubert Theatre.

4. What is African theatre about?

In Africa, traditional theatre is often not written, but memorized. In Nigeria, the story of Obatala, the Nigerian creator god, is played every year. Entire villages participate in the *ikaki* or tortoise play.

Q What is the earliest theatre we know of?

A The first theatre that we know of in Europe was in ancient Greece. It dates back to about 600 BC, when a poet named Thespis won the first drama competition. Theatres were built outdoors along a hillside that was cut into steps to seat people. The Greeks preferred tragedies – sad events, over comedy or laughter. Some Greek playwrights like Euripides and Sophocles are still studied and performed today. About 300 BC, the Romans began to write plays in Latin. They preferred comedies. But theatre was not an envied profession, so they chose slaves to act. The Romans loved theatre so much that they built 125 theatres in a period of about 200 years. To make theatre more exciting, their plays became violent. These Roman theatres were closed down with the spread of Christianity.

▼ **In classic style**
Dionysos Theatre below the Acropolis Hill in Athens, Greece, is typical of the style of ancient Greek theatres. In this open-air theatre, the audience sits at a level higher than the stage.

▲ **Kabuki theatre**
The Kabuki theatre of Japan has changed its form many times since it started in 1603. In the beginning, women played the roles of both men and women.

Q Was theatre allowed in medieval Europe?

A The dislike for theatre continued through the Middle Ages. Theatre buildings were not allowed, so actors or wandering minstrels stayed on the move. Soon, acrobats, jugglers and puppeteers joined them. They put up simple platforms to serve as stages wherever they went. They were frowned upon by the Church. However, Christians began their own simple form of theatre to explain the gospel better. Priests acted out events from the Bible, since not many people could read. These were known as Miracle plays.

Q When did theatre make a come-back?

A During the Renaissance people began studying the almost-forgotten ancient Greek and Roman texts. This led to a new interest in theatre. One of the new forms was the proscenium theatre in Italy, with a frame that divided the stage from the audience and a painted backdrop to make it more realistic. In England, the sixteenth century saw some of the best-ever plays being written by playwrights like Christopher Marlowe, Samuel Johnson and William Shakespeare. In France, playwrights like Molière and Racine wrote about ordinary people.

Q What is theatre like around the world?

A Kabuki is a form of Japanese theatre that began in the early 1600s. It was created by a woman named Okuni. It uses a particular kind of music and the actors are dressed in special costumes with thick, colourful make-up that resembles a mask. As something important happens, the actor stares and crosses his eyes in a special action. Make-up colour is important. A good character wears red and a bad character has blue paint. Different civilizations of Asia encouraged different forms of theatre. Asian theatre, unlike theatre in the West, often combines storytelling, dance, music, and mime but may not have a text. Masks, make-up and costumes are often important. The Peking opera of China even includes acrobatics. You know the character by the voice it sings in.

Q Was theatre popular in the United States?

A The first theatre in the United States was the Dock Street Theatre in Charleston, South Carolina that was built in 1736. The building did not last very long. In 1937, a new Dock Street Theatre was built exactly where the original one had stood. At the beginning of the twentieth century, the United States produced some of the most memorable modern theatre. Dubose Heyward became famous with *Porgy*, a play using the Creole language spoken by the African-Americans. It was the world's first international play and the first to run for over 300 shows. *Porgy* toured the United States and London. Heyward and music composers George and Ira Gershwin produced *Porgy and Bess*, which has been called the best Broadway opera. Vaudeville theatre of the United States influenced early film directors in Hollywood, and, through them, filmmaking all over the world. American plays include some of the classics of world theatre, such as *The Streetcar Named Desire* and *Cat on a Hot Tin Roof* by Tennessee Williams.

A series of globes

The original octagonal Globe Theatre was built by Shakespeare, actor Richard Burbage and others in 1599. Around the pit were three layers of balconies. The highest balcony had a thatched roof. In 1613 the thatch caught fire when a cannon was fired during a performance of Shakespeare's Henry VIII, and the building burnt down. It was rebuilt in 1614, but thirty years later, it was destroyed by the Puritans. In 1970 American actor and director Sam Wanamaker raised funds to rebuild the Globe. The latest Globe Theatre, based on the original, opened in 1996.

Q What is Broadway?

A New York's Broadway has over 39 theatres. Broadway was the centre of twentieth-century theatre. The two World Wars inspired realistic plays that told the stories of working class people. Eugene O'Neill, Arthur Miller and Tennessee Williams were among the most successful playwrights of this period. The West End in London is another hub of modern theatre. It has nearly 40 theatres along streets like the Strand, Drury Lane and Shaftesbury Avenue.

Try these too...

Ancient Greece (128–129), Ancient Rome (130–131), The Renaissance (142–143), Communication and Satellites (192–193)

▼ **Plush theatre**
Theatres such as this one in Vienna, Austria, have separate boxes. People who hire these boxes can watch a play without anyone being able to see them.

World of Sports

Sports have played a major role in every civilization. During the hunter-gatherer days, throwing a spear, shooting an arrow, running, wrestling, jumping and slinging a stone were part of the hunt. When people learnt to grow crops and breed animals, they did not have to hunt for food any more. But they have continued to hunt for pleasure and to compete in games.

Quick Q's:

1. Have we learnt any sports from early cultures?

Many popular sports have been learnt from earlier cultures. In 1778, Captain Cook found the people of Hawaii surfing. Native Americans played games like lacrosse. The Mayans and Aztecs played ballgames in a court, which inspired basketball.

2. What are team sports?

Sports played in a group or team, where two teams compete, are called team sports. Team sports like rugby, football, handball, basketball, throwball and volleyball are played with a ball. In cricket, hockey and baseball, a bat or stick is used to hit the ball.

3. What is athletics?

All running events, hurdles and race walking are athletics. All jumps and throws like shot-put, discus and javelin are also athletic events. Athletics also include cross-country runs, marathon and the steeplechase, which has a water barrier in its 3,000-metre course.

Q How serious were the ancient civilizations about sport?

A The Greeks believed that their gods liked humans to be strong and fit. They were especially fond of athletic events. There were several athletic competitions in Greece. The most famous is the Olympic Games and the Isthmian Games at Corinth. Young Greek men – mostly soldiers – trained for sports. Besides running and jumping, they trained to throw the discus and the javelin. All these sports were part of the Olympic Games. Girls were not allowed to compete in the physical games. They played dice, marbles and checkers. In ancient Egypt, people played a game like checkers. They also played games with dice.

▼ **Playing ball**
Baseball is very popular in North America and Japan.

▲ **Ancient sport**
A gladiator takes up a stance. In ancient Rome, gladiators were either mercenaries who fought for money, or slaves who were forced to fight, either with other men or with animals. It was cruel but very popular.

Q Who were the gladiators?

A By 300 BC, sports like chariot racing, horse racing and boxing were popular. The Romans in particular loved to watch sports where armed men and women, called gladiators, fought one another to death. Sometimes, men and women fought animals. Large stadiums were built for these games. There were some professional gladiators who took up this violent sport out of choice or economic reasons, but most of the people forced into the Roman stadiums were slaves. The Romans also played *ludi pilae* or ball games and athletics. Under several Islamic emperors, polo became popular in the Middle East. It soon spread to the Roman Empire and to China. Individual skill sports like gymnastics were popular in ancient China. In Egypt, where the Nile was an important part of life, swimming and fishing were popular.

Q What were the games played after that?

A Board games like chess and checkers became popular. With the glass industry growing, children began to play marbles. Chess, which was probably invented in India, spread to Europe and the Middle East. Gladiator sports came to an end but bull fights were fought in amphitheatres. Several team sports like football and hurling began in the Middle Ages. Horse racing became popular in England.

Five rings and an olive branch

The Olympic Games are named after Mount Olympus, where the ancient Greeks believed that the gods lived. The earliest recorded Olympic Games were held in 776 BC in ancient Greece. Since they were held every four years, they made sport more organized and very competitive. Winners were honoured with an olive branch. In 1896, French educator Baron Pierre de Coubertin revived the Olympics to encourage international diplomatic relations. Since then, the Olympics have been held every four years, except in 1916, 1940 and 1944, during the two World Wars. Even today, the Olympics are the most important sports contest, where the honour of the country matters most. The Paralympic Games, held at the same time and place as the summer and winter Olympics, is for those with physical disabilities and cerebral palsy. These were first held in Rome in 1960.

▶ **Indoor sport**
A gymnast on the parallel bars. Gymnastics is one of the more popular of the indoor games. It requires a superb combination of strength, fitness and flexibility. While many indoor games require the same level of physical fitness as outdoor games, others are less physically demanding.

▶ **Popular passion**
Many sports, such as pole vault (top), swimming (second from top), parachuting (centre), cricket (second from bottom) and boxing (bottom) are popular and are followed by thousands of people across the globe. Professional sports are run like multi-million dollar businesses.

Q Are sports still changing?

A In the nineteenth and twentieth centuries, cricket became popular in Britain and in the former British colonies. In the United States, baseball, a game similar to cricket, got its set of rules in the 1840s. Rugby, rather than football, became popular there. With the Industrial Revolution, better quality sports equipment flooded the market. With life becoming more urban and routine, exciting sports like hang-gliding, paragliding, bungee jumping and canoeing have become popular.

Q Are all sports played outdoors?

A Even sports like tennis and hockey can be played indoors, in a covered stadium. Games like chess, billiards and bridge are nearly always played inside a room. Gymnastics and table tennis are indoor games that require a lot of physical activity.

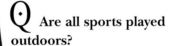

Try these too...

Ancient Greece (128–129), Ancient Rome (130–131), Incas and Aztecs (141), Communication and Satellites (192–193)

World of Movies

In the early nineteenth century, scientists noticed that if a series of still pictures is made to move, it seems as if the image is moving naturally. This moving picture is what developed into movies, also known as motion pictures or films.

▲ Movie history
Radio City Music Hall in New York had a famous movie hall in the USA from the 1930s to the 1970s.

Q What was the daguerreotype?

A One of the first moving-image devices scientists used was a slotted disk with a series of drawings, called the daguerreotype. When the disk spun in front of a mirror, anyone looking through the slots would see the drawings move. In 1839, the daguerreotype led to photography. In the 1870s French inventor Émile Reynaud developed the first projector using a reflector and a lens to enlarge the moving images. By 1892, he was showing his moving drawings at Théâtre Optique in Paris. Each show lasted for just 15 minutes. These were virtually the first film shows.

Q How did cinema develop?

A In the 1870s, Leland Stanford laid a bet on whether all four feet of a galloping horse were ever off the ground at the same time. He hired a British photographer Eadweard Muybridge who photographed a moving horse on 12 cameras. The photographs showed the horse with all four feet off the ground. In 1889, George Eastman introduced the celluloid roll. Celluloid, a material made from the chemicals camphor and nitrocellulose, was used as a medium for film photography.

◀ The clapper
Every shot in a film starts with the top of the clapper being brought down to make a sound. The board is used to record the details of the shot. The clapper has become one of the symbols of the film industry.

In the 1890s, Thomas Alva Edison and his assistant, William Dickson, invented the kinetograph and the kinetoscope. The kinetograph was a single camera that could record a succession of images on to a moving celluloid film. The kinetoscope was a large coin-operated box that had a peephole through which the 'movie' could be seen.

Q What are the Lumière brothers famous for?

A In France, Auguste and Louis Lumière ran a factory where they manufactured photographic equipment. In 1895 they developed a hand-held camera, the cinematographe. It could show large images on a screen when attached to a projector. Their first public screening was held in Paris in December 1895. They made several films during 1895 and 1896. They could even bring a story into films. *Waterer and Watered*, made in 1896, shows a boy playing a prank to drench a gardener. They also made films about real life, like *Workers Leaving the Lumière Factory*, 1895 and *Arrival of a Train at La Ciotat*, 1896. But cinema is not the invention of any one person. In Germany, Emil and Max Skladanowsky also designed a machine to project films in November 1895. In Britain Birt Acres and Robert W. Paul could project films by January 1896.

◀ The big prize
The Oscars are one of the main awards given for films.

Q Which was the first real entertainment movie to be shown?

A In 1901 American projectionist Edwin S. Porter began making longer films that told a story. His *The Great Train Robbery*, made in 1903, was the first film shown for entertainment. Nickelodeon theatres sprung up in converted storefronts and charged 5 cents for a show. The first colour films were hand-painted.

Q When did sound come in?

A Recorded sound was used in the late 1920s. Within just five years, sound was used in almost every film. Once sound could be recorded, musical films or musicals became popular. Warner Brothers made films which featured large groups of dancers. Their earliest films were *42nd Street*, *Gold Diggers of 1933*, and *Footlight Parade*.

Q What other types of films were encouraged by sound?

A With sound, directors could tell any story. Horror films, featuring monsters and murderers, became popular. During the 1930s, the films *Dracula* and *Frankenstein* were made. Action films and dramas also became popular with the introduction of sound. Colour films started in the 1920s.

But colour was only used widely in the 1950s to lure television audiences. Sound made animation films funnier. Walt Disney's first animated cartoon with sound was *Steamboat Willie* of 1928. By 1937, after adding colour to his films, he was making feature-length animation films in colour. The first such film was *Snow White and the Seven Dwarfs*, made in 1937. Animation films continued to be popular and contributed to the success of films like *Jaws*. In the 1990s, computer graphics speeded up the animation process.

▲ **Hollywood Hill**
Many of the world's biggest movies are made in this part of Los Angeles.

Try these too...

Scientific Revolution (150–151), The World after World War II (160–161), Light (180–181), Electricity (186–187), Communication and Satellites (192–193)

That's huge!

Imax or Image Maximum makes movies huge. Over 700 million people have watched an Imax movie. During Imax films, digital surround sound technology is used to make the sound seem more real and close. In an Imax theatre, the screen is high and wide enough to include the whole visual field of the viewer. A standard Imax screen is 22 metres wide and 16 metres high (72.6 x 52.8 feet). The world's largest Imax screen is in Sydney, Australia.

World Religions

Religion is a set of rules based on faith in a spiritual power. Every civilization has its religion. Religion can also mean faith in plants, animals, ancestors and spirits. Pantheism is the belief that there is something spiritual in everything around us. The word religion comes from the Latin noun religio, or rituals and faith. Most religions practiced today were started long ago.

▲ **Ancient Egyptian gods**
These gods were portrayed as half-human half-beast.

Quick Q's:

1. What is the meaning of Zoroastrianism?

Zoroastrianism is a religion founded in Persia around the sixth century BC by the prophet Zarathushtra. Arabs later banned the religion. Zoroastrians or Parsees fled to India. Zoroastrianism believes in one god, Ahura Mazda. Their holy book is the Avesta.

2. Who are the Amish?

The Amish are a Christian sect known for their shunning of modern technology. The Amish, who live in the United States and in Ontario (Canada), avoid the use of electricity and cars as far as possible. They do not join the military, nor do they take any money from any government. They place a high value on humility, and are strongly against pride.

Q What is Judaism?

A Judaism, the religion of the Jewish people, has about 15 million followers around the world. It began about 3,500 years ago in Palestine. Judaism is perhaps the earliest religion to preach belief in one god. The laws of God are known as the Ten Commandments, which God revealed to Moses on Mount Sinai. These laws are written in the Old Testament of the Bible. The Torah is the holy book of Judaism. This religion influenced later religions that began in the region, including Christianity, Islam and the more recent Baha'i faith. The Jewish temple is called a synagogue. Jewish people believe they should pray three times a day. Saturday or Shabbat is a day of rest and prayer, to remember that God rested on this day after creating the world in six days.

Q Did ancient Man believe in religion?

A There are signs that every ancient civilization believed in a higher power. The ancient Egyptians worshiped many gods like Anubis, Set, Osiris, Isis and Horus. Egyptian Kings, called Pharaohs, were believed to be God's representatives on Earth. The ancient Egyptians were the first to prepare the dead for an after-life. They buried kings and commoners with many things they believed would be needed in the after-life. The ancient Mesopotamians, especially the Sumerians, had a strong belief in several gods who took human form.

However, they believed that these spirits had superhuman powers and so they could not be seen. Four of their main gods were An, the god of heaven; Ki, the goddess of earth; Enlil, the god of air; and Enki, the god of water.

Q Which is the oldest religion in the world still practiced?

A Hinduism began before 1500 BC. It grew from the four Vedas – religious texts written by scholars. The Vedas contain hymns and information about rituals. Hinduism believes that the world was created by Bramha, and is maintained by Vishnu. Any destruction in the world is ascribed to Shiva. The two major sects of Hinduism are Vaishnavism, or the path followed by the followers of Vishnu, and Shaivism, where Shiva is the main deity. Apart from Bramha, Vishnu and Shiva, the mother goddess, in her many forms, is worshipped as Shakti, or strength.

▲ **Hindu god**
The elephant-headed god Ganesha is one of the most popular of the Hindu deities. As in other ancient religions, Hindu gods are often depicted in various supernatural forms that are symbolic.

Q Who started Buddhism?

A Siddhartha Gautama was born in 563 BC. Troubled by sickness, sorrow and suffering, he left his palace to meditate or think about life. When he found the answers to his questions, he became known as The Buddha – Enlightened One. Buddhism is practised in Nepal, India, China, Myanmar, Thailand, Japan, Korea and Sri Lanka, among others.

Q What is Christianity all about?

A Christianity is practised in every continent where humans live. There are over 1.9 billion Christians. They follow the teachings of Jesus Christ, who lived about 2000 years ago. The New Testament of the Bible, the holy book of the Christians written after his crucifixion, details the life and teachings of Jesus.

▲ **The headquarters of the Catholic Church**
St Peter's basilica in the Vatican – the seat of the Pope, who is the head of the Catholic Church.

Q When did Islam begin?

A The Prophet Muhammad founded Islam in the seventh century AD in Arabia. Islam is the second largest religion in the world. The holy book of Muslims is the Quran. Muslims believe that the Quran was revealed to Prophet Muhammad by God through the Angel Gabriel. Islam has one God. The word Islam means 'peace' and 'obedience to God'.

▲ **Shrine of the Báb**
The tomb in Haifa, Israel, of the founder of Baha'ism. Started in the nineteenth century, it is the world's youngest religion.

▶ **Old symbol**
The menorah, the seven-branched candlestick, is one of the oldest symbols of Judaism. It was used in the Temple of Jerusalem.

Try these too...

Ancient Mesopotamia (124), Ancient Egypt (125), Ancient India and China (126–127), Native Americans (133–135), Medieval Europe (136–137)

On the calendar

Each religion sets aside certain days as important. For Christians, Christmas, or the day Christ was born, is celebrated on 25 December. Easter, the day Christ rose from the cross where he was crucified, is commemorated on a Sunday in the middle of April. For Muslims, Eid ul-Fitr marks the end of a month of fasting during Ramadan. The date is decided by the cycle of the Moon. Eid ul-Adha marks the end of haj, the pilgrimage to Mecca. Jews celebrate their new year as Rosh Hashanah, which they believe was the day the world was created. Yom Kippur is the day of praying for forgiveness for mistakes committed. Hindus celebrate several festivals. Diwali, or the Festival of Lights, celebrates the victory of good over evil. Dussehra celebrates the victory of Lord Rama in his battle against the demon king Ravana. Buddhists celebrate Buddha Purnima as the Buddha's birthday.

Matter

Everything around us is matter. Anything that occupies space and has weight is matter. Matter is made up of atoms and molecules. It takes three main forms: solid, liquid and gas. All matter can change from one of these forms to another.

Quick Q's:

1. What is plasma?

Plasmas are super-hot atoms. A tube light glows because the gas inside the tube gets charged up by the flow of electricity and creates plasma that glows. The Northern Lights are an example of plasma occurring in nature. Stars also have plasma in them.

2. What is a super atom?

When some elements are cooled to a temperature just above absolute zero, the atoms begin to clump together to become one 'super atom'. Super atoms have only been made in laboratories for fractions of a second.

3. Can I look at an atom?

We cannot look at an atom directly, even through the most powerful optical microscopes, because atoms are much smaller than the wavelengths of light that optical microscopes detect. A human hair is as wide as one million carbon atoms. However, we can detect the position of an atom on the surface of a solid with an electron microscope, so we know it is there.

Q What does matter look like?

A Matter is found in different forms and shapes. It can be as huge as a mountain or as tiny as gravel. It can be hard like diamond, or as soft as silk. Even water is matter. A cube of ice is the solid state of water. At the melting point of water, or a little over 0 °C, the ice turns in to water. If the water is boiled, it turns in to steam or gas. When this steam meets a cold surface, like a tile on the kitchen wall, it cools and becomes liquid. Plasma, another form of matter, can be made from a gas.

◀ **Underground water**
A geyser blows steam into the cold air of Iceland. The temperature underground can be so high that the water turns into steam. This steam then expands and looks for ways out of its chamber. When it finds a pipe leading to a hole on the Earth's surface, it gushes out in the form of a geyser. On contact with the cold air outside, the steam cools down and turns back to water again.

Q What are solids?

A Anything that has a shape of its own and occupies space or has volume is a solid. An ice cube is a solid. When it melts in to water, it turns in to a liquid that has volume but no definite shape. If you pour the liquid in to a spoon, it takes the shape of the spoon. If you pour it back in to the ice tray, it takes the shape of the ice tray. If the water is heated to a certain temperature, it becomes vapour or gas and has no definite shape or volume. Gas expands to fill any container you put it into.

▼ **Crystal of carbon atoms**
A diamond is a transparent crystal of carbon atoms. It is one of the many forms in which carbon is found.

▲ **All three forms**
The ice cubes (top), the water in a cup (top right) and the vapour in front of the kettle (above) are the three forms in which water can be found – solid, liquid and gas. All three forms are interchangeable, by adding or taking heat energy away from the water. The chemical properties of water remain the same in all states.

Q What is matter made of?

A The tiniest part of all matter is an atom. Several atoms form a molecule. Matter in solid state, like the ice cube, gets its shape because the atoms are packed close and tight. In the liquid state, atoms are more loosely packed. In the gas state, the atoms are even more spread out and have lots of space between them.

Q How does an ice cube become water?

A Adding more energy or taking away energy from a substance changes its form. When you add heat energy to an ice cube, it turns to water. This is a physical change since its shape and state change but the chemical composition, or the atoms and molecules, do not change.

Tiny orbit

Atoms are made up of three parts called electrons, neutrons and protons. The neutrons and protons form the nucleus, or centre, of the atom and the electrons move around the nucleus. An electron has a negative electric charge, the proton has a positive electric charge and the neutron is neutral or has no charge. The atomic theory was first developed by John Dalton (below).

Q What are chemical changes?

A Sometimes, adding or taking away energy changes the substance so much that no amount of heating or cooling can turn it back to what it was. This is called a chemical change. When you heat or toast bread, it turns brown and finally gets burnt or black. No amount of cooling can turn this brown bread white again because the bread has been through a chemical change.

Q What is a compound?

A All matter is made up of some basic substances called elements. Elements are natural substances. They cannot be made artificially. Oxygen is an element. If two or more elements are combined in such a way that they can be separated again, it is called a mixture. When you combine two or more elements to make something new that cannot be changed, you get a compound. If you heat iron and sulphur, it will form iron sulphide, which is a compound.

◀ Different shapes
A liquid does not have a specific shape but takes the shape of the container in which it is poured. This is because the atoms that make up the liquid are freer than they are in solid form, so they move about more and occupy all the space.

▲ A chemical change
When you toast a slice of bread, it is a chemical change. The heat leads to chemical reactions in the bread, so that it hardens and changes colour.

Try these too...

Stars (8–9), The Sun (10–11), The Planets (12–13), The Moon (20–21), Comets and Asteroids (22–23), The Renaissance (142–143), The Industrial Revolution (148–149), Scientific Revolution (150–151)

◀ Plasma
This is matter in its plasma state, the fourth state of matter. When gases become very hot like in these neon tubes, they turn in to plasma and start glowing. In this state, electrons and protons move about freely, so that the matter is said to be ionized. Neon lighting is used widely in cities.

Light

Light is a very important part of our lives. Without light we would not be able to see the beautiful world around us, and it wouldn't even exist. Light is essential for life to thrive on this planet. Animals and humans depend on plants for their food. Plants make their own food, but they cannot do so without light.

Quick Q's:

1. What is a light year?

The distance that light travels in a year is called a light year.

2. What colour is light?

Light usually appears white, but is made up of various colours of the rainbow: violet, indigo, blue, green, yellow, orange and red (VIBGYOR).

3. Why does the Sun look like a red disc during sunrise and sunset?

During sunrise and sunset, the sunlight has to travel a much longer distance than during the rest of the day. The scattered blue light is not able to cover this extra distance and therefore does not reach our eyes. The red light reaches us, as the wavelength of red is longer. This helps red light travel further. This is why the Sun appears like a red disc.

4. What do the words 'opaque' and 'transparent' mean?

Solids are said to be opaque, as they do not allow light to pass through them, while water and glass are transparent as light is able to pass through.

▲ Source of light
Light is actually a form of energy that is produced by both natural and artificial sources. A light source is any object that gives off light. The Sun is the main natural source of light. Artificial sources of light include candles and electric bulbs.

Q How long does it take for sunlight to travel to the Earth?

A Light from the Sun takes about eight minutes to reach us on the Earth. This is because sunlight travels at an incredible speed of about 300,000 kilometres per second (186,000 miles per second). Nothing in this universe travels faster than that!

Q Does light always travel in a straight line?

A Light travels in a straight line unless an object is placed in its path. If the object is solid the light bends around the edges of the object, creating a shadow. If you place a mirror in its path, the light hits the surface and gets reflected. If you use a transparent object, the light goes through it, but its direction is altered slightly. This phenomenon is called refraction.

Q Why are we not able to see objects on the other side of a wall?

A We are able to see an object when light bounces off that object and reaches our eyes. However, solid objects like a wall block the light from passing through to the other side. Instead, the light hits the wall and bounces back. Therefore, we are able to see the wall but not the objects on the other side.

◄ A matter of colour
The colour of an object is determined by the colour of the light it scatters – an object appears green because it scatters green and absorbs the rest of the colours. A black object is black because it does not scatter any light.

Q Glass is also a solid object, yet how are we able to see through it?

A The molecules of solid matter are usually packed tightly together, and therefore do not allow light to pass through them. In liquids and gases, the molecules move about freely and there is a lot of space between them. That is why light is able to pass through these materials easily. Glass is made by first melting sand, and then cooling it. The substance made has the rigidity of a solid, but still has the free moving molecules of a liquid. So the space between the molecules of glass allows light to pass through, although glass itself is a solid.

Q How are rainbows formed?

A A rainbow is created by the refraction of sunlight by water droplets in the atmosphere. When sunlight passes through a drop of water, it is bent in such a way that the various colours that make up white light are split. Each colour is bent at different angles. Red bends the least, while violet is bent the most. It is this phenomenon that we see as a rainbow.

▼ A rainbow of colours
The rainbow is always formed on that portion of the sky that is directly opposite to the Sun. A rainbow is not composed of just seven colours. In fact, it also contains colours like infrared that cannot be seen.

Mirror, mirror!

Light usually bounces straight back when it hits a solid object. We can see the object, but it doesn't reflect anything. However, some objects also absorb a part of the light that falls on them and reflect it. Others reflect all of the light that falls on them. These objects create reflections. Reflections are seen best on mirrors as they have smooth, flat surfaces that reflect light better. When you stand in front of a mirror, the reflected light from it falls on you and therefore you are able to see an image of yourself on the mirror.

Q Why is the sky blue?

A The Earth's atmosphere contains tiny molecules of gas and dust particles. Sunlight entering the atmosphere hits these molecules and dust particles. Colours with longer wavelengths, like red and yellow, can pass through the atmosphere without being scattered by these molecules of gas and dust particles. But the colour blue, with its shorter wavelength, is scattered by the gas molecules and the dust in the upper atmosphere. This is why the sky appears blue.

▶ Blue water
Water is actually colourless. However, large amounts of water act like the sky and scatter blue light. This is why seas, lakes and rivers usually appear blue.

Try these too...

Galaxies (6–7), Stars (8–9), The Sun (10–11), The Industrial Revolution (148–149), Scientific Revolution (150–151)

Sound

Sound is a form of energy that is transferred by pressure waves in air or through other materials. These waves can be picked up by the ear, which is how we hear sounds. But there are many sounds around us that our ears do not pick up, and so we do not hear them.

Quick Q's:

1. What is the range of sound that the human ear can catch?

A young human being can hear almost all sounds from 15 Hz to 20,000 Hz. With age, you hear less, and find it difficult to catch higher frequencies. A human voice carries sound at about 60 Hz, but a shout can reach 13,000 Hz. Elephants, dogs and other animals can hear ultrasonic sound that we cannot.

2. How does ultrasonic sound help doctors?

Ultrasonic sound waves help doctors locate and diagnose medical problems, because different tissues reflect sound waves in different ways. Using this method, doctors can also monitor the development of a foetus during pregnancy.

3. How do I speak?

Human beings have vocal chords inside the larynx which produce sound. When air passes through a gap between the chords, these chords vibrate and produce a sound. All animals that can produce a sound have vocal chords, except birds which produce sound through a bony ring, called a syrinx.

Q How does sound move?

A Sound needs a medium like air, water or solids to travel through. When something moves through the air, it disturbs the molecules of gas in the air around it. The air vibrates or moves back and forth. This vibration is heard as sound. The greater the vibration, the louder the sound. Since sound travels in waves, it gets weaker the further it travels. That is why your voice cannot be heard beyond a certain distance. If you put in more energy and shout, the sound waves will be stronger and travel further so that your voice can be heard further. Sound cannot travel through a vacuum, because a vacuum is completely empty, and has no medium with which to carry the sound wave.

Q Can you measure sound?

A Sound is measured in several ways: frequency, wavelength and amplitude. Sound waves vibrate at different rates. These are called frequencies, measured in cycles per second or Hertz (Hz). 1 Hertz = 1 vibration per second. A wavelength measures the length of one cycle. Longer wavelengths have a lower pitch. The lowest tones that a human can catch are about 16 vibrations per second, or 16 Hz. Amplitude measures how loud the sound is. A sound wave of high amplitude will produce a louder sound. It is measured in decibels (Db).

◀ **Music to the ears**
Music generally conforms to eight notes or an octave. All other sound is noise. Although most of us agree on what music is, there can be disagreements. For example, people beating on pots and pans can create unusual music.

Q Does sound travel as fast as light?

A Sound travels far slower than light. Light travels at 299,337 kilometres per second, (186,000 miles per second) and sound travels at about 8 kilometres per second (5 miles per second). This is why we see lightning before we hear thunder. If you hear a clap of thunder ten seconds after you see a flash of lightning, then the lightning struck 3.6 kilometres (two miles) away.

Q What is an echo?

A Sound waves can be reflected off any reasonably flat surface like a cliff, high wall or mountain. When this surface is neither too near nor too far, a sound made by you hits the surface and comes back to you as an echo. The further the surface is from you, the weaker the echo and the longer it will take for the echo to return. The waves keep bouncing back and forth, getting weaker as they travel, until they lose energy and die out.

▼ Sonic boom

When an aircraft flies faster than the speed of sound, it is hitting the sound waves in front before those waves have moved away. So successive sound waves are getting mixed up. This creates the sonic boom.

How the ear hears

When sound energy reaches the outer ear, the eardrum that separates the outer and middle ears transmits this sound inside, where it is converted into nerve signals and sent to the brain. The brain tells us what we hear. We hear our own voice much the way we hear other sounds, and also by bone conduction. The vibration of the voice makes the bones in our skull vibrate. These vibrations are picked up by the inner ear. That is how some people with hearing problems can be helped with a hearing aid that transfers sound vibrations to the skull bones.

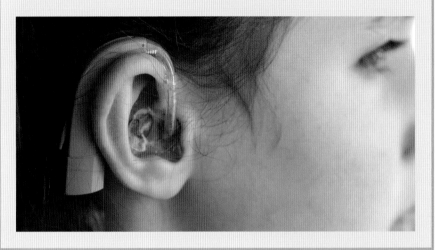

Q How does an aircraft break the sound barrier?

A Supersonic aircraft travel at a speed greater than that of the speed of sound, which is about 1,220 kilometres per hour (760 miles per hour). The first supersonic flight was in 1947 by a Bell X-1 rocket plane flown by Chuck Yeager. These aircraft measure speed in Mach. Mach 1 is the speed of sound. At less than Mach 1, the aircraft is flying at a speed lower than the speed of sound or is subsonic. At Mach 1, it is travelling at the speed of sound or is transonic. Speed between Mach 1 to 5 is supersonic. Above Mach 5 is hypersonic. At supersonic speed and above, an aircraft creates such a strong shock wave that it is heard on ground as a sonic boom. This can be so loud that most supersonic aircraft fly above Mach 1 only above the ocean, where few people outside will be troubled by the sonic boom.

Try these too...

The Industrial Revolution (148–149), Scientific Revolution (150–151), The World after World War II (160–161), Music (168–169)

▲ Sharp ears
Dogs can pick up a lower frequency than humans can. Dog whistles are made on this principle.

Heat

Heat is a form of energy that is created by atoms moving. Even things that are cold have some heat energy because their atoms move, albeit slowly. When we feel cold, we jump up and down for warmth to get our atoms moving! Heat energy is also known as thermal energy. Many types of energy like light, chemical, sound and nuclear can be converted into heat energy by increasing the speed of the atoms in the object producing the energy.

Quick Q's:

1. What is thermodynamics?

Thermodynamics is the study of heat and how it can help us.

2. Why do things expand when heated?

When you heat solids, liquids or gases, they expand because the molecules start moving faster. To move fast, they need more space, so they expand.

3. What is boiling point?

The temperature at which a substance changes from liquid to gas is called its boiling point. The melting point of a substance is the temperature at which it changes from solid to liquid.

4. What are good conductors of heat?

Metals are the best conductors of heat. That is why cooking pans are made of metal to carry the heat from the stove to the pan. Wood and plastic are poor conductors. That is why the handles of cooking utensils are often made of these materials, so we don't burn our hands!

Q Where do we find heat?

A The largest source of heat in nature is the Sun. The Sun is a burning ball of fire whose average surface temperature is 6,000 $^{\circ}$C (10,800 $^{\circ}$F), about 400 times the average surface temperature on Earth. In the kitchen, we need heat to convert raw food into something that is digested easily. We use gas or an electric oven to heat our food. Before stoves, heaters and ovens running on gas or electricity were developed, the heat for cooking was provided by burning wood or coal. Vehicles like cars move with the heat that comes from burning fossil fuels like petrol and diesel. Machines like a knife sharpener or an electrical saw generate heat. Our bodies get heat energy from the food we eat. But ultimately, the source of all this heat is the Sun. Even the fires that burn under the Earth's crust produce heat that originally came from the Sun.

◄ From heat to light
The heat energy produced by the burning of the matchstick also produces visible light. The lighted match is used to light the wick of the candle. As the wick catches fire, it produces heat. Some of this heat energy is converted into light energy that we see. Another portion of the heat energy melts the wax to provide fuel, so that the entire process can continue.

Q How is heat measured?

A Heat is measured with a thermometer. A thermometer is a glass tube that ends in a bulb containing mercury. Numbers are written on the tube. The mercury in the bulb heats up when it touches something hot, like the inside of your mouth. As a result, the mercury expands and rises up the tube. If we do not have a fever and are resting, the mercury will stop at 37.0 $^{\circ}$C (98.6 $^{\circ}$F). When we are unwell and have a fever, the mercury rises further, and the doctor knows how high the fever is.

Q What is heat energy used for?

A We use heat energy every day. Electrical energy is converted into heat energy in appliances like electrical stoves, toasters, hair dryers and light bulbs. When you boil water, heat energy from the stove makes the molecules in the pan move faster. This heats up the pan. This heat from the pan, in turn, makes water molecules inside it move faster and heat up. That is why the water heats up only after the pan is hot. Heat energy does a lot of work for us. The earliest trains ran on thermal power from burning coal.

◄ Using heat
One of the most common uses of heat energy is for cooking food. The heat leads to chemical changes, which turns raw food into cooked food that we can digest.

Q How is heat transferred from one thing to another?

A Heat is transferred by conduction, convection and radiation. Conduction means the transfer of energy from one molecule to the next molecule. Whenever two substances come close to each other, heat flows from the warmer to the cooler substance through conduction. Convection is when a source of heat warms up a liquid or gas due to movements of currents inside the liquid or gas. This is how water boils. Radiation is the transfer of heat in straight lines like the rays of the Sun. Direct radiation from the Sun can be dangerous because it contains ultraviolet rays that damage our skin.

Q How can I light a fire?

A When two things rub against each other, it is called friction. This generates a lot of heat, sometimes enough heat to light a fire without matches. People struck pieces of flint to light a fire before matches were developed. Even today, when you light a match, it is friction that causes the matchstick to catch fire.

▼ Transfer of heat in a microwave oven
Microwave radiation passes through the food inside this oven. Some molecules in the food absorb energy from the microwave beam and start moving around. This movement produces heat that cooks the food.

The largest source of heat energy

Heat energy from the Sun is known as solar energy. Rays from the Sun heat the surface of the Earth, the oceans and the air above. Taking a hint from the Sun's natural heating capacity, scientists have made solar cells from which we can get electricity. When sunlight touches a solar cell, it causes a chemical reaction and electricity is generated. Solar panels can heat water and cook food and solar cells can even run a car. Fossils fuels like petroleum have to be mined from the Earth, and one day we will use them all up. But solar power will not run out for millions of years.

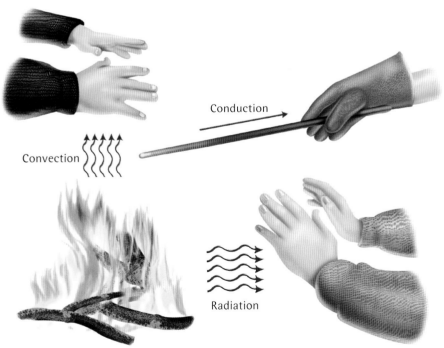

Conduction

Convection

Radiation

▲ Ways of heat transfer
Heat travels through solids by conduction. Most metals are good conductors of heat, while wood is a poor conductor. That is why frying pans are made of metal, but often have a wooden handle. As the diagram shows, convection currents first move upwards. Heat transfer by radiation takes place in all directions.

Try these too...

The Sun (10–11), The Industrial Revolution (148–149), Scientific Revolution (150–151)

Electricity

Electricity is a secondary source of energy. We have to generate electricity from primary sources of energy like moving water, nuclear power, coal or natural gas. It can be converted in to other forms of energy like light or heat. Electricity is used for lighting and heating or cooling our homes. It runs machines to wash clothes and dishes and to cook. It brings us information through computers and television.

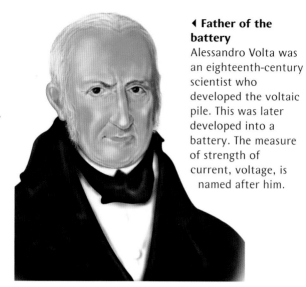

◀ Father of the battery
Alessandro Volta was an eighteenth-century scientist who developed the voltaic pile. This was later developed into a battery. The measure of strength of current, voltage, is named after him.

▲ Electric animal
One of the large electric eels of South America can deliver a shock powerful enough to kill a human.

Quick Q's:

1. If electricity lights a bulb, does it also light my torch?

A bulb is lit with electricity from a power generator. Another source of electricity is the battery. It has chemicals that react and produce a small amount of electricity, enough for a torch.

2. How do power stations generate so much electricity?

Power stations convert the kinetic energy of moving water (hydroelectricity), heat produced by burning coal (thermal electricity) or by a nuclear reaction (nuclear power), the kinetic energy of wind that turns a windmill, tide movements (tidal power) or heat from inside the Earth (geothermal power) to generate electricity.

Q Who discovered electricity?

A Ancient Greeks knew that electricity could be produced by rubbing two pieces of felt together. But the first use of the word electricity was by Sir Thomas Browne in his 1646 book *Pseudodoxia Epidemica* (Vulgar Errors). In 1752, Benjamin Franklin proved that lightning was created by electric charges. He tied an iron key to a kite string during a storm and showed that the lightning hit the key. For this reason, Franklin is said to have discovered electricity. Today, we know that lightning is the most commonly seen form of natural electricity. It is caused by clouds carrying a negative charge that bump in to positively charged objects on Earth.

Q What is electricity?

A Everything is made of atoms. At the centre of an atom is the nucleus made of protons and neutrons. An atom also has tiny electrons which spin around the nucleus. Electrons have a negative electrical charge, and protons have a positive charge. The electrons don't stay in one place. They move around to different atoms, so some atoms have more protons, some have more electrons. An atom with more protons is positively charged. One with more electrons is negatively charged. When the electrons pass from one atom to the next, it creates an electric current.

Q Can electricity make my hair stand on end ?

A Static electricity is created when you rub against a charged surface. The extra electrons move from your body or the other way around, and a tiny spark of electricity is created. Static makes dry hair stand on end after you run a plastic comb through it.

◀ Natural electricity
The lightning that transfers electrons from negatively charged clouds to positively charged substances on the surface of the Earth is the biggest source of natural electricity we know of. Lightning can be dangerous to someone caught outdoors. Anyone caught outdoors during a thunderstorm should keep as low as possible.

Q How is electricity measured?

A Voltage is the measure of the strength of an electric current. The unit for measuring voltage is the volt. A voltameter tells us how many electrons are sent from one end of the circuit and how many are received at the other end. The distance electricity travels affects its quality, especially if it is prevented from flowing freely because of resistance. Resistance is a material's opposition to the flow of electric current through it. Resistance is measured in ohms. Scientists are always looking for materials like copper that are good conductors of electricity and have a low resistance. Silver is the best conductor, but it cannot be used in wires in our homes because it is too costly. Most metals are good conductors.

Q How does a light bulb work?

A The electric bulb is made of transparent or translucent glass and has a delicate wire called a filament. It has to be thin so that its atoms collide more often when an electric current is passed through it. That is how it glows. Thomas Alva Edison made the first practical, workable bulb for home use. Compact fluorescent lamps that use less energy than other bulbs have become increasingly popular since the 1980s.

▶ **Inside a bulb**
Scientists experimented with the conversion of electrical energy to light throughout the nineteenth century. In 1801, Humphry Davy made platinum strips glow by passing an electric current through them. Seven different types of light bulbs were patented in that century before the first could be used at home.

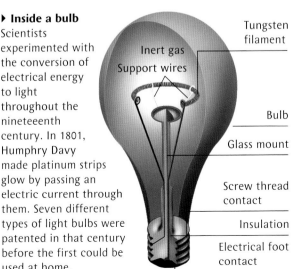

Tungsten filament

Inert gas

Support wires

Bulb

Glass mount

Screw thread contact

Insulation

Electrical foot contact

Electric brain

Without electricity, we wouldn't be able to feel anything! The human body has a continuous flow of electric current through our nerve cells. That is how the nerve cells convey messages to the brain, and we know that our back is hurting, or that someone is standing on our foot. In its turn, the brain uses these tiny electric currents to send commands to the rest of our body. Your hand turns the page when the brain commands it to do so.

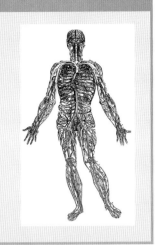

▲ **Changing skyline**
The night skyline of almost every city in the world has changed dramatically in the last 100 years or so, after electricity came into widespread use for lighting.

▼ **A hydroelectric power station**
Water is held in a dam. Then a bit of the water is allowed to run through a channel, turning the blades of a turbine connected to a generator.

Try these too...

The Industrial Revolution (148–149), Scientific Revolution (150–151), Magnets (188–189)

Magnets

Any object that attracts metals like iron, cobalt, nickel or steel to itself is a magnet. A magnet can push away or repel other magnets. Some magnets, like iron, are very strong, while other magnets are much weaker.

Quick Q's:

1. Why do things stick only to the poles of the magnet?

Magnets are strongest at their poles so objects stick to one of the poles most easily.

2. How can you destroy a magnet?

Though magnets can be natural or man-made, dropping, heating or hammering them can destroy them, especially if they are small and weak.

3. Can you store a magnet?

Magnets get weaker with time. The best way to store them is to keep them in pairs with the unlike poles next to each other and placing keepers or pieces of soft iron across the ends. The keepers become temporary magnets themselves and keep the magnetic force stronger.

4. What is an electromagnet?

Winding an electric wire around a piece of iron can make electromagnets. When electric current runs through the wire, a magnetic field is created. The iron piece picks this up and becomes a magnet.

Q How did people find out about magnets?

A The magnet was discovered in China as early as 200 BC. Around the same time, the Chinese found that from a magnet, one could find out directions like north and south. Sailors in most civilizations began to use a certain type of magnet called a lodestone to navigate. It is the most magnetic substance on Earth. In the sixteenth century, Sir William Gilbert discovered that a piece of iron could acquire the properties of a lodestone if you rubbed it with a lodestone. That allowed scientists to create many more magnets. People were no longer dependent on the few natural lodestones they could find. Today, magnets are made of a blend of different materials that contain some or all of iron, nickel, copper, cobalt and aluminium.

Q What are poles of a magnet?

A Just as the Earth has two poles – the North and the South poles, a magnet also has two poles. It is easiest to find the two poles of a bar magnet where the poles are at either end are equally strong. The north seeking pole of the bar magnet points towards the Earth's North Pole. The other end points towards the South Pole. But if you use the magnet for navigation, you must remember that the magnetic poles of the Earth are not in exactly the same positions as the geographic poles of the Earth. Also, if you hold two bar magnets next to each other the poles will not point in the same direction because the magnets interfere with each other. The like poles repel each other while the unlike poles attract each other.

▲ **Magnetic scientist**
Michael Faraday (1791-1867), an English scientist, led the study of electromagnetism. He showed that magnetism could affect rays of light.

Q What is a magnetic field?

A The area around a permanent magnet has a force that can affect other magnets or magnetic materials that come near it. This area is called a magnetic field. Even the Earth has a magnetic field. It is like a huge bar magnet. Even if you cut a huge bar magnet into tiny pieces, each piece is still a magnet with its own small magnetic field.

▲ **Fridge magnets**
Most of us are familiar with the pretty and useful magnets we stick on the refrigerator.

Paper clip power

Any magnetic material in touch with a magnet starts behaving like a magnet itself. If you hang a paper clip from a magnet, it becomes a temporary magnet. You can prove it by hanging a second paper clip from the first and then another and another. However, if you remove the first clip from the magnet, all the clips below fall apart since they lose their temporary magnetism.

▶ **Horseshoe magnet**
You can play a variation of the paper clip game with a horseshoe magnet, which has its two poles adjacent to one another. Since the opposite poles are much closer, a horseshoe magnet produces a relatively strong magnetic field – you can stick many more clips to the magnet, starting with one that is stuck to both poles.

Q **Are mariners the only people who need magnets for their work?**

A Magnets are used almost everywhere in modern life. Most electrical appliances, from power stations to the little hair dryer at home, use a magnet to convert electrical energy into mechanical energy. Cassettes are coated with magnetic material that allows sound to be recorded on its surface. Credit cards have magnetic strips that contain encrypted information and enable us to use them. Motors found in dishwashers, fans, washing machines, refrigerators, CD, DVD and audio players use magnets. Magnets are also used to hold false teeth in place. And they help you remember too – by holding your notes to the refrigerator!

This way to the North

Try these too...

The Poles – The Arctic and Antarctica (122–123), The Industrial Revolution (148–149), Scientific Revolution (150–151), Electricity (186–187)

◀ **The compass**
Even a small pocket compass can show you the exact direction in which you are travelling. Remember that it is not the point marked North but the needle that is always pointing to the magnetic North Pole. In some compasses you can rotate the dial and align it with the needle to help you find which way is true north. The Earth's magnetic poles shift periodically. The needle points to the current pole.

Forces and Motion

Force can change the state of an object. If an object is stationary, force can get it to move. Once it is moving, force can make the object accelerate or pick up speed. It can also stop a moving object. A stationary object cannot move without force, nor can a moving object stop without force.

Quick Q's:

1. What is net force?

When more than one force acts on an object, the total of all forces acting on that object is called the net force. When more than one force acts on an object in the same direction, the object moves faster. If the forces act in opposing directions, they cancel each other out to a certain extent.

2. What is lateral deflection?

It is a force that makes a bullet spin to one side, or a football curl through the air. During the Soccer World Cup in France in 1998, Brazilian Roberto Carlos scored a free kick with a perfect lateral deflection. He kicked the ball to the far right of the defenders and made it suddenly curve round and zoom into the goal.

Q. **Where is force used?**

A Force is used in all our activities from brushing our teeth to walking, lifting and writing. Every one of our actions requires some force. You need energy to create force. Machines use force to move something or to build something.

Q. **What is inertia?**

A An object tends to carry on doing the same thing, whether it is at rest or moving, unless a force acts on it to change that. This is called inertia. Your pencil box lies on the table until you push it. This state of rest is called inertia of rest. Then, with the force of your finger, it moves on until it meets another force that stops it. This movement is called inertia of motion. If the force you push the object with is too much, it will go beyond the point where you wanted it to go.

Q. **What is gravitational force?**

A Gravity is the force that Sir Isaac Newton discovered, as he watched an apple fall off a tree on to the ground. It is a force that draws everything in the Earth's atmosphere and beyond towards the centre of the Earth and it keeps us on the ground. Gravity does not just act on the Earth; it is the force of attraction between all bodies (things) in the universe.

◀ **The science of a kick**
The force of the kick makes the ball move. The force used by someone else's foot makes it stop.

▲ **The discoverer of gravity**
Sir Isaac Newton (1643–1727) is supposed to have discovered gravity after seeing an apple fall from a tree.

As bodies get closer together, the force of gravity gets stronger, and as they move apart, gravity gets weaker. Bigger, heavier bodies are affected more by gravitational force. They also exert a greater force of gravity themselves. Gravity holds the solar system together and keeps the Earth close enough to the Sun for us to get the warmth we need.

Q. **How do I stay on a merry-go-round without flying off?**

A You stay on a merry-go-round because of centripetal force. When you feel you are going to fly off into the air, it is because your body wants to keep moving in the same direction all the time. This feeling is the inertia of motion. But the centripetal force keeps attracting you to the centre of the merry-go-round, making sure you stay on board! Objects set in motion normally move in a straight line because of inertia of motion, unless some other force acts upon them and changes their path. When a ball tied to a piece of string is swung round, the centripetal force acts upon the ball, attracting it to the centre of the circle. The centripetal force from the string pulls the ball to keep it on its circular path.

Q What is the difference between speed and velocity?

A Speed is the distance travelled by an object in a particular time. Velocity is speed in a particular direction. Suppose you sat in a train that was moving eastwards at 60 kilometres per hour (37 miles per hour). You would say that the speed of the train was 60 kilometres per hour (37 miles per hour), while its velocity was 60 kilometres per hour (37 miles per hour) east.

Q What is friction?

A Friction is a force that opposes the movement of an object by acting on it in the opposite direction. The force of friction comes into effect when two surfaces are in contact, and force is applied to make one or both of the surfaces move. Suppose you roll a ball on the floor. The ball will come to a halt after travelling a certain distance, even if it has hit nothing or no one has stopped it. The ball stops because the friction exerted by the floor acts against the motion of the ball. The soles of your new shoes probably have cuts in them to make an uneven surface.

Torque

The force that causes rotation is called torque. Torque can be measured in opening or closing a door, and it is applied when you turn a racquet from side to side. An archer applies torque to move the bow to one side when aiming an arrow. Ideally, the archer should hold the bow loose enough so that when the arrow is released, it shoots straight ahead. If the archer applies unnecessary pressure, the bow will twist upon release, the arrow will not fly straight, and the shot will miss the bull's eye.

When you run, the uneven surfaces of the shoes and the road rub against each other. This friction makes sure you do not slip while you are running. Lack of friction also causes us to slip on a wet floor since the water makes the floor smooth, which means friction is reduced. Friction produces heat. That is why when you rub a matchstick against a matchbox, sparks fly.

Try these too...

Galaxies (6–7), Stars (8–9), The Sun (10–11), The Moon (20–21), Hurricanes and Tornadoes (40–41), The Industrial Revolution (148–149), Scientific Revolution (150–151)

▼ **Sitting pretty**
We stay on the merry-go-around instead of flying off in one direction because of the centripetal force that holds us to its centre. The force that wants to make us fly off is called the centrifugal force.

Communication and Satellites

A satellite is an object that orbits other objects in space. This includes natural satellites like the Moon and artificial satellites made by people. The term satellite came to be used after Galileo Galilei discovered the four main moons of Jupiter.

Quick Q's:

1. When was the first artificial satellite launched?

Sputnik 1 was launched by the then USSR on 4 October 1957. It reached a height of about 250 kilometres (150 miles) and collected information about the furthest reaches of the Earth's atmosphere. Three months later, it burned up completely as it came back to Earth.

2. Who owns the satellites?

The first satellites were owned by countries. Today, with satellites becoming cheaper and doing more work, companies also own satellites. The area on the surface of the Earth covered by the satellite's signal is called its footprint.

3. What is a constellation?

Groups of satellites doing the same kind of work are called a constellation. The Global Positioning System is one such constellation made up of twenty-four satellites. GPS works in any weather condition, anywhere in the world, 24 hours a day. A GPS instrument can tell you exactly where on Earth you are.

Q What does an artificial satellite do?

A Artificial satellites have been put to a wide range of uses. Some satellites send and receive television signals so that we can watch many television channels. If there are enough satellites in space, one television programme can be seen all over the world at the same time. Weather satellites help scientists called meteorologists predict what the weather will be like. These satellites can save hundreds of lives by warning fishermen not to sail before a storm, and predicting when a hurricane will strike. Some satellites take photographs of the Earth's surface so that scientists can study changes in the world. This is how scientists know that glaciers that are millions of years old are melting because of global warming. Some others are communication satellites that deal with telephone, fax, internet and computer communications.

▼ **Watching a live game**
The images captured by the television camera are sent instantly around the world via satellites.

▲ **Satellite television**
Satellites bring television signals from all over the world instantly into our homes.

Q What is an orbit?

A Artificial satellites are given a definite path around the Earth. The Earth's gravity holds the satellite in a path called an orbit. There are several kinds of orbits. One is Leo or Low Earth Orbit. A Leo satellite circles 160–480 kilometres (100–300 miles) above the Earth's surface. It has to travel very fast to avoid being sucked back to the Earth by gravity. Leos travel at about 28,164 kilometres per hour (17,500 miles per hour) and can circle the Earth in less than two hours. Medium Earth Orbit or Meo satellites are placed 9,656–19,312 kilometres (6,000–12,000 miles) above the Earth. They are often used for communications of all kinds. Geos or Geostationary Earth Orbit satellites circle the Earth in 24 hours, which is the time the Earth takes to rotate once on its axis. So they seem to be fixed above one spot on the Earth. Geo satellites orbit 35,859 kilometres (22,282 miles) above the Earth. They carry television signals across the world, telephone calls between countries and internet messages. They also help predict the weather.

Q How does the satellite get into space?

A A satellite is launched into space on a launch vehicle which is driven by a rocket engine. There are special launch stations for satellites like Cape Canaveral in the USA, Baikonur in Kazakhstan, Kourou in French Guiana and Xichang in China. To start with, launch stations were run by countries or national organizations. Nowadays there are large private companies that also run some launch stations and provide the service of launching a satellite on a commercial basis. These launch stations must be far from human habitation so that the falling launch vehicle lands in water or on desolate land. Some satellites are launched from a portable platform on the Pacific Ocean. The launch vehicle's rockets carry the satellite into a temporary orbit. The rockets and the launch vehicle drop off. Then the satellite is ready to take off on its own motor. When it reaches its permanent orbit, the antennae and solar panels open up and the satellite starts sending and receiving signals.

Q What is a Comsat?

A Communication satellites or Comsats help in long distance communication by receiving and redirecting radio, television and telephone signals. Today, satellites provide a cheaper and better global communication network compared to many land networks. Comsats help large countries like China keep in touch with their remotest parts. They also help countries like Indonesia, which is a country of 13,677 islands, stay connected much more effectively than it would have been possible with wires and telephone poles. Navigation satellites provide information for navigation on Earth. They provide signals to moving objects, helping them identify their exact location. These satellites are mostly used by the military and provide information on speed, distance from target or destination and travel time.

▲ **Orbiting the Earth**
A satellite with its solar panels extended orbits the Earth.

◄ **Satellite signals**
Dish antennae are used to receive satellite signals.

Try these too...

The Moon (20–21), Humans in Space (24–25), The Industrial Revolution (148–149), Scientific Revolution (150–151), Computer Revolution (162)

Satellites for tomorrow

Since 1968, research has been conducted to develop solar power satellites or SPS. The project has been delayed by the high costs to build it. Once taken to a High Earth Orbit, it will beam solar power to Earth for use in place of fossil fuels like coal and petroleum, which are getting depleted quickly.

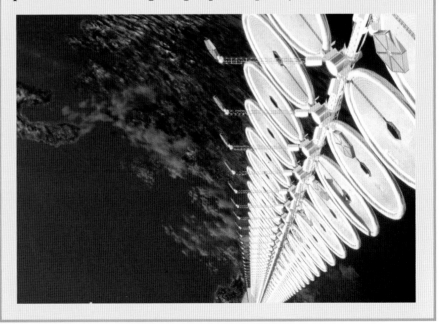

Land Transport

The earliest travel was on land. At first, people just walked. Then, they learnt to tame animals for travel. They rode on horses, mules and oxen. Gradually, they made themselves more comfortable, making carts and carriages. Modern transport on land includes a wide range of vehicles such as bicycles, cars, buses and trains.

Quick Q's:

1. When was the first wheel invented?

As early as the fifth century BC, the Mesopotamians invented the wheel. At first it was used to make pottery but later people realized that wheels could be attached to carts and used to move things and people easily.

2. When were the first cars produced in a factory?

In 1896, thirteen Dureyas cars were made in a factory in Springfield, Massachusetts (USA). These were the very first examples of mass-produced cars.

3. What is the record speed for land travel?

The latest record speed for land travel was achieved on 15 October 1997 by Andy Green of Britain in a Thrust SSC car. He travelled at a speed of 1,233.738 kilometres per hour (766.609 miles per hour)!

▶ **Moving in luxury**
Land transport has made much progress in the twentieth century after the development and mass use of the motor car.

Q Why did early man need to travel?

A People have always needed to travel to hunt or to trade with other people. Sometimes they needed to shift home when the rains failed. At first, they tamed animals to carry them. Later, when the wheel was invented, the animals were attached to vehicles. Until recently, even human beings were used to transport others. They carried litters or sedan chairs in which the rich sat.

Q When did roads improve?

A As civilizations grew, people needed more and better roads to trade and to conquer new lands. The Romans were the first to put time and money into making all-weather roads. Rather than just smooth over a clay surface, they dug beds and filled them with crushed stone for a firm support.

▲ **Penny farthing**
One of the early bicycle models that has gone out of use.

The stone chips acted as a filter for rain water to flow through so the roads did not flood. On busier routes, they added paving stones to ensure that the roads were firm and dry for their chariots to move on. These roads were used to connect up the huge Roman empire. Over time, even chariots and carts were improved with springs and shock absorbers to make the ride smoother.

▲ Modern train
Modern passenger trains can carry hundreds of people in comfort over all sorts of terrain.

Q Where were the first railroads?

A The first railroads were built in Germany around 1550. Horses pulled wagons along wooden rails and brought minerals out of mines. After the Industrial Revolution, rails were made of iron and so were the wheels. The development of the steam engine made rail transport easily available to carry people and goods over long distances.

Q When did people start to use buses?

A People travelled in stagecoaches and omnibuses pulled by horses from the early sixteenth century. The first horse-drawn tram cars came in the nineteenth century. The invention of engines that ran on steam and on fuel such as diesel and petrol led to the development of buses as we know them.

Q When did the first cycle roll?

A In 1680, German inventor Stephan Farffler made a hand-cranked tricycle. Later, he gave it another wheel to improve its balance. In 1817, Baron Karl von Drais of Germany made the *draisiennes*, a wooden bicycle with a seat and handle bars. But since von Drais didn't think of pedals, the rider had to push with his feet on the ground. The first modern bicycle was built by Kirkpatrick Macmillan of Scotland in 1839.

Q When was the motor car made?

A The first car was designed by Nicholas Joseph Cugnot and constructed by M. Brezin in France in 1769. It ran on steam and on rails. The first non-rail automobile was made by Etienne Lenoir, also of France, in 1860. He drove the very first gas-powered car from Paris to Joinville in 1862.

Try these too...

The Industrial Revolution (148–149), Scientific Revolution (150–151), The World Wars (158–159), The World after World War II (160–161), The New Millennium – 21st Century (163), Forces and Motion (190–191)

A road to drive on

Roads had to keep up with the development of technology for surface transport. McAdam designed the first highways lined with soil and stone, which is still known as macadam. The highways were higher than the land around, so that rain water could drain off. Later, these highways were tarred and the surface was called tarmacadam or tarmac. Modern roads are built of asphalt cement or concrete.

Water Transport

The idea of travelling by water probably came to people when they watched logs and leaves float down a river. After land, water has been the second most popular medium of transportation used by humans. Early humans built simple rafts, which were improved upon in every way over thousands of years.

▲ **Galleon**
Huge sailing ships called galleons carried people and goods across the seas of the world during the Age of Exploration. The Spanish galleons were the most famous.

Quick Q's:

1. What are modern ships made of?

Boats and ships continued to be made of wood for centuries. With the start of the Industrial Revolution, people began to use steel to build ships. Today, ships are also made of aluminium and fibreglass.

2. Who was the first person to sail around the world single-handedly?

American seaman Joshua Slocum was the first man to sail around the world single-handedly. He started off from Boston on 24 April 1895, and returned to Newport, Rhode Island on 27 June 1898, having sailed 74,000 kilometres (46,000 miles) in over three years.

3. What is a hovercraft?

The hovercraft can travel on water and land. It stays suspended a few centimetres above the ground or water surface with the help of an air cushion that it creates by the thrust of its jet engines. It is used as a fast patrol boat by the police and military of several countries and also for water sports.

Q What were the first boats like?

A Rafts or planks of wood were probably the earliest modes of transportation by water. The earliest boat found dates back to 6300 BC. The boat was a hollowed-out tree trunk, also called a dugout. Some people sailed coracles, which were boats made of animal skin stretched over a wooden frame. Oars changed water transport. They allowed people to decide where they wanted to go, rather than depend on the current. Around 4000 BC, the Egyptians made long narrow boats powered by many oarsmen.

Q When were the first sails used?

A By 3000 BC, people knew how to tie a cotton sail. Sails allowed people to use wind power instead of muscle power. Now people used ships for trade. By 1200 BC, the Phoenicians and Greeks built trading ships that had special places to store the cargo. By 500 BC, they had ships with two masts.

Q How did ships navigate?

A Early ships had to sail close to shore as the sailors could not find their way in open sea. By about 100 BC, technology improved and the sailors could navigate with gadgets like the astrolabe. The early Chinese used a spoon much like a compass. Sailors from other countries also used a lodestone, which is a natural compass. By the twelfth century, the magnetic compass was in use. As the science of cartography (mapping) improved in the Middle Ages, getting lost was less of a risk for sailors. In 1757, the sextant, a device to measure latitude, was invented.

◀ **Luxury cruiser**
Modern cruise ships carry tourists in luxury and are very popular.

Q What was special about the Viking ships?

A By the late 1000s, the fierce Vikings of Scandinavia ruled the seas. Their famous longboats were about 24 metres (80 feet) long and 5 metres (17 feet) wide and were rowed by 40–60 oarsmen. Vikings also used small rowboats called *faering* for swift attacks on their enemies. By the twelfth century, the Vikings knew how to use a rudder to steer the ship. This gave them more control than the side steering oar. All the Viking ships were slim and fast, so they could launch deadly attacks on merchant ships and coastal areas.

Q Was inland water travel different?

A While sails came in handy on rivers, streams and canals required special technology to get boats on the move. Around 984 AD, the Chinese discovered how to make an inland canal lock. This connects canals at different levels and needs sound engineering skills. By 1373, Holland had a system of canal locks. On canals and rivers, boats were often drawn by horses against the flow of water, and tow-paths were made on the banks for the horses to walk on. As engineering skills improved, sometimes canals were made by tunnelling under a mountain instead of going around it. Today, many canals that were earlier used for industry are tourist sites and nature reserves.

Q How did water travel develop?

A During the Industrial Revolution, water travel entered a new era. The development of the steam engine in the eighteenth century led to the first steamboats, which had paddle wheels to move against the current. By the late 1800s, the first iron ships came in, driven by the screw propeller. Vehicles for travel on water have now become very specialized, from the huge tankers that carry oil to luxury yachts and small speedboats.

A titanic disaster

The *Titanic* was a British luxury liner that weighed 46,000 gross tons. It was one of the grandest ships ever built, and was believed to be unsinkable. On its first voyage from Southampton to New York City, it struck an iceberg about 153 kilometres (95 miles) south of Newfoundland around midnight on 14 April 1912. It sank in less than three hours, taking about 1,513 of the 2,220 people on board with it.

Q What are submarines?

A A submarine is a ship that can be entirely submerged underwater. Submarines became popular during World War II since they could launch surprise attacks on enemy vessels. Early submarines had to surface often to replenish their oxygen supply. Today, submarines use nuclear power or liquid oxygen to propel their engines and can stay underwater for several months.

Q What are ships used for today?

A Water craft can be used for virtually any purpose now. There are car ferries and tugboats and water sports vehicles like rowing boats, kayaks, yachts and motorboats. Most big ships carry cargo from one port to another, but there are luxury ships called cruisers which carry many tourists at a time.

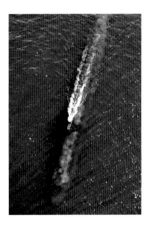

▲ **Rarely above water**
The sleek shape of the submarine allows it to move fast under water.

Try these too...

Oceans (34–35), Discovery of New Lands (144–145), The British Empire (146–147), Scientific Revolution (150–151)

Air Transport

Man has always wanted to fly. Early experiments with air travel included fancy kites, gliders and even artificial wings. Two types of aircraft can be used for air travel. Those that are lighter than air, such as hot air balloons, and aeroplanes and helicopters which are heavier than air.

◀ **Faster than sound**
The Concorde was a commercial plane that flew faster than the speed of sound.

Quick Q's:

1. What is the Concorde?

In the 1960s, jets that could travel faster than the speed of sound were developed. These were called supersonic jets. The Concorde was a commercial supersonic jet which could fly at a height of 17,500 metres (60,000 feet) at more than twice the speed of sound.

2. What are airships?

Airships were among the earliest aircraft. They were filled with hydrogen gas or helium, which helped them to float. Engine-driven airships, called Zeppelins, were widely used by Germany in World War I to launch bombing attacks on enemy territory. Today, flexible airships are used in advertising.

3. What is a seaplane?

Seaplanes, developed by Glenn H. Curtiss, can land on and take off from the surface of water. They are useful for reaching areas where no other transport is available. There are two types of seaplanes. Floatplanes are planes with large floats instead of wheels. Flying boats are planes that float on their bellies when they land.

Q **Who were the first scientists to study air travel?**

A In the thirteenth century, Roger Bacon declared that he was sure air could support aircraft. At the beginning of the sixteenth century, Leonardo da Vinci studied the flight of birds and invented the propeller and the parachute. He made designs for three heavier-than-air craft, including a helicopter with a rotor that helped it rise vertically, and a glider with a wing fixed to a frame. None of these was practical at that time. But they were based on the science of flight.

◀ **Joseph Michel Montgolfier**
Joseph Michel and his brother Jacques Etienne Montgolfier invented the hot-air balloon. While watching wood chips rise over a fire, they realized that the burning created a gas that caued any light material over it to rise. The same principle was later used in airships.

Q **What were the first aircraft like?**

A Hot air balloons were the first 'aircraft'. In 1783, the Montgolfier brothers successfully launched an unmanned hot air balloon in France. The balloon was a large linen bag filled with hot air. The light, hot air carried the balloon over a distance of 2 kilometres (1.3 miles) in a flight that lasted 10 minutes. Later, with improved designs, hot air balloons could reach a height of nearly 2,400 metres (8,000 feet) and travel a long distance.

Hydrogen-gas balloons were an improvement on the hot air balloon. Hydrogen could lift the balloon easily without being heated, as it is lighter than air. In 1785, Frenchman Pilatre de Rozier tied a helium-filled balloon and a hot air balloon together to fly across the English Channel. Unfortunately, Rozier died when the balloons exploded.

Q **Who made the first flight in a powered aircraft?**

A The nineteenth century was important for the development of aviation. Sir George Cayley experimented with kites and gliders that could carry people, and he designed a helicopter. But it was not until the twentieth century that the first flights were made. Brothers Wilbur and Orville Wright designed and constructed an aircraft. On 17 December 1903, in North Carolina in the USA, each brother made two flights. The longest, by Wilbur, was 260 metres (852 feet) in 59 seconds. The next year, the brothers made 105 flights. One of them lasted more than five minutes. In September 1908, Orville Wright flew for more than one hour. All around the world, inventors were racing furiously to develop the first heavier-than-air plane that would fly successfully, but the Wright brothers had beaten everyone to it. Shortly after the first flight of the Wright brothers, people across the world were starting to make successful flights. In 1906 Traian Vuia made a flight in Paris and Jacob Christian Ellehammer made one in Denmark.

Q Who was the first passenger in an aircraft?

A The Wright brothers continued their research. In 1908, Orville carried the first passenger, Lieutenant Frank P. Lahm, on a flight that lasted 6 minutes and 24 seconds. Shortly afterwards, Orville's plane crashed, killing another passenger, Lieutenant E. Selfridge.

Q Are aircraft used only for travel?

A Air transport is used for commercial aviation, which includes travel and ferrying cargo. It is also used by military forces to fight enemy aircraft, and for dropping bombs on enemy targets. Some aircraft are used for dusting crops with pesticides from the air, sowing clouds for rain and flying for sport.

Q What is a jet plane?

A Jet engines fly with the power from the discharge of a jet from the tail of the aircraft. They can fly at heights between 3,048 and 4,572 metres (10,000–15,000 feet). The first jet plane was flown in 1939 in Germany. Jets were used extensively during World War II to drop bombs and to fight other aircraft. Since then, jet planes have made travel by air a reality for millions of people. They can carry up to 600 passengers and fly at 680–900 kilometres per hour (420–580 miles per hour).

Try these too...

Earth's Atmosphere (26–27), The Renaissance (142–143), Scientific Revolution (150–151), The World Wars (158–159), The World after World War II (160–161), The New Millennium – 21st Century (163), Forces and Motion (190–191), Communication and Satellites (192–193)

◀ Deadly plane
This is the famous SR-71 Blackbird of the US Air Force. The black coating of the aircraft is made out of a special material that makes it difficult to be seen by radar. At the same time, there is a special fire-control radar on the nose of the aircraft.

Strange bird

The helicopter was designed by Ján Bahyl in 1905. Helicopters are propelled by rotating overhead blades. They are slower than planes, carry fewer people and can only travel short distances. But they are an advantage in places where there is not much space, since they can land and take off vertically. They are widely used for military purposes and for rescue operations, aerial photography and fire fighting.

▼ Aircraft carrier
Many military planes operate out of large ships called aircraft carriers, a practice that developed in World War II.

Index

Picture Credits

L: Left, R: Right, M: Middle, C: Centre, T: Top, B: Bottom
6t: **NASA Marshall Space Flight Center**, 6b, 7t, 16bl, 17br: NASA/JPL-Caltech, 7b, 109br: sgame, 8t: **Stephen Shields and George Greenfield/Adam Block/NOAO/AURA/NSF**, 8b: **H. Richer/NASA**, 9mc, 9br, 10t, 12m, 12b, 14t, 14bl, 14br, 15t, 15br, 16br, 17t, 18tl, 18tr, 18bl, 18br, 19tl, 21b, 22b, 23t, 23m, 23b, 24tl, 24tr, 25t, 27b, 32t, 37b, 39b, 40m, 40b, 110t, 121t, 123br, 163br, 193tr, 199t: **National Aeronautics and Space Administration (NASA)**, 9mr: **The SINGG Survey Team and NOAO/AURA/NSF**, 10b: **Michael Bischof**, 11tl, 13b: **ESA/NASA**, 11bl, 17bl, 19bl, 20b, 22t, 26b, 30m, 31b, 33t, 33b, 36m, 36b, 37t, 41m, 43br, 46t, 46m, 46b, 48t, 49tr, 51m, 52b, 53m, 54t, 54b, 55bl, 55br, 59t, 60br, 61t, 62t, 62bl, 62br, 63t, 65m, 65b, 67t, 69t, 69bl, 71t, 75br, 80t, 82t, 82b, 83m, 85t, 85b, 86m, 86b, 87bl, 88b, 89t, 89b, 90b, 91b, 92b, 93t, 93b, 95b, 102b, 111m, 111b, 119t,119b, 120t, 121mr, 121bc, 122b, 123t, 123m, 123bl, 126t, 126m, 126bl, 132m, 132b, 138m, 140m, 140b, 145t, 151b, 155bl, 155br, 164l, 165br, 185br, 187bl: **Q2A Media**, 12t: **NASA/JPL**, 13t: **NASA's Planetary Photojournal**, 15bl: **Cassini Imaging Team, Cassini Project, NASA**, 16tr: **ESA**, 16c: **USGS Astrogeology Research Program**, 19m: **NASA, ESA, and A. Schaller**, 20t: **John C. Panella Jr.**, 21t: **Taipan Kid**, 24b, 25b: **European Space Agency**, 27t: **Uli**, 27m: **Pascaline Daniel**, 28b, 29t, 34m, 41t, 43t, 44b, 48b, 54m, 55t, 57tl, 64tl, 73tl, 75t, 76bl, 76br, 77t, 77bl, 78t, 78b, 79m, 79b, 94t, 117bl, 120t, 127t, 127b, 134, 141mc, 142bl, 142tr, 146b, 147bl, 149m, 150tr, 153t, 157t, 157b, 168b, 169tl, 169m, 172m, 176b, 179bl, 186tl, 186tr, 188t, 190t, 198m: Illustrations by Robert Frederick Ltd, 29m: **Keith Levit**, 29b: **Stephen Inglis**, 30t: **Galyna Andrushko**, 31m: **Tony Sanchez-Espinosa**, 32br: **Mary Lane**, 36t: **Barbara A. Harvey**, 37m: **pdtnc**, 38t, 38b: **U.S. Geological Survey**, 41b, 181t: **Tad Denson**, 42t: **Martina Berg**, 42bl, 173br: **WizData, inc.**, 42br, 49l, 53bl, 66t, 97b, 173mr: **Vova Pomortzeff**, 43bl: **Fleyeing | Dreamstime.com**, 44t: **Gary Unwin**, 45t: **Simone van den Berg**, 45bl: **Dnadigital | Dreamstime.com**, 45br: **Mb-fotos | Dreamstime.com**, 46m, 47m: **kristian**, 48t: **Mateusz Drozd**, 49br: **Hermann Danzmay**, 50tl: **Mark Atkins**, 50-51t: **Ron Hilton**, 50b: **Heiko Grossmann**, 51b, 135m: **Nici Kuehl**, 52t: **Jody Dingle**, 52c: **Yan Vugenfirer**, 53t: **Grigory Kubatyan**, 53br: **TheThirdMan**, 56t: **Håkan Karlsson**, 56b: **Jami Garrison**, 57tr: **Eray Haciosmanoglu**, 57m, 57b, 65t, 12lt: **National Oceanic and Atmospheric Administration (NOAA)**, 58t: **Sjanie Gonlag**, 58m: **Andrea Leone**, 59m, 63m: **Tammy Wolfe**, 59b: **Appletat | Dreamstime.com**, 60t: **Smileyjoanne | Dreamstime.com**, 60bl: **Mark Van**, 61m: **Garnite7 | Dreamstime.com**, 61bl: **Department of Defense**, 61br: **Natasha Chamberlain**, 63bl: **swepri**, 63br: **Michele Perbellini**, 64tr: **Jason Stitt**, 64bl: **Sword Serenity**, 64br: **Xaviermarchant | Dreamstime.com**, 66m: **Drbouz | Dreamstime.com**, 66b, 115b: **Ian Scott**, 67t: **Paul Vorwerk**, 67bl: **Dan Lee**, 67br: **Stephen Boyd**, 68t: **Peter Heiss**, 69br: **Hiroyuki Saita**, 68b: **Qldian | Dreamstime.com**, 70t: **Katrina Brown**, 70b: **TerrainScan**, 71bl: **Lori Skelton**, 71br: **Daniel Hyams**, 73tr: **Paul Piebinga**, 73m: **Daniel Cooper**, 73bl: **John Billingslea jr**, 73br: **javarman**, 74t: **Teardrop | Dreamstime.com**, 74b: **Constance McGuire**, 75bl: **Lebedinski Vladislav Evgenievitch**, 76t: **Timothy Craig Lubcke**, 77br: **Thorge Berger**, 79t: **Brad Thompson**, 80b: **kevdog818**, 81t: **F2 | Dreamstime.com**, 81m: **Andreas Meyer**, 83t: **John Arnold**, 83b: **Grace True**, 84t: **Andrey Armyagov**, 84bl: **Ljupco Smokovski**, 84br: **pixelman**, 86tl, 198t: **Johann Hayman**, 86tr: **Stefan Klein**, 87t: **Steve Shoup**, 87bl: **Tan Hung Meng**, 88t: **risteski goce**, 89b: **Chung Ooi Tan**, 90t: **Ralf Juergen Kraft**, 94b: **mjones**, 96t: **Ramona Heim**, 96bl: **Janehb | Dreamstime.com**, 97tl: **Travis Klein**, 97tr: **CoverStock**, 97br: **Eric Patterson**, 99t: **Devonyu |**

Dreamstime.com, 99br: **Monika Adamczyk**, 100t: **Soo Jen Ric**, 100b: **Chen Wei Seng**, 101t: **Pryzmat | Dreamstime.com**, 101bl: **Loretta Hostettler**, 101br: **Steffen Foerster Photography**, 102bl: **Daniela Andreea Spyropoulos**, 102tr, 103, 104, 105, 106, 107, 108, 110t, 112t, 114t, 118t, 124r, 125, 128, 129, 130, 131, 132t, 136, 137tr, 137br, 138t, 140t, 141t, 144t, 146t, 150tl, 164r, 176t: **Arcturus Publishing Limited**, 109ml: **Thomas Mounsey**, 109mr: **Chris Ryan**,109bl: **Giorgio Gruizza**, 110b: **Stephen Mcsweeny**, 111t: **Peter Weber**, 111m: **Nancy Nehring**, 112b: **Zina Seletskaya**, 113t: **Johnny Lye**, 114bl: **Eldad Yitzhak**, 114br: **Marc Prefontaine**, 115tl: **Jeff Chandler**, 115tr: **David Maczkowiac**, 116tl: **Cornishman | Dreamstime.com**, 116m: **Elena Korenbaum**, 116b: **Kevin Lings**, 117t, 161bc: **R. Gino Santa Maria**, 117m: **Dragan Trifunovic & LockStockBob**, 117br: **Elena Sherengovskaya**, 118b: **Wessel du Plooy**, 119br: **EcoPrint**, 120b: **ARTEKI**, 124l: **B. Speckart**, 126br: **J.M. Kenoyer, Courtesy Dept. of Archaeology and Museums, Govt. of Pakistan**, 133m: **Steve Reed**, 134tr: **SGC**, 135tl: **Robert**, 135tr: **Judy Crawford**, 135bl: pmphoto, 135br: **Marcus Tuerner**, 138b: **Jeff Cleveland**,139t: **Jason**, 139m: **Allan Morrison**, 139b: **Gina Goforth**, 141mr: **Vladimir Korostyshevskiy**, 142t: **Tilman Reinhardt**, 142b, 144b, 145b, 148b, 152, 153b, 154b, 155t, 156b, 158, 159, 173tl: **Library Of Congress**, 144m: **William R. Hutchison Jr.**, 148t: **Brent Pizzato**, 149b: mbusa.com, 150b: **Tischenko Irina**, 151tr: **Ron Kloberdanz**, 156t: **Bryan Busovicki**, 161t: **Billy Lobo H.**, 161br: **Ronen**, 162l: **Jakub Semeniuk**, 162r: **Norman Chan**, 163r: **Oleksandr Gumerov**, 163bl: **Rafa Irusta**, 165t: **Hu Xiao Fang**, 165bl: **The British Library Board**, 166t: **Brasil2**, 167t: **Tan, Kim Pin**, 167b: **Copyright Estate of Robert Smithson/Licensed by VAGA, New York**, 169tr: **David Davis**, 170b: **Michael Palis**, 171t: **Presiyan Panayotov**, 171b: **Izim M. Gulcuk**, 172b: **Richard Paul Kane**, 173mt: **Chad McDermott**, 173mb: **Lance Bellers**, 173bl: **Galina Barskaya**, 173mr: **LockStockBob**, 174tl: **emin kuliyev**, 174tr: **James Steidl**, 174b: **Oliver Uhrig**, 175t: **Cary Kalscheuer**, 175b: **BMPix**, 177tm: **Joy Powers**, 177tr: **Stephen Coburn**, 177m: **Mike Liu**, 178t: **Shawn Roberts**, 178ml: **Stefan Glebowski**, 178mr: **Julie Ten Eyck (JTeffects)**, 178bl: **Lise Gagne**, 178br: **Ivan Stevanovic**, 179tr: **Konstantin Andryukhin**, 179m: samantha grandy, 179bm: **Kovalev Serguei**, 180t, 191t: **Joe Gough**, 180b: **Nsilcock**, 181bl: **Julian Barkway**, 181br: **Mark Yuill**, 182: **Rene Jansa**, 183t: **Oktay Ortakcioglu**, 183bl: **U.S Airforce**, 183br: luchschen, 184t: **Robert St-Coeur**, 184b: **Suhendri Utet**, 185t: **Richard Schmidt-Zuper**,185bl, 195b: **Maciej Noskowski**, 186b: **Dan Eckert**, 187t: **Suzan Oschmann**, 187m: **Natalia Bratslavsky**, 187br: **Matthew Cole**, 188b: **Jim Jurica**, 189t: webking, 189b: **Todd Taulman**, 190b: **NorthGeorgiaMedia**, 191b: dwphotos, 192t: **Sean Locke**, 192b: **Mitch Aunger**, 193tl: **Manuel Fernandes**, 194t: **Maciej Feodorâ_w**, 194b: rarpia, 196t: **Margaret Smeaton**, 196b: **Denis Pepin**, 199bl, 199br: **U.S Navy.**